To you the earth yields her fruit,
and you shall not want if you but
know how to fill your hands.

—KAHLIL GIBRAN, *The Prophet*

BILLY JOE TATUM'S WILD FOODS COOKBOOK AND FIELD GUIDE

EDITED BY HELEN WITTY

PLANT DRAWINGS BY
JIM BLACKFEATHER ROSE

WORKMAN PUBLISHING COMPANY, NEW YORK

Library of Congress Cataloging in Publication Data
Tatum, Billy Joe.
Billy Joe Tatum's Wild foods field guide and cookbook.

Later ed. of: Billy Joe Tatum's Wild foods
cookbook and field guide. 1976.
Includes index.
1. Cookery (Wild foods)
2. Wild plants, Edible—Identification.
I. Witty, Helen. II. Tatum, Billy Joe.
Billy Joe Tatum's Wild foods cookbook and field guide.
III. Title. IV. Title: Wild foods
field guide and cookbook.
TX823.T39   1985   641.6   85–5360
ISBN 0-911104-77-1(pbk.)

Cover illustration: Ed Lindlof
Cover design: Paul Hanson
Occasional plant drawings: Bee Robinson

Workman Publishing Company, Inc.
1 West 39 Street
New York, New York 10018

Manufactured in the United States of America
First printing February 1976
6 8 9 7 5 4

To Dad Taylor, who unconsciously taught me
to love what the land yields,
and to Mom Taylor, who taught me
that every meal can be a feast,
I dedicate this book

CONTENTS

Garlic
Allium vineale

Bur Oak
Quercus macrocarpa

Plantain
Plantago lanceolata

Chinquapin Oak
Quercus prinoides

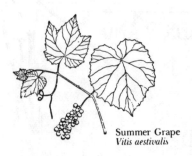

Summer Grape
Vitis aestivalis

ACKNOWLEDGMENTS

Every book would be less good without the help of many people, and this book is no exception. Among those who have helped me are the friends who encouraged my foraging and cooking interests and who gathered recipes and wild foods for my testing. I also want to give just due to my family—to my husband, Hally, who "allowed" me to be liberated and who washes his own socks and fixes his own breakfast; to Angel, my eldest daughter, who corrects my sentence construction and continues to think I'm just great, although a bit "kooky;" to Lisa, the foremost taster among all my girls; to Lori, who knows mushrooms so well; to Maury White, who may not like the taste of all the wild foods, but who can always make them look prettier; to Toby, my only boy-child, who is a tireless forager and a great tea maker . . . These six have been my real salvation in the writing of this work.

The warmest thanks are also due to Ann Taylor Packer, my sister and personal "editor," who makes me think and helps me say what I feel; to Idavonne Rosa and Sammy Denhoff, also my sisters, who have for years been my clipping service, my tasters, and my ego boosters; to my eldest brother, Orville W. Taylor, who encouraged me to start keeping notes; to Jamie Taylor, who always knew I would someday write a book; to Ira White Taylor, who took me foraging in Spain; to Jack and Mary Jean Taylor, whose foraging land I share with their children, Susan Blue and "Steven too."

There are others whom I'd like to thank by name, as they have been extra-special in many ways . . . Bob White, my son-in-law; Ora McCollum, Edna Greenstreet, Joan Mabrey, Glen and Helen Hunt, Harry and Hazel Elberg, LaNelle Davidson McCollum, Donnie Wylie II, Bob Matthews, Robert Batson, Crescent Dragonwagon, and Bob Fraser; Annie and Walter Smith and the Jay Harrises, for sharing their asparagus patches; Ellen Dunnaway and Gretchen Kopert, who checked my manuscript; and Renee Finley, the greatest secretary. And I also thank Carrie Elliott, Dr. James Hutcheson, at Arkansas State University, and Clay Anderson, who first published my writings; the University of Central Arkansas Biology Club, led by Dr. Jewel Moore; Dr. Joe Griffin, who gave me my final push toward finding a publisher; and Payton Kolb, who helped me keep my sanity . . . And I say thanks for their inspiration to those who have gone before me in writing about wild foods, especially Bradford Angier and Euell Gibbons.

FOREWORD

Each of us is many in one: poet and scholar, hermit and sociable friend, artist, adventurer, miser, and spendthrift. Who among us has not heard a bird sing and yearned to sing as well, or seen a field of goldenrod in the sun and wanted to paint a picture? Who has not listened to an old-timer or to a world traveler and not yearned for adventures? Do we not all, at times, require the solitude of the hermit and at other times clamor for companionship?

In field and forest I have found satisfaction for these and many other needs. Living in a rural area, I have been surrounded with things of nature, but other environments offer many of the same satisfactions I have found. One can be conscious of the poetry in the rhythmic clack-clack-clack of the wheels of a commuter train, or find adventure in looking for the first flowers of spring in the midst of megalopolis. In a large city library we are more easily able to satisfy a scholarly curiosity than perhaps anywhere else, and either friendship or the hermit's solitude can be found on a park bench. Have you not felt wonderfully thrifty at the local junk shop, and just as wonderfully spendthrift when buying a boutonnière that will wither by evening?

Artistry need not be confined to poetry or painting. Cooking can also be a form of artistry—not just the boiling of a pot of greens and setting them out to be eaten, though there are times when even this is sheer beauty. After a busy day, however spent, a simple meal of greens well seasoned and tastefully served can indeed be a work of art. And the contents of that pot of greens can be gathered outdoors by the city dweller or a suburbanite as well as by someone who lives in deep country.

There is something deeply exciting about embarking on a new venture, whether it be a trip, a new job, or a new hobby—foraging for wild foods, for instance. Something new is to be learned, new emotions are evoked, and many interesting questions arise. Will the new hobby be expensive? Will I understand the terms and activities involved? Will the rewards be sufficient?

Let me assure you that foraging indeed has its rewards, both in learning and in the wild-food hunting itself. And perhaps the greatest reward comes in cooking the new and interesting finds you have made. This book will help you to find plants worth gathering and will tell you how to cook them in ways I'm sure you'll enjoy.

I find it challenging as well as helpful to learn the botanical names of the plants I find. Knowing botanical names isn't a luxury or a scholarly quirk—these Latin names are universally recognized, unlike common names, which often vary from one place to another even within the United States and which are often duplicated—there are three "pigweeds," for example, among the plants in this book. The "real" names of plants—their botanical names—help you to know exactly which plant you're reading or talking about and make it possible to converse intelligently with others interested in wild foods or in botany. They also help you to find other plants that are related to the ones you know.

The field-guide section of this book lists plants first by their best-known common names for the convenience of those who may still be learning the more formal scientific names. It also identifies each plant botanically, by its genus or by its genus and species, and the entries often discuss several species that are closely related. Further, I have included other well-known common names in the entries so that, with the aid of the index, you will be able to find a given plant under at least two and often many more names.

The forager's hobby need not be expensive. A book or two, a spade, a knife, a basket, and some spare time are about all you'll need for your expeditions. (You'll also need some pots and pans and a means of cooking your harvest when you get it home—and you'll want to try the recipes in Part Two.) An open mind and an eagerness for new experiences are invaluable. After you have foraged for a time you will become more aware of your surroundings, more knowledgeable about

ecology and the needs of the environment, and I'll promise that you will develop greater sensitivity in many areas of life. The fascination of wild foods has even caused some foragers to consider a new life style. Whether that happens to you or not, you'll find great rewards in the search and in the finding.

Billy Joe Tatum
Billy Joe Tatum

Wildflower
Melbourne, Arkansas
October, 1975

PART ONE
THE FORAGER'S SEASONS:
A FIELD GUIDE TO EDIBLE
WILD PLANTS

THE FORAGER'S SEASONS

SPRING

In those vernal seasons of the year, when the air is calm and pleasant, it were an injury and sullenness against nature not to go out and see her riches, and partake in her rejoicing with heaven and earth

—MILTON

Greening-up time is here—the season awaited with more anticipation and longing than any other. The very name of spring is a word-picture of the seasonal intent—the springing up of things that have been dormant for a time. Young poke and asparagus stalks are beginning to peek up out of the warming earth, as are milkweed and the tiny fronds of bracken and other ferns. Flowers of the violet look out among the fallen leaves, dandelions appear, and the first mushrooms of the year push up miraculously between one day and the next. Yes, the awaited spring has come, and we have only to get knife, spade, and basket and set out for the nearest wild garden spot.

If you live in a rural area, as I do here at Wildflower, in the Ozarks of Arkansas, your wild garden spot is all around you. If you live in a suburb or a largish or small town, it's not far away, and even in the central city you need not despair. Where there is soil, there are plants growing from it. Often the cracks in a stretch of city sidewalk offer the making of a great dish of wild greens. Look around your neighborhood. Is there a vacant lot, an unpaved playground? How about the city park or the local golf course? (Be sure to check with the golf pro—not every time may be the right time to wander around within range of players' drives!) Check the grassy areas around the tennis courts. Have you looked for an overgrown parking lot, or near the drive-in movie? How about the sides of a jogging track or an equestrian trail? Prowl, leave no avenue unexplored, no stone unturned, and, believe me, you will find wild foods.

Standard reference works list thousands of edible plants of the world, wild and tame, and books dealing with the United States alone list hundreds of wild foods. I have not made a statistical check of the works of such popular saints of wild-food foraging as Euell Gibbons and Bradford Angier, but they and others who have written on this subject have presented far more than a mere smattering of the edible plants growing wild for the taking.

Today there is a new interest in wild foods, perhaps promoted by the back-to-the-land movement of the young members of the counterculture—and by older people, too, who either remember gathering delicious wild fruits, nuts, leaves, and shoots, or who wish to learn about them. There are many books, too, that range in their coverage from the fundamentals of locating, identifying, and cooking wild foods to those of much wider botanical and culinary scope.

It's spring, and you're not really tied to the house just because there's a wash to be done, or obligated to play bridge or go bowling just because that's what you usually do. Maybe it's worth a try to find out if a country outing with the family might be even more fun than bridge or bowling. Laundry will wait, bridge is always with us, and the bowling lanes won't disappear.

Now's the time to go down to the park to see if there are greens growing there—greens sure to be more delectable than canned or frozen "tame" ones, or the fresh kinds sold in markets. If you live in the suburbs, in the time it takes your washer to run a cycle it's likely that you can pick enough dandelion blossoms for a batch of superb fritters for supper. Or, going a bit farther afield, you can find the makings for poke pickles, or for candied violets, or for a pot of mixed greens. Maybe you'll find your first mushrooms—which you shouldn't venture to eat until you have carefully identified and cross-identified them to establish their edibility—but at least you will have *found* them. Can it be possible that foraging is actually more fun than bowling or bridge?

Today foraging is fun (and rewarding in terms of taste and nutrition), but once it was almost a necessity. The old-timers who had lived for many months on game, salted meat, dried fruits and vegetables, and the contents of the root cellar—turnips, potatoes, and rutabagas—were more than ready for the edible wild greens, shoots, blossoms, and mushrooms that follow the first warm days of this vernal season. With these it was not necessary for them to wait for the ground and weather to warm up enough for a garden to be planted, and it was not necessary to wait for a crop to mature. The spring was a harvest season as well as a beginning—the many plants that had begun their underground growth in late winter had appeared above the earth and were soon ready to be gathered.

And this is still true for those who know what to look for. Now is the time for the first fruits of spring, the plants that require only a few days of warm sun before they're ready. Let's look for some of them—see the descriptions in Part One for help in finding and identifying them, and see the

recipes in Part Two for ways to prepare and enjoy them. Among the plants to look for before June are these:

Amaranth	mushroom, morel,
Asparagus	oyster mushroom,
Bracken and other	shaggy mane
ferns	Mustard
Burdock	Onion
Cat-tail	Pepper grass
Chickweed	Plantain (leaves)
Chicory	Pokeweed
Chives	Prickly pear (pads)
Dandelion	Purslane
Day lily	Sassafras
Dock	Sow thistle
Elderberry (flowers)	Spring beauty
Garlic	Violet
Henbit	Watercress
Lamb's quarters	Wild ginger
Leek	Wild rose
Milkweed	Wild strawberry
Mint	Winter cress
Mulberry	Wood sorrel
Mushrooms:	Yucca
chanterelle, meadow	

SUMMER

Steep thyself in a bowl of summertime.
—VIRGIL

As the warm days get warmer and the sun sets later each day, a languor seems to overtake us. Spring is the swift season, the newness of its green fairly jumping out at us. The summer seems more leisurely—perhaps it is the lengthening daylight of late May and early June, or perhaps it's the heat of the sun that makes us feel we have forever to do anything we choose and that this is therefore a slowing-down season.

Not so, if you want to keep up with the time of plenty. There are many new wild foods to gather now and there are new offerings from some of the plants you have been harvesting in the spring. There will perhaps be less variety in the greens pot, but there will be enough. If you have kept cutting back your wild pokeweed patches, you will have ample poke shoots and greens. Both lamb's quarters and watercress can be depended upon for the pot, and new greens appear now. Look around for sorrel to add to a salad, and expect upcroppings of mushrooms after warm summer rains . . . look for puffballs, meadow mushrooms, chanterelles, and shaggy manes especially, and be sure that you have identified and cross-identified them with more than one reliable mushroom field guide before you eat them—when you know your mushrooms as well as the face of an old friend, you'll be an old hand, and can dispense with formal identification of each batch. (These four mushrooms are often found in urban places and so are worth looking for in city parks, on golf courses, and on suburban lawns as well as in rural fields and pastures.)

There will be summer berries galore to feed us now and to put up for later use. We can look forward to marvelously busy days picking berries in the cool of the morning or the late evening, and even busier days making jams and jellies for winter. Whatever you do with your berries, it's a delight to come in, buckets laden, to wash enough for breakfast, then to enjoy the fruit covered with cold milk and accompanied by cinnamon toast—an unforgettable feast. Look at the buckets of berries and know that the preserves you put up today will provide for other breakfasts, for cobblers and other baked goods, for pies, syrups, for a dozen delights. These are the fruits of the forager's labor.

Besides the best-known wild fruits, such as blackberries, strawberries, blueberries, huckleberries, raspberries, plums, and so on, summer brings fruits that will be new to many—ground cherries and wild black cherries should not be overlooked, nor should maypops or passion fruit, papaws, and such delicious but little-known fruits as mulberries. Often in May, when we think that summer has really begun here at Wildflower, the season can have its interruptions. "Is it winter again?" I wonder as the smell of cold weather hits me. No; it's "blackberry winter," about as regular here as Indian summer in the late fall. I am not the only creature slowed down by the touch of unseasonable chill. The butterflies are not flitting with their usual vigor—they loiter on the blackberry canes, as if dallying there will warm them. Even busy ladybugs, usually eager to show off their red-lacquer coats with black spots, seem to be affected. I always try not to worry about the wild strawberry crop while I'm worrying about the blackberries—somehow the growing habits of strawberries seem to protect them from untimely cold weather. Nevertheless I find myself going off to my own private strawberry patch when I'm satisfied that the blackberries will make it through these few cold days. My favorite place for strawberries is off the beaten track, safely away from any berry hunters less ardent than I. In a coppice of pines, the lovely plants grow thickly and fruit for me alone. I will begin gathering the full, rich fruits in late May, but today I'll just sit in the spotty sun after checking them out. The music of the wind swishing through the pine branches is an invitation to rest from my springy walk over the carpet of needles that has lain here so long, undisturbed by any other human.

As I watch the phoebe bird working with frenzy to feed its young, I think about the sweetness of the promised fruit, the delight of my children in eating the first berries they pick, straight from their favorite patch. I think that I am somewhat like the phoebe, hurrying to feed my young. I think of the fun we have making jam from this fragrant fruit; and this year we'll make a special strawberry cake for a new friend who has never eaten the wild berries, though his name sounds as if it has been translated from the French *fraises*, which means "strawberries," to the staid English "Fraser." I think of our best strawberry hunter, who lives nearby at Tameweed. She is ten years old, has sparkly eyes, is black and white spotted, and stands about one foot high. Tinker Bell loves all fruit, and being so close to the ground she often sniffs out and eats the strawberries before the rest of us can even see them. We know the berries are ripe and ready when this dog stays an unusually long time in our roadside patch. Other thoughts pass through my mind—childhood memories of slipping off to wade the creek even before barefoot weather and finding the first ripe fruit of summer. In these memories I can hear the same breezes and hum of bees, I smell the same fruity fragrance. I resolve that this year I will pick enough berries to dry as my grandmothers did, for the Christmas cakes. Blackberry winter has not harmed either blackberries or strawberries, and the plants will fulfill their reason for being, and I will fill my larder with the berries.

After the strawberries, other summer fruits will be ours for the picking, as I hope they will be yours. Try as we may, we can't keep up with the production rate of the summer, but I do try to plan ahead for picking and preserving, thinking of the hot cobblers, pies, and muffins that today's canning will make possible next winter. If you have never canned foods or preserved jams and jellies and juices, you are in for a new approach to living when you try it—or you may prefer to use your freezer to store the fruits and wild vegetables of summer, and find equal pleasure in your harvest. (You'll find that standard directions for canning and freezing, such as those in the *Ball Blue Book*, published by the jar manufacturers, the Ball Corporation, Muncie, Indiana 47302, work perfectly for wild foods as well as tame.) From late May to early September, nature's bounty is at its height. Here is a list of the wild foods in this book that are to be looked for and gathered now:

Amaranth	mushroom, puffball,
Bee balm	sulphur shelf, oyster
Blackberry	mushroom, shaggy
Black cherry	mane
Black raspberry	Mustard
Blueberry	Onion
Burdock	Papaw
Cat-tail	Plantain
Chickweed	Pokeweed
Chicory	Prickly pear (pads)
Chives	Purslane
Dandelion	Sassafras
Day lily	Sorrel
Dittany	Sow thistle
Elderberry	Spring beauty
Garlic	Sumac
Grape	Sweet goldenrod
Ground cherry	Violet
Huckleberry	Watercress
Lamb's quarters	Wild ginger
Leek	Wild plum
May apple	Wild rice
Maypop	Wild rose (hips)
Milkweed	Wild strawberry
Mint	Wood sorrel
Mulberry	Yucca
Mushrooms: meadow	

AUTUMN

What more glorious to behold
Than autumn's bounty, autumn's gold?
What reward can one ask more
Than to feast from nature's store?

—A.T.P.

Autumn slips in on us here at Wildflower with a subtlety of colors—when frost appears, the summer tints give way to deeper colors in all the fall leaves, flowers, fruits, and grasses. The yellows and golds of plums and maples deepen to shades of rose and then to reds and maroons. The fields gradually turn golden as honey with sagebrush, foxtail grasses, and wild oats. The foliage of the May apple changes from green to a yellow that rivals the tint of its ripening fruit. The wild flowers of this season are mainly in the yellows and golds of sunflowers and goldenrod, but many mints bloom in bright lavenders and blues. The dogwood and sassafras trees surprise many with their fruit — the deep-red seed clusters of the dogwoods are, to me, even more beautiful than the spring flowers, and the sassafras fruit is a real beauty, with its clear red stem and cap holding the blue-black oval seed. My poet friend Frank Wood beautifully and aptly describes this young season in the title of his song "Butterscotch Autumn." How this catches the feeling of the season — golden, sweet, soft, and good!

We now slow down in our foraging fervor, though there is still much to collect. Many seed plants, such as sumac, with its spires of closely knit, ruddy, velvety seeds, are now begging to be gathered as the days shorten and we feel crispness in the night air. The tea plants are ready to be picked,

dried, and stored to last a whole year. Many mints are blossoming now in shades of blue, lavender, or purple, and these are at their best for tea when picked at the flowering stage. Fragrant bee balm—wild bergamot—will be blooming in a brilliant show of cardinal red and lavender, if indeed it hasn't blossomed earlier. Sweet goldenrod, dittany, and rose hips are all ready to gather, dry, and store away beside the scarlet sumac fruits, ready to make teas, punches, or other beverages.

But above all autumn is nutting time. Left alone, the nuts (including acorns), which are the seeds of the trees, will drop from the branches with the rains, winds, and other falling weather and will eventually be buried beneath the leaves. Gradually the husks will rot, then the nuts will sprout, splitting their shells. The new roots will sink deep into the humus of the woods and new forest trees will have made a start.

But now the black-walnut and hickory and butternut and pecan trees are laden with their crop of goodness for us and the creatures of the forest. If you, too, live in a deciduous forest area of the South or the Southeast, you may be fortunate enough to fend off the squirrels and get your share of the almost forgotten chinquapins, which can be compared in flavor only to Old World chestnuts, now that virtually all native American chestnut trees have died of blight.

Except for acorns, we hull all of our nuts—which means removing the outer casing—and let them dry for a few weeks before they are used. If kept in their shells in a cool place and cracked when they are needed, hickory nuts, black walnuts, butternuts, and pecans keep well and seldom dry out; I have sometimes kept them in their shells for several months. Usually, however, we spend many winter evenings cracking nuts and picking the kernels from their shells. Chinquapins and any shelled nuts that aren't needed immediately can be frozen and so be kept fresh.

Our larders are full of the harvests of spring and summer—the jars are lined up row upon row, promising good eating for the coming months. How lovely the pickled chanterelles look—how unusual the poke dills, stored away four months or more ago. How beautiful the golds, reds, roses, and purples of the jams and jellies—besides the many familiar kinds such as strawberry, grape, plum, and blackberry, there are also such delicacies as maypop jam and ground-cherry jelly and violet syrup to amaze those who have never tasted them. Here are the caper-like pickled elderberry buds, meant to be served with fish dishes, and the spiced relishes, venison jelly, and other preserves made to go especially with the wild game we expect to see on our table now that hunting season is at hand.

There are still wild foods to be gathered as autumn draws on. The fall mushrooms are abundant for those who know what to look for. Here at Wildflower we find an abundance of chicken of the woods, oyster mushrooms, and the odd fungus the Chinese call "tree ears," better known to American mushroom hunters as Judas's ears; meadow mushrooms, too, are still to be found.

Yes, winter is coming, as the nippy nights and brilliant foliage warn us. But let it come—it won't catch us unprepared. As we wait for the cold weather, we can find, for the taking, many of these wild foods:

Acorn	Black walnut
Amaranth	Butternut
Bee balm	Chickweed
Black cherry	Chicory
Black haw	Chinquapin

Chives	sulphur shelf
Dandelion	Mustard (seed)
Day lily	Papaw
Dittany	Pecan
Dock	Persimmon
Elderberry	Prickly pear (fruit)
Garlic	Purslane
Grape	Raspberry
Ground cherry	Sassafras
Hickory nut	Sumac
Huckleberry	Sweet goldenrod
Jerusalem artichoke	Violet
Lamb's quarters (seed)	Watercress
Mint	Wild ginger
Mushrooms:	Wild plum
chanterelle,	Wild rice
Judas's ear,	Wild rose (hips)
meadow mushroom,	Winter cress
oyster mushroom,	Wood sorrel
shaggy mane,	Yucca

WINTER

They laugh and eat and are warm. Their food is ready at hand.

—ELIZABETH COATSWORTH

With Indian summer, autumn has given its last brilliant splash; with its passing, winter is at hand. The sun is in the sky for fewer hours and we on earth somehow seem to be farther away from it than at other seasons. The skies are less often blue and more often grey, shadowed, and cold. The nights are long and dark, but clearly etched with stars that seem more brilliant in the deepness of a winter night than in the softness of summer.

The chill and dampness of the weather keeps us much indoors. I am often drawn to the large window which overlooks my valley and the range of mountains beyond. This window frames a picture of the outside world that differs from hour to hour, day to day, as the changing seasons make up the changing years. Outside today, the ground around the sundial bird feeder is a fairyland of frost, the crystals sparkling and twinkling on the dry grasses. There is a frost flower on a broken milkweed plant near the edge of the bluff—a rare sight, this phenomenon: a hard frost and a chilling wind came at the same time and the plant's stem was broken, allowing the rising sap to freeze and flower outward into a cascade of ice. The frost flower is a sure sign that winter is here to stay.

I smell snow in the air and the birds are flitting on the feeder, many more of them than usual. The ground squirrel is filling his jaw pouches with sunflower seeds pilfered from the birds' supply, and yesterday I saw a fox squirrel come from his tree hole and dig under a rotting log for his fall-stored acorns. There will be snow soon, I hope.

It's the next day, a December morning, and I get up early to see if the snow has come. Yes, the mountains are white to the top, where the sentinel trees march against the leaden sky. The valley lies still beneath the snow with seldom a sign of the life which nevertheless goes on within it. Often, on early mornings in winter, mist fills the valley and swirls upward until the hills vanish, or until only their tops appear in a fantasy sea. Today this is not so. The cold and the blanket of snow have prevented a mist, so my familiar hills and valley are clear to the sight. I'll add dry wood to the banked logs in the fireplace and bake mouth-watering biscuits to be eaten before the fire with jam made from June's

strawberries. And I'll put on some Chopin records to awaken my young gently to this new winter covering.

As I measure the flour for the biscuits, I hear the powerful hammering of the pileated woodpecker on the large oak that grows in the valley, its top stretching up above my lichened rock on the edge of the bluff. I run to my window to get a good view of this master of all woodpeckers, his red crest and hard, strong beak moving in a quick crescendo to get at a larva or a beetle beneath the bark. With a flash of black and white he darts deeper into the forest with his strange undulating flight.

What is growing for us to forage during the winter? Not a lot in the regions which, like ours, have four distinct seasons, including one of cold during which all nature seems outwardly to rest. But even here, after a few warm days, we can often find enough winter cress or even watercress for a spicy salad or a sandwich. There are mushrooms that appear in spite of the cold, such as Judas's ears and oyster mushrooms, and that are good even if they should freeze. The Jerusalem artichoke became available in the late fall, and its tubers still lie in plenty beneath the ground, ready for use whenever they are dug until spring moves them into growth again. Some nuts still cling to the trees, and there are prickly-pear fruits to be found for the making of confections.

Because we have been busy foraging through spring, summer, and fall, now is a time we've looked forward to with anticipation. We are indoors more and we'll have time to try out new ways of serving the foods we have put by. We can grind the seeds and acorns and make breads and cakes and muffins to serve with our collection of wild teas, or we can roast some dried chicory or dandelion roots for a pot of delicious "coffee." We can read about the mushrooms we want to hunt next year. We can put on some winter music, stoke up the fire, get out our recipes, and decide what new and exciting fare we can prepare for tonight's dinner.

Winter is a time of rest for all. The roots and seeds for next year's greening-up time are now dormant, revitalizing themselves to spring up when the seasons change. We're doing the same, preparing for next season while we are enjoying the harvests of the last.

Chickweed	oyster mushroom
Day lily (roots)	Pecan
Hickory nut	Persimmon
Jerusalem artichoke	Prickly pear
Mint	Sassafras
Mushrooms:	Watercress
chanterelle,	Winter cress
Judas's ear,	

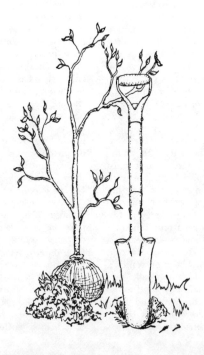

A FIELD GUIDE

ACORNS—THE NUTS OF THE OAK

Various species of the *Quercus* genus
Other common names: Bread Stuff (and, in the Winnie-the-Pooh books, "hay-corns.")

Where to find them: In every region where temperate-zone forest trees grow.

Parts used: Kernels, extracted after the ripe acorns are gathered in the fall.

How used: Fresh or frozen, after leaching and, usually, roasting; eaten as a nut, or ground into flour or meal.

"Mighty oaks from acorns grow" to produce more oaks, and acorns, for all creatures. Not only the wild animals, but the people inhabiting all of the many parts of the world where oaks grow, have used the nourishing kernels of acorns as food. There are hundreds of oak species in North America, and all are similar in producing edible nuts, although their sizes, shapes, appearance of the bark, and leaf forms vary enormously from species to species. (To me the most unusual oak is the cork oak, which grows in Spain and Portugal and whose bark yields most of the world's cork supply.) Acorns all look more or less alike, although they vary a lot in size. They are always held to a twig of the tree by a scaly cup. The acorns themselves are oval to roundish and have a thin, slick brown shell with a tiny pointed tip. When opened the shell reveals a divided nut-meat, the edible part.

For acorns to become palatable the large amount of tannic acid they contain, which makes them astringent, must be removed. The simplest method of doing this is to leach out the tannin by cooking the acorns. First slip off the cup, then either crack the hull with a nutcracker, hit the pointed end of the acorn with a hammer, or slit the hull with a knife, then remove the shell.

Put the decupped, cracked, and hulled acorns in a pot, cover them with boiling water, and boil from 2 to 4 hours, changing the water for fresh, already boiling water whenever it becomes dark. When you change the water, taste an acorn —they are leached enough when all astringency has gone. They will darken as they cook. Drain the acorns and let the surface moisture dry off, then spread them in a shallow pan and roast them for about an hour in a 300° oven. The acorns are then ready to be eaten like other nuts or to be ground into coarse flour or meal to be used in bread, muffins, or cookies. (You can use a food grinder, with the fine plate in place, and grind the acorns twice; or use a small grain mill.) The roasted acorns or the flour may be stored in airtight cans, or else frozen for future use. Uncooked acorns, too, freeze well—they will keep indefinitely.

Perhaps the directions "decupped, cracked, and hulled" seem superfluous, but my friend Gretchen cooked her first acorns fully clothed and capped—needless to say, the astringent tannin was deeply embedded in the kernels. The Indians used to extract the tannic acid from acorns by leaching them in the cold running water of a stream. This sounded like a romantic adventure, so I tried it, and it does work. The acorns are considerably less darkened when the tannin is removed in this way, but it took many days for them to become sweet. The acorns of white oaks (*Quercus alba*) are sweeter than almost any others except the acorns of bur oaks (*Q. macrocarpa*), which are huge, almost golf ball-sized. Bur oaks are not common in my area, as they have been cut for timber, so I get the smaller acorns from other oaks. You can do the same, gathering and en-

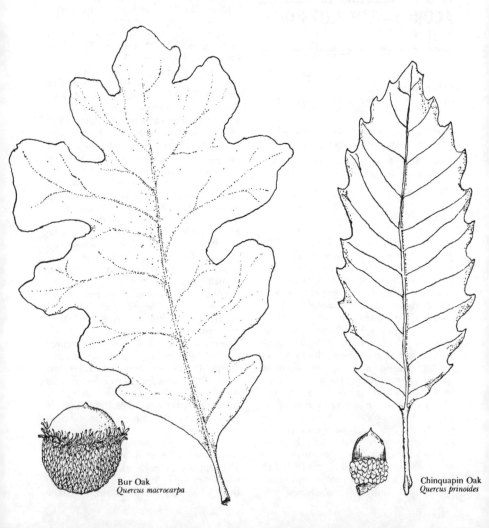

Bur Oak
Quercus macrocarpa

Chinquapin Oak
Quercus prinoides

joying whatever kind of acorns you come across in the fall—all are worth trying. Some are even sweet enough to roast and eat without leaching—you can find out which these are only by trying the ones you find. The illustration shows the leaves and acorns of four of the more common oaks.

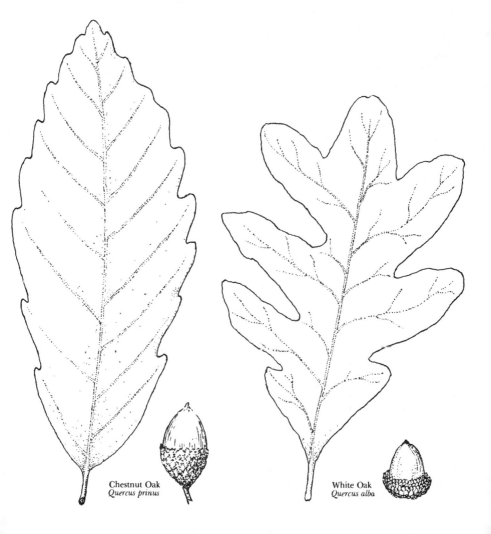

Chestnut Oak
Quercus prinus

White Oak
Quercus alba

AMARANTH

Various species of the *Amaranthus* genus

Other names: Careless Weed, Pigweed, Redroot Pigweed, Green Amaranth, *Amaranthus retroflexus;* Prince's Feather, Red Amaranth, *A. hybridus.*

Where to find it: These two species and closely related ones are found as weeds throughout the United States, but especially in the eastern half. Found in fields, yards, fence rows, and waste ground.

Parts used: Young leaves in spring; seed in late summer and fall.

How used: Leaves as greens, fresh or frozen; seed dried and ground into meal.

Green amaranth shares the ubiquitous common name of "pigweed" with lamb's quarters and purslane, among other plants. The green or "pigweed" amaranth, often called "careless weed," is one of the commonest weeds of gardens and old garden plots. Its pointed-oval leaves are medium green and a little downy underneath. The greenish, feathery flower spikes, not very showy, are borne at the leaf axils and at the top of the plant. In the fall there are abundant tiny black seeds for the gathering. The plant tends to be prickly to the touch, which makes it bothersome to pick leaves or harvest seed, but the bother is repaid by the value of the plant as food.

Amaranthus hybridus, or prince's feather, is the red amaranth. This flower is sometimes grown in today's gardens, but it was indispensable in our grandmothers' flower gardens. The leaves are not only edible but particularly tasty, lending a slight beet flavor to the greens pot. Orientals prize them; my first knowledge of amaranth as a Chinese delicacy was when Hazel and Harry Elberg up at Twin Hills brought me some seed from a Chinese friend in St. Louis. When I planted the seed in my kitchen garden, it turned out to be that of my old faithful *A. hybridus.*

The plant, leaves, and flowers of careless weed and prince's feather are generally shaped alike. However, red amaranth will grow 4 to 5 feet high, but careless weed seldom grows more than 3 feet. If it's uncrowded, however, it may grow taller. Gardeners hate the careless weed. It is careless about dropping its seed everywhere, careless about sending up countless little new plants. Gardeners fight it with fervor, not realizing that it can be as important a vegetable as the spinach from which they are weeding it.

Careless Weed
Amaranthus retroflexus

ASPARAGUS

Asparagus officinalis

Other common names: Asparagus Fern, "Grass," "Sparrow Grass."

Where to find it: Along roads, railroads, and fence rows; in fields and meadows and wasteland throughout the United States and southern Canada.

Parts used: Young shoots, in spring. Foliage used in flower arrangements, summer.

How used: Fresh, frozen, canned.

The warm, humid spring weather brings us this familiar vegetable, whether in our own gardens or in the many places where it thrives as an escape from cultivation, often growing from seeds scattered by the birds. The part we eat is the young shoot arising from the perennial root, or rhizome. Left alone, the shoot will burst into the ferny foliage that the countrywoman likes to put into her vases of summer flowers.

The stalks you'll find may range from the thickness of a pencil to that of the handle of a toy broom. All sizes are good, so long as they are tender enough to break easily; actually, it's better to cut them when harvesting, making the cut at or slightly below the soil surface. I try to pick my wild spots every three days or so, at the same time breaking back any spears beginning to "fern out." This will assure more yield; sometimes I have picked a patch for as long as six weeks. My son Toby did a little study of our "asparagus route" not long ago. He counted the sprouts picked from the plants where we removed all growth and compared the count with that from

plants where we picked only what was then edible; the clean-picked plants produced considerably more for the pot.

Asparagus is fairly easy to transplant; just lift the rhizomes (early fall is a good time) and move them into good soil in the garden. They appreciate plenty of fertilizer once they're established, and a mulch in winter will increase the spring yield. To find a source of roots, look for the ferny tops while they're still green, or after they turn yellow-beige with frost.

If you have more asparagus than you can use—see our recipes—it freezes wonderfully, and it can be canned, too.

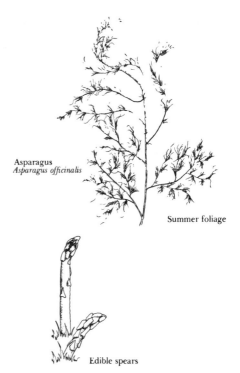

Asparagus
Asparagus officinalis

Summer foliage

Edible spears

BEE BALM

Various species of the *Monarda* genus

Other common names: Wild Bergamot, Oswego Tea, Horsemint.

Where to find it: In open meadows and wastelands and on roadsides, from Quebec to Saskatchewan and south to Florida and Arizona.

Parts used: Flowers and leaves, gathered in summer and early fall.

How used: Fresh or dried, for tea.

This tea plant is a member of the huge mint family, although its flavor is all its own, not "minty" in the usual sense. It is a late summer and early autumn bloomer, providing many of the lavender and crimson hues in the fields of late flowers.

The stem is square, as all mint stems are. The leaves are oval with a pointed tip and grow in opposite pairs on the stiff stems. The dark-green leaves have a central vein from which lateral veins branch toward the saw-toothed edges of the leaf.

The flower head is a botanical mess to describe, but it looks like this to me: The center is like a round pincushion about the size of a nickel. The many single blossoms surrounding the center are tubular, each with a drooping beardlike tongue below and a split petal above. The throat of the tube is sometimes speckled. *Monarda didyma*, Oswego tea, is brilliant red to beet-colored. *M. fistulosa* has pale lavender flowers, and its flowers and leaves are smaller than in the red-flowered monarda. Both red and lavender bee balms are often grown in flower gardens.

Both these monardas are excellent tea plants. As they begin blooming, start your collecting. Break the stiff stems 6 or 8 inches from the ground, where the leaves begin growing thickly. Tie 20 or 30 stems together loosely and hang them in a dark, warm, dry place for a week or two. When the leaves crumble to the touch, they are ready to be stripped.

I pluck off the leaves singly if they are large, or run the stem between my thumb and forefinger and strip them off. I use the flower heads too, as the blossoms add flavor as well as color to the tea. Store the dried tea airtight.

Make this tea with about a half-teaspoon of dried leaves per cup of water, and sweeten it to taste. If you make tea with fresh leaves, use about twice as much.

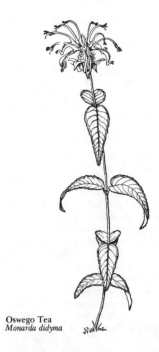

Oswego Tea
Monarda didyma

BLACKBERRY

Rubus allegheniensis

Other common names: Allegheny Blackberry; Common Blackberry; Bramble; Running Berry.

Where to find it: Grows widely from eastern and southern Canada as far west as Minnesota, then southwards, especially in mountain regions. Closely related species are found in temperate environments throughout the United States.

Parts used: Fruits, in summer.

How used: Fresh, canned, or frozen, in desserts; preserved in jams and jellies.

The blackberry is such a common plant that almost everyone knows it by sight. There are uncounted members of its parent genus, *Rubus,* and many of them are also called "blackberry," but the one I will discuss is *R. allegheniensis,* perhaps the one most commonly found in our area. It is related to *R. occidentalis,* the black raspberry, as well as to all the other raspberries, dewberries, wineberries, cloudberries, and other members of the huge *Rubus* genus.

Blackberries are found in all sorts of places—along fence rows, in old gardens, in clumps among shrubs and bushes in fields, in the deep woods as well as open meadows. I've seen them spring up in city gardens, too. They are a favorite food for birds, which help to spread the seeds.

The branching plants have long, thick, rather woody canes covered with very prickly thorns of various sizes. The leaves are palmate, with 3 to 5 leaflets—usually 5—with serrated edges. The flower is a delicate white five-petaled bloom; the many stamens make the center noticeably yellow. The flowers look like clusters of tiny wild roses, which isn't surprising—both the blackberry and the rose belong to the very large Rose family.

The flowers are followed by hard green fruits which ripen from June onwards into many-seeded, black, juicy berries, usually borne very abundantly. Some berries are as small as a pinto bean, while other plants may have fruit the size of a marble. Often blooms and berries are on the canes at the same time, promising a long season of picking of this delightful and useful fruit.

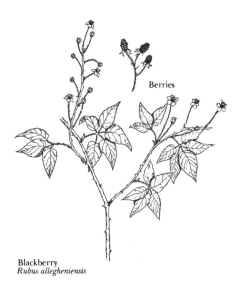

Berries

Blackberry
Rubus allegheniensis

BLACK CHERRY

Prunus serotina

Other common names: Rum Cherry, Sweet Black Cherry, Wild Cherry.

Where to find it: From southeastern Canada to North Dakota, and southward to Florida and Texas and into Mexico.

Parts used: Fruit, from early summer through early fall, depending upon locality.

How used: Fresh, frozen, or canned, for desserts, pies, beverages, jam, and jelly.

One of the several "wild cherries," the black cherry grows into a long-lived tree as high as 75 feet tall; it often bears when

Black Cherry
Prunus serotina

quite small. It is valued for its fine wood, used in cabinetmaking. The black cherry is a lovely sight when it bursts into fragrant white blossoms after its leaves are about half grown.

The black cherry has reddish bark with white speckles. The inner bark is aromatic—it was long used medicinally, especially in cough syrup. The leaves are broadly lance-shaped and finely toothed, looking much like those of other cherries. In fall they turn yellow and rose-colored and shine as if they were made of enameled metal.

The fruit, about half an inch in diameter and purple to black in color, ripens in loose clusters. If the tree is producing fully, it is easy to gather a large supply of slightly puckery but basically sweet and tasty fruit. Black cherries are especially good for making a fine tart jelly; many people like them in pies; and a punch made from them is unforgettably delicious.

Among the other wild cherries are some that have escaped from cultivation, such as the sweet cherry or wild sweet cherry, *P. avium,* and the sour cherry, *P. cerasus.* Real wildings include the shrubby sand cherry, *P. pumila;* the pin, bird, or fire cherry, *P. pensylvanica;* and the chokecherry, *P. virginiana.* Some trees of a given species will produce better fruit than others, so it's a good idea to taste and compare fruit when you can.

Don't fail to look for wild cherries when you go foraging. It's easy to gather them in abundance, and if you have a real surplus, you might can them according to the directions for "tame" cherries in cookbooks.

BLACK HAW

Viburnum prunifolium

Other common names: Stag Bush, Stag Brush, Arrow Wood, Nannyberry, Sheepberry, Wild Raisin.

Where to find it: In both moist and dry areas, in woods, thickets, and along roadsides, from southern New England west to the Great Lakes and Kansas and south to Georgia and Texas.

Parts used: Ripe fruits, in the fall.

How used: Fresh or dried, as a nibble; frozen or canned; preserved in chutney and fruit butter.

This showy shrub or small tree, with its heavy clusters of pure-white blossoms, blooms with abandon in the spring, soon after the dogwood bloom is over. The leaves are slick, finely serrated, and gently pointed. The bud clusters, surrounded by a few small leaves, soon open into full, flat-topped clusters of sweet-smelling little flowers. Each cluster looks like an old-fashioned nosegay of Granny's time. The flowers are a welcome sight to many a rural horticulturist who has transplanted black-haw bushes to grow near the house as ornamental shrubs. There, as well as in the woods, wildlife will be tempted to come and browse. I have seen fox squirrels, white-tailed deer, ruffed grouse, brown thrashers, cedar waxwings, and wild turkeys enjoying this plant.

The black-haw berries grow in clusters. They are blue-black and oval in shape, flattened on one side, and are overlaid with a grey mist of bloom. They ripen in the fall and are even sweeter after frost touches

them lightly, shriveling the smooth skin. As this plant seldom grows more than 15 feet high, the fruit is an easy crop to harvest.

To use the black haws, cook them in a small amount of water until soft. Then rub the pulp through a colander to remove the seeds. The pulp is black, as black as a prune, thick and tasty, good for chutney and fruit butter. Black haws are also a delicious nibble when dried. One of the loveliest sights in the kitchen at Wildflower in the fall is the clusters of black haws hanging from the open beams to dry. We simply hang the clusters on cords from nails in the beams, to pluck and nibble when they have shriveled to sweetness. They can also be stemmed, then dried on wire trays in a dry, dark place. When they are thoroughly dry, store them airtight.

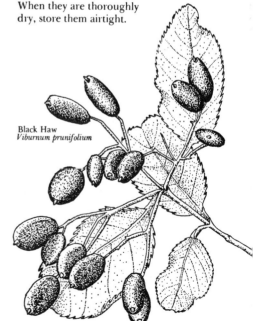

Black Haw
Viburnum prunifolium

BLACK RASPBERRY

Rubus occidentalis

Other common names: Thimble Berry, Hindberry.

Where to find it: Dry or moist woods, old fields and garden places, and in burned-over areas, Quebec to North Dakota and Colorado and south to Georgia, Arkansas, and Oklahoma. Other species of raspberries are widely distributed throughout the country

Parts used: Fruit, in midsummer.

How used: Fresh, canned, or frozen, or in preserves.

The black raspberry is common in open wooded areas, and it often springs up after a forest fire. It likes the company of its own kind and, like all the other raspberries as well as the blackberries, which are all in the *Rubus* genus, it usually grows in large thickets. The thick, reddish-brown stems are sparsely covered with hooked briers which are strong and very prickly. The leaves are divided into 3 or 5 leaflets each, and these are toothed on the edges. The flowers appear in loose clusters and are white to pink, with 5 petals. The fruit, at first green, then red, then very deep purple or, more usually, black, is very juicy and mildly tart to the taste.

One name for black raspberries, "thimbleberry," came about because when the berry is plucked from the stem the cap comes away and there is left a space inside the berry where the finger can be placed.

Black raspberries are easily transplanted to the garden and do well there, growing in a row. When watered regularly and kept

pruned—the old woody canes should be cut off after bearing—they will produce an abundance of fruit conveniently at hand. However, if you don't have a garden or don't care to transplant this berry, do go out hunting for it. The fruit ripens in June or July, depending upon the locality and the weather.

Raspberries are a particularly cooling fruit and less acid than most berries, so they tend to alleviate thirst. The recipe section has some of our favorite ways of using this berry, but don't fail to experiment on your own, too.

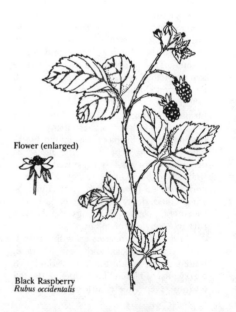

Flower (enlarged)

Black Raspberry
Rubus occidentalis

BLACK WALNUT

Juglans nigra

Other common names: Walnut, Jupiter's Nut. Timber called "gun wood."

Where to find it: From Massachusetts to Minnesota, South Dakota, and Nebraska; south as far as Florida, and westward to Texas. Look in rich woods, in valleys, along streams and in old fields and pastures.

Parts used: Nutmeats as food; hulls for dyeing yarn. Nuts ripen in fall.

How used: Nuts used fresh or frozen.

It was once not unusual to see a black-walnut tree 100 feet high, with a straight trunk clear of branches for half its height; but old trees are growing rare, as they are valuable for timber. The leaves are compound, having from 15 to 23 leaflets growing alternately on a stem. Yellowish-green in color, the saw-toothed leaflets are up to 5 inches long and taper to a point. The bark of the tree is dark brown and is marked by a network of rounded ridges.

The nuts mature inside a green, grainy husk a bit larger than a golf ball. In late fall the hull turns dark and the ripe nut falls, ready to be picked up by the harvester. To get to the hard-shelled nuts, the hulls must first be removed. My grandfather had an ingenious method: He got a flat board with knotholes about the size of a nut without its hull. He set each nut over the hole and forced it through with another board or a hammer, and the nut would come out clean. We still use this method, boring 1½-inch holes instead of looking for a board with knotholes of the right size.

There doesn't seem to be an easy way to extract black-walnut kernels from the hard, thick shells. We put the nut on a hard surface with the pointed end up and hit it hard with a hammer; this cracks it fairly well. (A friend of mine puts hulled nuts in a burlap bag on her driveway and runs a car over them a few times.) After the nuts have been cracked, simply pick away with a sharp nail or a nutpick until you have extracted the meat.

In good walnut years we gather bushels of these nuts, and often we store the surplus nutmeats in the freezer to keep them fresh. They are particularly strong-flavored, with a unique taste. Use them in our favorite recipes (Index), or whenever pecans are called for.

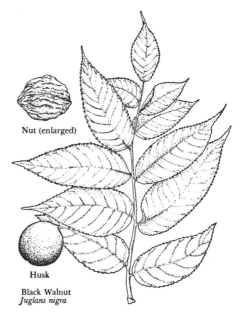

Nut (enlarged)

Husk

Black Walnut
Juglans nigra

BLUEBERRY

Various species of the *Vaccinium* genus

Other common names: Whortleberry, Highbush Blueberry, Lowbush Blueberry, Bilberry, Hurts, Whorts.

Where to find it: All blueberries prefer acid soil. Look on upland slopes and ridges, burned-over areas, in open woods, especially oak, and sometimes in low moist areas. They range over much of the United States, and also much of Canada.

Parts used: Fruit, ripening in summer.

How used: Fresh, canned, frozen, in preserves.

If this berry grows in your area you are lucky, as it is a profuse producer and the berries are delicious, either raw or cooked in many ways. They ripen in clusters from June onwards, depending upon species, region, and altitude.

In the Southern states the highbush blueberry is the more common one. Cultivated forms of this one are sometimes 6 feet or more tall. In the North, however, the lowbush forms are more common; they may be only a few inches high, like the ones growing in cracks in the rock in front of my house, or may reach 2 feet or so. To identify the many distinct species is the job of a trained botanist; however, they are enough alike that with the following guidelines you are quite safe in picking them.

The shrub has somewhat shiny small leaves of medium green, sometimes with finely toothed edges. The flowers are a joy to look at: sometimes drooping gracefully from the slender twigs, they are bell-shaped and often pink at their edges. They appear in May or June and are followed by ripe berries in a couple of months. I have picked blueberries, which can range in color from pale powder blue to almost black and which almost always have a coating of powdery bloom, from the Fourth of July to Labor Day. As they can be tedious to pick and clean if you're getting a lot, it is good that the task can be spread out over the long fruiting period.

There are many ways of cooking this berry (see the recipes), although it's delicious eaten fresh with sugar or honey and cream. Huckleberries and blueberries can be interchanged in any recipe. In a good year, be sure to pick enough to can for pies in the winter. They may be frozen with ease: I simply wash and drain them well and freeze them without sugar in plastic boxes or ice-cream cartons with tight lids.

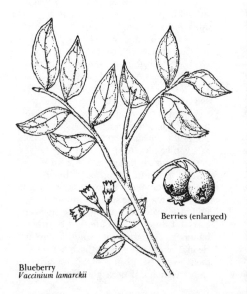

Berries (enlarged)

Blueberry
Vaccinium lamarckii

BRACKEN AND OTHER FERNS

Bracken, *Pteridium aquilinum;* Cinnamon Fern, *Osmunda cinnamomea;* Ostrich Fern, *Matteuccia Struthiopteris.*

Other names: Bracken—Brake Fern, Pasture Brake, Hog Brake, Eagle Fern, Wa-ra-be (Japan). Eastern Bracken— *Pteridium aquilinum* var. *latiusculum.* Western Bracken—*P. aquilinum* var. *pubescens.* Southern Bracken—*P. aquilinum* var. *pseudocaudatum.* Ostrich Fern is also called *Pteritis nodulosa* and *Onoclea Struthiopteris.*

Where to find them: Bracken in most of North America, in open woods, old fields, burned-over places. Ostrich fern in moist soil, in woodlands or along streams or in swamps, across southern Canada and the northern United States and south to Virginia and Missouri. Cinnamon fern in moist areas throughout the country.

Parts used: The "fiddleheads" or young fronds that are still tightly curled, gathered in spring when only a few inches high.

How used: Raw, in salads. Cooked, as a vegetable, in soup, and in salad. Frozen or canned. Preserved as a pickle.

Ferns for gathering in the spring can be found by locating last year's dry, brown, broken fronds, then watching for the fiddleheads before they uncurl to make the lacy leaves. Gather them while they are tender, brittle, and juicy. I seldom pick any that are over 10 inches high—they get stringy and bitter when larger.

Fiddleheads are covered with fuzz or scales, depending on the kind you have, and this covering should be removed by rubbing them between your hands. I sometimes use a bit of nylon net for clean-up of the fronds before washing them.

Bracken is one of the first ferns to appear in spring, often growing in huge patches. It continues to produce new shoots, covered with thick "velvet," into summer. As its fiddleheads uncurl, the frond is at first forked, then grows to a knee-high compound leaf composed of several smaller frondlike sections set opposite to each other on the stem and ending in a pointed tip. It can vary in height, sometimes growing to only a foot, sometimes to 5 feet.

While we were going to press we learned that recent laboratory tests have shown that bracken contains substances that are cancer-causing when large doses are given to experimental animals. What this means to someone who enjoys an occasional dish of bracken greens I'm not sure, but I think it should be mentioned. I might point out that the laboratory tests involve much higher concentrations of these substances than any of us is ever likely to eat.

Cinnamon ferns, often 3 feet high at maturity, and ostrich ferns, 6 feet, are highly prized for eating at the fiddlehead stage, especially in New England. Cinnamon-fern shoots are covered with a greyish-silver coating that gradually turns cinnamon-brown. Ostrich-fern fiddleheads are drier and less mucilaginous than the other two, and have a scaly coating rather than fuzz.

Raw fern fronds add a new texture to a salad of wild greens. Cooked, they are a little mucilaginous, like okra, but this is often desirable, particularly in soups. I often tie the fronds in small bunches before cooking them to make it easy to remove them from the pot.

Too often we think of ferns only as

background for a bouquet, or as the plant
Grandmother always set outdoors after a
winter on the fern stand. More of us
should take up the habits of the first
people of our land, the Indians, and add
this succulent vegetable to our list of usable
plants.

Bracken
Pteridium aquilinum

Cinnamon fern
fiddleheads

Ostrich fern
fiddleheads

BURDOCK

Various species of the *Arctium* genus

Other names: Great Burdock (*Arctium lappa*); Common Burdock (*A. minus*); Clotbur, Beggar's Button, Gobo, Wild Gobo, Cuckold, Harlock.

Where to find it: In waste places, along roads and railroads, and around dwellings throughout most of the United States and Canada, except for the deep South, the Southwest, and the western Great Lakes region.

Parts used: Leaf, early spring; stalk, spring and summer; root, spring and summer; flower stems, summer.

How used: Fresh, either raw or cooked; frozen; canned.

Great burdock has the largest leaf of any greens used for the pot; at maturity the leaf is often as large as a dinner plate. It is dark green on top and the underside is greyish-green and as soft as lamb's wool. It is the new texture as well as the new taste that makes burdock welcome in our assortment of greens for the pot. When picking leaves, take only the small young spring leaves.

Burdock is a biennial plant that reproduces by seed only. Its large taproot lives through one winter and produces new leaves and a flower stalk the second year. The flower stalk on second-year plants is edible. Great burdock, *Arctium lappa*, may reach 10 feet; common burdock, *A. minus*, is at most 6 feet tall. The best way to locate this plant, which is often a bothersome weed, is to look for last year's seed stalks, with their heads of burrs. Then watch for the new growth in the spring. When cooking the leaves, add soda to the first cooking water, then finish the cooking in fresh water. Give the same treatment to the flower stems, picked when young, before they show color. Strip off the rind, which is bitter, then cook the pith, which is delicate, tasting somewhat like celery.

Getting the edible taproots to the top of the ground is quite a feat, as they grow deep and are brittle. In April or May, after the leaves have begun to grow and preferably after a heavy rain, choose first-year plants—those with flower stalks are second-year plants and the roots are too tough to eat.

The best tool I have found for digging burdock is a sharpshooter spade or shovel, which has a long, tapering blade. When digging, start about 6 inches away from the base of the plant and make a circle of deep cuts all around, then lift the root and shake off the soil. Now split and remove the outer layer of the root; inside is a smooth, white core, crisp, crunchy, and tasty enough to devour on the spot. Try it in a salad.

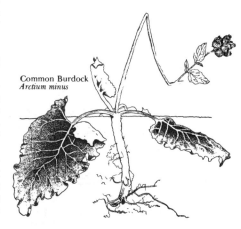

Common Burdock
Arctium minus

BUTTERNUT

Juglans cinerea

Other common name: White Walnut.

Where to find it: The eastern United States, from northern Mississippi, Alabama, and Georgia north into Canada and as far west as Oklahoma.

Parts used: Nutmeats, in fall and winter.

How used: Fresh or frozen.

Closely related to the black walnut is the butternut or white walnut, *Juglans cinerea*. This medium-sized tree has compound leaves 15 to 30 inches long; in each there are from 11 to 19 leaflets, finely toothed and slightly hairy.

The nut is from 1½ to 3 inches long and, like the black walnut, grows in a thick-walled hull. The butternut hull is slightly pointed and irregularly ridged. The nut, when dried, then hulled and cracked, offers a sweet, oily kernel which is every bit as delicious as the black walnut, although less emphatic in flavor. To hull the nuts, see the directions for black walnuts.

In our part of the world, a butternut tree is quite a find, and its location is often kept secret by anyone who finds it. The delicious nuts can be used in any recipe calling for pecans or black walnuts or English walnuts.

The Indians are supposed to have known how to boil down the sap of the butternut tree to make a sweet syrup. I haven't tried this, although it might be worth an experiment in the late winter or early spring.

Hull

Butternut
Juglans cinerea

Nut

CAT-TAIL

Typha latifolia

Other common names: Common Cat-Tail, Cat o'Nine Tails, Cossack Asparagus, Reed Mace, Swamp Bullrush, Bullrush.

Where to find it: In slow streams, ponds, and swamps throughout North America.

Parts used: Sprouts, leaf shoots, flower buds, pollen; in spring and summer.

How used: Sprouts, shoots, and buds fresh or frozen, as vegetable or in salad; pollen used in baking.

Even if you have never gone foraging for this well-known water plant, you will recognize it easily by its flower heads, those large wieners on their own sticks that are a common sight in florists' dried plant arrangements.

The plant, with long, lance-shaped leaves, often grows as tall as 6 feet, but may be much lower. The flower heads arise on a stiff, pencil-sized stalk sheathed by the leaf bases. When the flower heads are ripe they produce much yellow pollen.

In the early spring before the cat-tails begin to grow above the surface, take a hoe or a rake and pull the roots from the water. On them you'll find the swollen sprouts ready to start upward to form "Cossack asparagus" as spring advances. Cut off, scrub, and peel these sprouts, then use them in salad or cook them as a vegetable.

Once the long "asparagus" shoots begin to appear, cut them, then slip off the sheath of each, consisting of a tough outer leaf. You will be left with a crisp whitish or greenish core that is often 18 inches long. Like the sprouts, the shoots can be eaten raw or cooked. Gather the "asparagus" before the cat-tails are more than 2 feet high.

Because it will take a pond of cat-tails as long as a month to green up, one pond will give you food aplenty over an extended period. Don't fret over getting your feet wet—just splash out there and harvest your cat-tails at whatever stage.

While the flower is still sheathed, cut it to cook as a vegetable—see the recipe section. Later, as the pollen forms on the flower heads, it is easy to collect enough to use in place of flour in pancakes or muffins: simply bend the heads over a container and shake them.

Roots and shoot

Flower head

Cat-Tail
Typha latifolia

CHICKWEED

Stellaria media

Other common names: Common Chickweed, Starwort, Stitchwort.

Where to find it: Abundant in waste ground, in lawns and gardens, as well as along roadsides, in light woodlands, and along streams throughout North America, but especially in the east-central states and the upper South.

Parts used: Leaves and stems, most of the year.

How used: Fresh, cooked as a vegetable or raw in salads; frozen; canned.

Chickweed, which shares its common name with two nonedible low plants of the *Cerastium* genus, grows in virtually every country of the world which has seasonal changes and adequate rainfall. In the South and other mild-climate regions it can be picked as readily in January as in August, and it can often be found green in midwinter in cold-climate regions, too, where fallen leaves have protected it. It is probably the most commonly found edible weed, although few people consider it for the table.

The plant is weak-stemmed and low-lying, growing in dense mats. It has tiny oval leaves that have pointed tips and are a pale green that appears almost opaque. The leaves grow in opposite pairs on the stems, and the very small flowers grow in clusters. The flowers are five-petaled and white; the flower bud makes me think of a nosegay that fairies and elves might choose to carry on party occasions.

This plant continually produces its juicy crop of leaves and is an extremely tasty addition to the greens pot. Because it is so productive, it can be an important addition to the wild-foods list. It needs no special preparation for cooking—just wash and drain it. It cooks down to about half of the original quantity, so get twice as much as you think you'll need. It's a good mixer when cooked with the more pungent greens—dock and poke, for instance—which seem to me better if their flavors are "cut down" a bit.

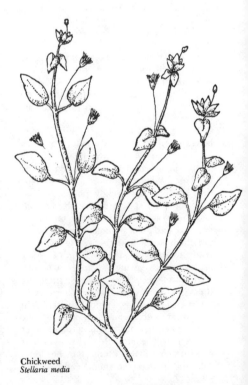

Chickweed
Stellaria media

CHICORY

Cichorium intybus

Other common names: Succory, Blue Sailors, Ragged Sailors, Witloof; Barbe du Capucin (Europe).

Where to find it: Along roadsides and in pastures, fields, and waste places throughout the United States, but especially in the eastern and central regions, and also on the Pacific Coast.

Parts used: Roots in summer and fall; leaves in spring.

How used: Leaves, fresh, frozen, or canned, as vegetable; roots, dried, roasted, and ground, for "coffee."

Chicory is a blue-flowered perennial plant from 1 to about 5 feet tall, with a deep-growing taproot that is often branching. The leaves are alternate, clasping the hollow stiff branching stems of the plant and mainly clustered low on the plant near ground level.

The flowers are many-petaled, each straplike "petal" being actually a complete flower. They are almost always emphatically blue, the same clear blue as the sky on a hot summer day, but pink or white flowers sometimes turn up. The blooms are short-lived and wilt almost immediately when picked. The flower heads grow from the axils of the leaves on the upper part of the stems.

Find the growing places of chicory when it is in bloom and easily recognizable, and return next spring to gather the tender young leaves for eating, before the flowers appear. Later they are tough and bitter.

After the flowering season is over, get your trusty sharpshooter spade and dig the roots to make a coffeelike beverage. Scrub them well, then lay them out on a wire rack and let them dry for a couple of weeks. An attic is the perfect spot, but I know of one lady who puts hers on a closet shelf. Now chop the dried roots and roast them in an oven set at 300° until they are crisp—about 3 hours. Grind them moderately coarse in a coffee grinder or grain mill, then make "coffee" by the recipe listed in the Index.

Chicory flowers

Chicory
Cichorium intybus

CHINQUAPIN

Species of the *Castanea* genus

Other common names: Chinkapin, Chinkypin.

Where to find it: From Maine to Michigan and west to Illinois and southwest to Texas; down the East Coast to northern Florida. Grows in acid soils, both moist and dry.

Part used: Nuts, gathered after burrs split open in the fall.

How used: Fresh, roasted, or frozen for future use.

The chinquapins are members of the chestnut genus, which is all but extinct in North America because of the chestnut blight. Most chinquapins now found belong to *Castanea pumila*, a species that is more shrubby than treelike and is often no more than 6 feet or so tall. This species produces nuts quite profusely here in the Ozarks. The tree chinquapin, *C. ozarkensis*, which may grow to 60 feet, is native to Arkansas and Missouri and is scarcer than the shrubby form.

Chinquapin bark is light brown with a definite tinge of red. The pale-green leaves are oblong to lance-shaped, and the edges are serrated, coarsely in the case of *C. ozarkensis*. Leaves of both forms are heavily veined, slick on top and slightly furry underneath.

The nuts are borne in prickly greenish burrs which turn brown and split open in the autumn to offer smooth, shiny, dark-brown nuts to those lucky enough to beat the woodland creatures to them. The nuts are thin-shelled and about the size of a large marble. One end is flat and the other is pointed like an acorn. The nutmeats are sweet, tasting much like the European chestnut.

To get the nutmeats, crack the shells, remove the kernels, and pour boiling water over them, allowing them to stand for 2 or 3 minutes. When the skins begin to split, plunge the kernels into cold water, then slip the skins off. I usually roast my chinquapins for about 45 minutes to an hour in an oven set at 250°. They are done when they are the texture of a roasted peanut, slightly hard. They make an excellent addition to dressing for poultry and game birds, are a good nibble, and make a great candied treat.

If you can beat the squirrels to a great number of these nuts, be sure and freeze the surplus, as otherwise they will turn rancid within a month or so.

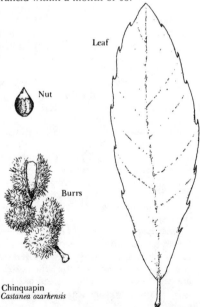

Leaf

Nut

Burrs

Chinquapin
Castanea ozarkensis

CHIVES

Various species of the *Allium* genus

Other common name: Wild Chives.

Where to find it: In temperate-climate areas throughout the United States and Canada.

Parts used: Leaves, spring through fall.

How used: As seasoning, fresh, frozen, or dried.

This little member of the onion or *Allium* genus is common all over the United States and, in fact, all over the world in temperate regions. Chives are those little dark-green, hollow-leaved clumps of onion-scented weeds that can either be a treasure in the garden or an eyesore to the lover of the weedless lawn, where their fluffy lavender flower heads are not considered as decorative as they are in the herb garden. Cultivated chives are sold at garden centers and can also be grown from seed. They are quite hardy and even a beginner can grow them successfully. The chives most often seen are *Allium Schoenoprasum;* botanists also distinguish a species called wild chives, *A. Schoenoprasum* variety *sibiricum.* They look very much alike.

Whether wild or in the garden, chives are available fresh over a long season; you can pot them up in the fall, let them go dormant in the pot, and bring them indoors in midwinter to green up and supply fresh herb flavoring.

It is a simple matter to dry chives for winter use. Here is how we do it at Wildflower. With kitchen shears, we cut a cluster just above ground level (they'll grow back if not cut too low). Tie the stems together with a bit of twine and wash thoroughly. Now snip off any brown tips, untie the bunch, and clip into short pieces, $^1/_{16}$ to ¼ inch long, and to spread them on a wire drying rack or in a colander. Let them dry in a dark, dry, warm place for about a week, or until brittle. Store airtight.

At Tameweed next door, Ann freezes chives after preparing them the way I do for drying. She simply dips out a spoonful from the jar of frozen chives. Use frozen chives in the same amount as fresh; use about three times as many dried chives.

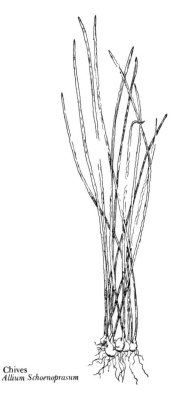

Chives
Allium Schoenoprasum

DANDELION

Taraxacum officinale

Other common name: Priest's Crown.

Where to find it: In lawns, fields, meadows, on roadsides, along railroads, in waste places, throughout the United States and southern Canada.

Parts used: Root, young leaves, buds or crowns, flowers; spring through fall.

How used: Leaves, flowers, and roots fresh, as vegetable; leaves in salads; roots dried, roasted, and ground to make "coffee."

Dandelion derives its English name from the Latin *Dens leonis*, lion's tooth. In its botanical name, *officinale* indicates that it has long been considered a medical remedy.

This golden-flowered menace to lovers of weedless lawns begins growing from its perennial taproot in the very early spring, not only on home grounds but in fields and along roadsides over most of the country. There will be, growing close to the ground, a rosette of irregularly lobed or toothed leaves from which a brilliant yellow-gold, many-petaled daisylike flower pops up on a slick, leafless hollow stem. The flower is surrounded by a necklace of green, reddish-tipped bracts. The lovely flowers yield in time to seed heads that are puffy orbs of silken down. The seeds are easily blown from the stalk by the slightest breeze, accounting for the plant's tendency to spread far and wide.

The dandelion offers many delicacies to those willing to stoop down for them. There's the delicious wine made from the flowers (see the Index for our recipe), but don't neglect the leaves gathered before the flowers open, used in a salad, in a bread-and-butter sandwich, or cooked alone or with other greens. The flower buds can be included in a choice omelet, or fried, or made into fritters. The root, if dug while young, can be boiled as a vegetable. The roots of any age can be scrubbed, dried in a warm, dry place, then roasted in a slow oven—200° to 250°—until crisp and shriveled and deep brown, about 3 to 5 hours. Then grind them coarsely and use them to make dandelion "coffee"—see our recipe (Index).

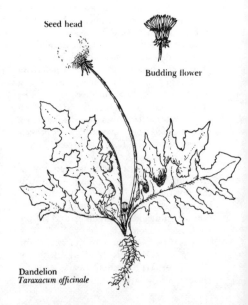

Seed head

Budding flower

Dandelion
Taraxacum officinale

DAY LILY

Various species of the *Hemerocallis* genus

Other names: None.

Where to find it: Day lilies have escaped from cultivation to grow along roadsides, on woodland borders, and near old home sites from New Brunswick west to Ontario and south over much of the United States. They are likely to be found wild wherever they grow in a garden.

Parts used: Buds and flowers, spring and summer; roots, fall and winter.

How used: Buds and flowers fresh, frozen, canned, and dried; buds can be made into pickles. Roots are cooked as a vegetable.

Hemerocallis fulva, the orange day lily, and *H. flava*, the lemon day lily, are common garden plants in a genus that has many hybrids and special varieties. They are often seen outside gardens, from which their strains originally escaped. The name *Hemerocallis* is from the Greek *hemera*, meaning day, and *kallos*, meaning beauty. Indeed each blossom of this beautiful plant survives only for a day, but the blooms come in succession for several weeks from early summer onward. Each flower has 6 petals that overlap slightly and curve backwards as the flower faces upward towards the sun. The long, pale-green, lance-shaped leaves grow in abundance from the perennial rhizomes (roots), which are edible.

The flower buds are the most delicious part of this plant. All sizes of buds may be eaten, although I prefer the smallest ones, picked before the color shows. They may be cooked in any manner in which green beans are fixed, or may be pickled, sautéed, or fried in fritters.

The flowers are prized by the Chinese, who call the dried flowers "golden needles" and use them in several dishes. Here is how to dry either the young buds or the open flowers: String them on a heavy thread, using a darning needle, and hang them in a high, dry place for a week or ten days, until thoroughly dry. Then store the buds or flowers in an airtight container. The open flowers are more easily dried if the petals are picked off and spread in a single layer on a cookie sheet and oven-dried for 4 or 5 hours in a very low oven (130° to 150°). They may also be sun-dried by placing them on a drying rack in the sun for several days, turning them once a day. To reconstitute the buds or flowers for cooking, just soak them in warm water for a few minutes.

In late fall or winter, try digging the edible roots, thinning out your picking patch a little (it will be good for it). Scrub, scrape, and cook the roots until tender. Delicious.

Day Lily
Day Lily leaf

DITTANY

Cunila origanoides

Other common names: Stone Mint, Fever Plant, Headache Tea.

Where to find it: Dittany ranges from southern New York and Pennsylvania as far west as Illinois, Missouri, Oklahoma, and Texas, and as far south as South Carolina, Tennessee, and Arkansas. Look for it on dry rocky soils, in open woods, and occasionally on prairies. Around Wildflower I find it mostly on rocky bluffs and slopes.

Parts used: Leaves and flowers, summer and fall.

How used: Fresh or dried for tea, and as a seasoning or condiment.

This small but showy member of the Mint family should be sought out for its value as a tea plant, even if you don't try the other uses I suggest. It has a characteristic pungent, somewhat minty fragrance when crushed. It isn't easily confused with the other plants commonly called "dittany"—Cretan dittany, or dittany of Crete (*Origanum dictamnus*), which is a garden herb, and the "bastard dittany," fraxinella (*Dictamnus albus*).

Dittany flowers between July and late fall, depending upon the locality; the blooms range from whitish to pale lavender to medium purple. Each tiny flower is clustered with others at the tip of a stiff, square stem or at the base of a pair of small oval or pointed-oval leaves along the stem. The whole plant is branching, low, and woody. It is usually about a foot high, but it may grow to only a few inches or to as much as a foot and a half.

Dittany leaves, either fresh or dried (dry until crisp, then store airtight), make an interestingly strong-flavored herb tea. In taste dittany is only distantly related to the "true" mints such as spearmint and peppermint, and some find it to be closer kin, in flavor, to oregano, for which I sometimes substitute dittany in recipes.

In the past dittany was often used medicinally to relieve fevers and headaches. Sam, a student at the University of Central Arkansas, says that where she grew up in Palestine this herb was used with hot olive oil and salt to make a dip. You'll find her recipe for Palestinian Dittany Dip farther along in the book.

Flower head

Dittany
Cunila origanoides

DOCK

Various species of the *Rumex* genus

Other names: Curly Dock, Common Dock, Sour Dock, Yellow Dock, *Rumex crispus;* Patience Dock, Herb Patience, or Spinach Dock, Passion's Dock, *R. patientia; Water Dock,* Great Water Dock, *R. orbiculatus.*

Where to find it: One or another species of dock is found almost everywhere in the country. Look for great water dock, which can grow to over 6 feet, in swampy areas and around lakes or ponds. Other docks grow in open fields, gardens, vacant lots and other waste spaces, and along roadsides or streams. Curly and patience dock may grow 3 or 4 feet tall under good conditions.

Parts used: Young leaves, gathered mainly in the spring, but also, in sheltered places, in the fall.

How used: Cook as greens.

The docks I'm writing about, all good for the greens pot, are members, along with the true sorrels such as *R. Acetosa*, of the large *Rumex* genus, which includes about 150 species of plants, many edible. Curly dock is probably the best known to foragers, but no matter which dock you find, you have a good edible plant. Some kinds are sweeter in taste than others, but all are desirable if the leaves haven't turned bitter with age.

The young leaves are what we're interested in. They are large, either oblong or lance-shaped, and rather coarse. Some are smooth-edged, but the leaves of curly dock are, naturally, wavy. Dock leaves can be up to a foot long when mature, and

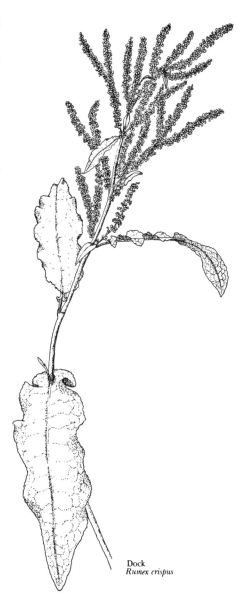

Dock
Rumex crispus

sometimes they show a bit of pink along the veins and near the stem. As the plant matures it puts out a many-branched flower stalk. The seeds, when they develop, are tiny, and each is enclosed in a winged arrangement that allows it to "fly" when ripe to reseed the dock patch. Flowers are a light chartreuse; as seeds develop they range from soft sand color to deep russet, as dark as the darkest brown bear's coat. When ripe they can be gathered and dried as bird feed.

Because dock is a large plant and grows in great patches, one gathering can furnish many meals. Cook dock alone or mix it with other spring greens. It doesn't cook down much, so it's particularly good for canning—just follow standard directions for canning greens. It also freezes well—I enclose it, after blanching, in plastic bags, then wrap it again in freezer paper.

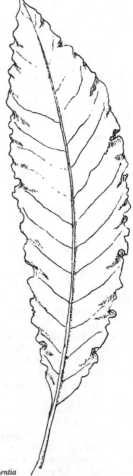

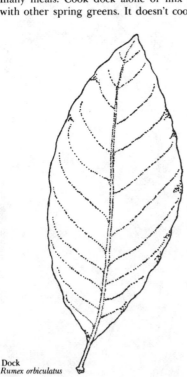

Dock
Rumex orbiculatus

Dock
Rumex patientia

ELDERBERRY

Sambucus canadensis

Other common names: Common Elder, Sweet Elder, Black-berried Elder.

Where to find it: In thickets, open woods, fields and meadows, along streams and fence rows and roadsides in the eastern part of the United States.

Parts used: Flower, in spring. Fruit, in summer and fall.

How used: Flowers in fritters and for wine; fruit, green as a pickle, ripe as juice, in jelly, in desserts, and for wine.

The elder shrub is seldom over 20 feet high, usually much less, and is bushy. Its botanical name may have come from the Greek *sambuce*, the name of a musical instrument—whistles and flutes are easily made from its pithy stems.

The compound leaves of this shrub are reminiscent of sumac, in that there are 5 to 7 pointed and toothed leaflets in each leaf. The leaves grow in opposite pairs on the stems.

The white flowers grow in flat-topped clusters that crown the top of the shrub; their heaviness causes them to droop. They are a mass of fragrant goodness—they may be made into elder-flower wine, or dipped in batter and fried into sweet fritters. The greenish flower buds may be picked before the blooms open, or the green berries picked later; both may be pickled for a condiment much like capers.

The full, dark-blue heads of berries ripen from August, in the South, to October in the North. The ripened berries may be taken off the stems by combing with a very coarse comb, or they may be simply stripped off by running the stems between the fingers. Because elderberries grow in thickets, the harvest is usually plentiful; also, as the shrub transplants easily, you can grow elderberries in your own yard.

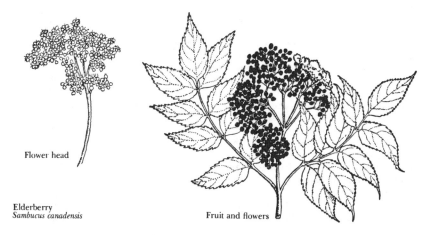

Flower head

Elderberry
Sambucus canadensis

Fruit and flowers

GARLIC

Allium vineale

Other common names: Field Garlic, Wild Garlic, Crow Garlic, Sauce-Alone, Jack-by-the-Hedge, Hedge Garlic.

Where to find it: In meadows, waste places, and along streams, roadsides, and railroads from southern New England south and west to New Mexico, but especially from Pennsylvania to Georgia and west to the Mississippi valley. Also found in the Northwest and in Wyoming.

Parts used: Bulbs and leaves, spring, summer, and fall.

How used: Fresh, frozen, or dried, as seasoning.

This species of wild garlic is often mistaken for chives because both have cylindrical leaves. This garlic leaf is often solid for part of its length, whereas chive leaves are completely hollow. It is brighter green than the bluish chives, and it is fatter and taller, sometimes reaching 2 or 3 feet when in bloom. The flavor is definitely oniony, as is true of all edible members of the *Allium* genus. The bulbs of commercially grown garlic, *A. sativum*, are a good bit larger and fleshier than those of this wild one, but their flavors are alike and they may be used interchangeably. I often use the tops of wild garlic as well as the bulbs. You can dry the tops or freeze them, as directed for chives; and, of course, if you harvest the bulbs, you dry them in the sun for a few days, then store them just as you would onions.

In Spain a few years ago I came upon a farmhouse that had several strings of wild garlic hung around the house and farm buildings. I was told that the family ate the garlic raw and cooked, made a broth of it in the early spring to "purify the blood," and that it also acted as an insect repellant as it hung around the house. In Afghanistan an acquaintance whose grandmother was the village "granny woman," learned in herbs, told us that garlic juice is good on stings of insects and that it is also supposed to cure many ailments, from bad coughs to toothaches.

In the Great Plague of the seventeenth century in England, garlic was believed to prevent the disease. Today, scientists believe that allyl disulfate in the garlic may have served as a germ killer to some degree.

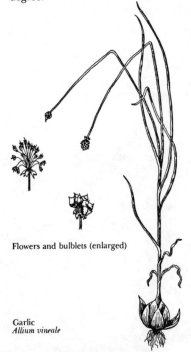

Flowers and bulblets (enlarged)

Garlic
Allium vineale

GRAPE

Various species of the *Vitis* genus

Other names: Summer Grape, *Vitis aestivalis;* Fox Grape, *V. Labrusca;* Frost Grape, *V. cordifolia* and other *Vitis* species; Muscadine and Scuppernong grapes, both *V. rotundifolia.*

Where to find it: Throughout the United States in temperate-climate regions. Found climbing over trees and shrubs, on roadsides, in fence rows.

Parts used: Fruit, late summer and fall.

How used: Fresh or canned for desserts, jams, jellies, beverages.

I shall not even begin to enumerate the innumerable kinds of native grapes. The vines are all similar in looks, though the fruit varies in flavor. Once you have identified a grape vine you'll always know grapes—wild or tame.

Grape leaves are slightly heart-shaped but deeply lobed and generally broader at the base, where the stem joins the leaf. They are heavily toothed and veined, and often the underside is paler than the upper surface of the leaf and is velvety in texture. The plant is usually a heavily vining one, with long woody stems held by curly tendrils to the trees, shrubs, or old fences that support them. The loose sprays of tiny white flowers are rarely noticed when they bloom in early summer, although there are kinds of grapes that send out a pleasant fragrance to heighten the pleasure of a summer night—the scent is more noticeable after the dew has fallen. The flower sprays gradually yield to tiny green grapes, usually in bunches (except for muscadines and scuppernongs) that gradually swell and ripen to the color typical of the particular kind, whether pinkish, blue, or purplish-black. Most grapes have a bloom, or powdery coating, on the fruit; again, the muscadines and their relations, the scuppernongs, lack this.

Wherever you find your grapes, taste them—if they taste good, they'll be fine for use. In a good year you can preserve enough juice, jellies, and jams to last until grape season comes around again. In the Ozarks we can usually expect to have our first grape picking by Labor Day. If you use grapes in as many ways as we do, you will find the picking more fun than labor.

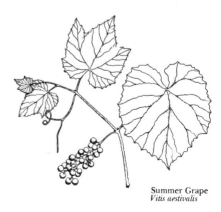

Summer Grape
Vitis aestivalis

GROUND CHERRY

Various species of the *Physalis* genus

Other common names: Husk Tomato, Winter Cherry, Japanese Lantern, Chinese Lantern, Strawberry Tomato, Cape Gooseberry, Bladder Cherry.

Where to find it: From New York and southern New England westward to Minnesota and Iowa, throughout much of the Midwest and southwest to Texas; also in coastal areas and in various scattered regions throughout the country, in both moist and dry soil, in woods and on prairies.

Parts used: Fruits, in late summer or fall, after husks begin to dry.

How used: In jams, jellies, and other preserves; in pies and sauces.

The ground-cherry genus, *Physalis*, contains scores of species, all with edible fruit, distributed all over the mainland United States and in Hawaii too. They differ from each other in details, but all are alike in producing small round fruits inside papery bladders or husks that look like little Japanese or Chinese lanterns. Some ground-cherry plants are annuals, some perennials; some are low and branching, some erect, some vining. The leaves may be smooth or hairy, toothed or lobed, or fairly smooth-edged, and may be tiny or as much as 3 inches long. The flowers, white, yellow, or greenish-yellow, nod from slender stalks at the bases of leaves. They are so slightly lobed that they resemble morning-glory blossoms. The calyx of the flower enlarges into the husk that encloses the fruit. A familiar or-namental plant, the Chinese-lantern plant, with red-orange "lanterns," is a *Physalis*.

The fruits are about the size of small marbles and are pale or golden yellow, or sometimes deep blue, when ripe. The tight-skinned "cherries" have numerous seeds that are soft enough to be no problem. At Wildflower I have picked ground cherries as early as August and as late as mid-November. Elsewhere some kinds may be ripe in early summer, and the fall season may be longer, too. Once you have found them, you may want to plant a row nearby for easy picking. Some seedsmen offer seeds of this plant; and many "wild" ground cherries are descended from garden escapees.

If you gather more ground cherries than you can use at once, spread them out in a cool place and let the husks dry. You can then store the ground cherries for several weeks in a cool, dry place. And you can also freeze them out of the husks—no sugar is necessary.

Flower

Ground Cherry

HENBIT

Lamium amplexicaule

Other common names: Dead Nettle, Dumb Nettle, Archangel.

Where to find it: In moist, rich soil in fields, lawns, and along roadsides throughout most of the United States and parts of southern Canada; commonest from the Great Lakes south, and southeast to Florida.

Parts used: Whole plant above ground level, harvested in early spring.

How used: Fresh in salads; cooked as a vegetable, alone or with other greens.

Henbit is a member of the *Lamium* or dead-nettle genus, which in turn is in the very large Mint family. It is one of the earliest spring greens—it appears as early as mid-February, its leaves at first clustered close to the ground. As the somewhat sprawling square stems begin to grow upward to the ultimate height of less than 18 inches, one becomes more aware of the ruffled leaves, the upper ones partially clasping the stem. The tiny flower buds look like beet colored velvet beads, as small

as a pinhead at first. As the buds open you see silken purplish flowers with long corollas, looking like Jack-in-the-pulpits in miniature. Sometimes this or a closely related species has flowers that are pale purple, pink, or occasionally almost white.

This common dooryard weed can be an important one for the greens pot if you like the distinctive flavor. We serve it both cooked and raw—in a salad using leaves, stems, flowers, and all, its color is enjoyed as much as its flavor. Because this is one of the earliest greens, it should be considered for the table if you have never tried it.

Flower (enlarged)

Henbit
Lamium amplexicaule

HICKORY NUT

Carya species

Other names: Hicker-Nut Tree, Shagbark, Shellbark, or Scaly-Bark Hickory, *Carya ovata;* Pignut, *C. ovalis;* Big Shellbark, *C. laciniosa.*

Where to find it: One or another species grows throughout most of the eastern and midwestern United States; also in the Northwest, from northern California to Canada.

Parts used: Nuts, gathered in late fall and winter.

How used: Fresh or frozen.

The hickory tree produces what we in the South call a "hicker nut," sweet and delicious. Large species may grow 75 to 100 feet tall, but smaller hickories are often found. The hickories called shagbark or shellbark have deeply furrowed bark that separates into shaggy loose plates, giving them their name.

The hickory leaf is compound, with 5, 7, or 9 leaflets to a leaf stem. They are finely toothed and of a dark yellowish-green. They are shiny above, hairy below. The unripe nuts are encased in a thick green hull divided into four sections. When the nut is ripe the hull turns dark and splits open, releasing the thick-shelled nut, which has angles rather than a smooth shape.

The nutmeats are very tasty but hard to remove from the shells. I have a method that makes it less difficult: I fill my pressure cooker three-quarters full of nuts and add water to about a quarter of the depth of the pot. I bring the pressure to 5 pounds and pressure-cook the nuts for 10 minutes.

I let the pressure return to normal, remove the gauge, and let the nuts cool. If you use a pressure pan without an indicator, just pressure-cook for 15 minutes, then let the pressure drop before opening the pot. The shells are now much easier to crack and the meats come out more easily. The nutmeats, which are partially cooked, will be soft. Toast them in a 300° oven for a few minutes if you want crisp nuts. Sort carefully for any bits of the hard shell, which can break a tooth.

If you have a bird feeder, save all your hickory shells to be portioned out in the winter months; titmice and chickadees like nothing better than pecking out any crumbs you have missed, and I have seen a tiny downy woodpecker fight a large red-bellied woodpecker for hickory-nut leavings. I don't blame the birds—this nut is the most flavorful, the nuttiest, of any kind growing wild.

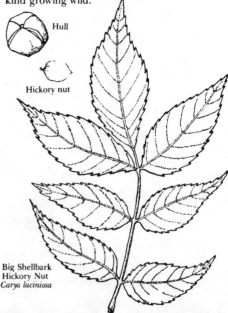

Hull

Hickory nut

Big Shellbark
Hickory Nut
Carya laciniosa

HUCKLEBERRY

Various species of *Gaylussacia* genus

Other names: Dangleberry, Summer Huckleberry, Winter Huckleberry. Sometimes called Farkleberry, Sparkleberry, Squaw Huckleberry, all common names more properly belonging to species of the *Vaccinium* (blueberry) genus.

Where to find it: Widely distributed in the eastern and southern states and on the West Coast from northern California north to Canada and east to the Rockies. Look for it in acid-soil areas, including oak woods and bogs as well as sandy and rocky places, in moist woods, clearings, and burned-over areas.

Parts used: Berries, from early summer to fall.

How used: Fresh or cooked; in desserts, pies, fritters, muffins. Frozen, canned, and preserved in jelly, jams, conserves, syrup.

Many people confuse blueberries (in the *Vaccinium* genus) with huckleberries (*Gaylussacia*). They are somewhat alike, but the one reliable difference between them is the presence of 10 hard little seeds in huckleberries, which are usually black-skinned or nearly so, while blueberries are some shade of blue, often with a powdery bloom on the surface. Blueberry seeds are so soft as to be almost unnoticeable.

Some of the many species of huckleberries can grow to 10 or 12 feet, but most of them prefer to grow in the shade of trees, especially in acid-soil areas, and tend to spread into colonies by means of shoots arising from the roots. Most such huckleberries are small shrubby plants,

some less than a foot high but sometimes up to 3 feet tall. Here in the Ozarks there is one we call summer huckleberry that blossoms in April and fruits in June and July. The fruit is often as large as a green pea and very sweet. Our winter huckleberry fruits in late September after blooming in July. We often have to fight the birds for the late fruit.

Huckleberry leaves are shiny green and oval to lance-shaped and grow on rather twisted branches with reddish-brown, thin bark. The flowers are pinkish white, sometimes green-tinged or reddish, and are bell-shaped and gracefully drooping. The fruit is considerably more mealy in texture than blueberries. Its flavor, too, is different—both berries have their partisans, but both are treasures to be looked for.

Huckleberry
Gaylussacia baccata

JERUSALEM ARTICHOKE

Helianthus tuberosus

Other common names: Artichoke. Sometimes sold in markets as "sun choke."

Where to find it: Throughout most of the country in places with fairly moist soil. Look along roadsides, in fields, along fence rows and in old gardens, and in sunny open areas near streams and ponds.

Parts used: Tubers, dug in late fall after killing frost and throughout the winter.

How used: Fresh in salads, cooked as a vegetable. Combined with fruit in desserts; pickled.

This tall perennial sunflower is less showy than the giant kind with a disk of large seeds in the center. It is sometimes as much as 12 feet high, although plants may not grow past 4 to 6 feet. The yellow flowers, 2 to 3 inches across, appear toward the top of the plant in late summer and through the fall. The leaves are mostly alternate on the stem, but may be entirely or partly opposite; they are broadly lance-shaped. The stalk is sometimes the size of a broom handle at its base.

The tubers don't form until autumn, but it's wise to locate your sunflower patch while the plants are in bloom. Mark it well and return after killing frost for the bounty of tubers, which are easily dug. They look like small, knobby, thin-skinned white potatoes. I have found up to a peck of them under a single plant—they grow so profusely that it's easy to get all you need. The ground where the plant is growing is the best place to store your future supply—just leave them there, and dig what you need from time to time through the winter. In spring the tubers will sprout again and be unfit for eating. At Wildflower we like this vegetable so much that we grow it in our kitchen garden; tubers for planting can be bought from seedsmen, if you can't find them wild.

The Jerusalem artichoke—no kin to the green globe artichoke—is unusual in that it contains the carbohydrate inulin instead of starch, so it can be eaten safely by people who have diabetes. Because of this, as well as its nutlike flavor, it is a favorite of foragers. As a raw snack it is unsurpassed; it pickles well; and it can be fried, boiled, creamed, or scalloped as a vegetable, baked with fruit for dessert, or even made into a pie. Is it any wonder that this is such a find?

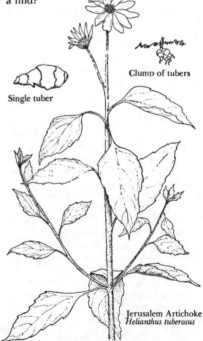

Single tuber

Clump of tubers

Jerusalem Artichoke
Helianthus tuberosus

LAMB'S QUARTERS

Chenopodium album

Other common names: Common Lamb's Quarters, Goosefoot, Pigweed, Wild Spinach.

Where to find it: Along roadsides and railroads, in cultivated fields and waste places and gardens throughout the United States and much of Canada; most common east of the Rockies, except for New England.

Parts used: Leaf, in spring and summer; seed, in early fall.

How used: As greens, fresh, frozen, or canned; seeds are used dried, roasted, and ground.

The leaf is the best means of identifying this plant. It is shaped somewhat like the print of a goose's webbed foot, hence one of its common names. It shares the common names "wild spinach" and "pigweed" with a number of other greens. The lamb's-quarters leaf is blue-green on top and has a white mealy coating on the underside that makes it almost impossible to wet the plant—the water simply stands in droplets, or runs off like "water off a duck's back."

The plant grows as tall as 6 or 8 feet hereabouts, although in places it may be only 3 or 4 feet or so high. The stalk, leaf, and flower heads are often tinted with red late in the season. Gather the whole leaf clusters and tender stems in the spring; then, through the summer, as it puts out new leaves on the sprawling plant, pick those, too, for the pot. The plant is unique in that the leaves stay tender until seed is set in late summer.

The seed heads yield a good cereal food—see the Index for a recipe. In the late summer and early fall, when the seeds begin to dry, I collect them—I just hold them over a cloth spread under the plant and rub the heads to free the seeds. Then I winnow away the husks and trash by pouring the seed back and forth between two baskets in front of a fan or in a good breeze. The hard black seeds should be roasted in a 300° oven for an hour, cooled, then run through a grinder until they are of a fine or medium consistency. Cook the meal as a breakfast cereal, or mix it with regular flour for baking.

Lamb's quarters is gentle by birth, an aristocrat among wild greens; it tastes much like spinach, though it's considerably milder. It can be cooked alone or mixed with other greens, and it cans and freezes well—I use the canning process suggested for spinach in the *Ball Blue Book.* Like other greens, it cooks down, so gather about twice as much as you anticipate using.

Lamb's Quarters
Chenopodium album

LEEK

Allium tricoccum

Other common names: Wild Leek, Ramp.

Where to find it: In rich soils, including rich woods, from southern Quebec through New England, as far west as Minnesota and as far south as Tennessee and Georgia.

Parts used: Leaf and bulb, spring and summer.

How used: Fresh or frozen, as a vegetable and as a seasoning.

The wild leek has little in common with the garden leek (*Allium porrum*) other than the taste. It's much smaller, with leaves seldom more than a foot or so high, and much slimmer. It is much sought after as a vegetable and as a seasoning and is used like the other members of the large *Allium* genus. I use it interchangeably with the garden variety, and it has been transplanted into my kitchen garden and into the rose bed, too, where it's supposed to act as a deterrent of rose diseases.

Wild leeks have the largest leaves of any of the wild onions. They are flat and wide, almost lance-shaped, widening upward from the almost cylindrical bulbs. It is not unusual to find large patches of leeks. The leaves die back before the heads of white flowers, on stems up to 2 feet tall, appear in July. In the South, leeks tend to come into growth again when a few warm days follow the cold of winter, and then they provide tender new leaves for our use.

An intriguing colloquial name for wild leek is "ramp." My friends Martha Hill and Lytholia Norman have told me about a festival called the Ramp Romp that is held in West Virginia, a sure harbinger of spring there in the mountains. The season is celebrated with a ramp hunt and a dinner featuring ramps served in numerous ways, and the Romp is finished off with an evening of storytelling and good old mountain music.

Though this leek is strong smelling, the flavor is mild. I find it the most palatable of all wild onions, and the fragrance of creamed leeks or a leek casserole from Wildflower's kitchen means that spring has arrived. If you like the flavor of garden leeks, you'll love wild leeks.

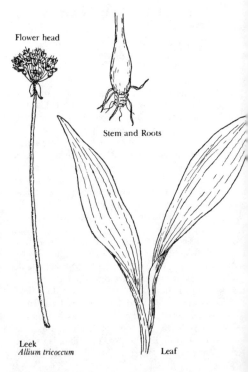

Flower head

Stem and Roots

Leek
Allium tricoccum

Leaf

MAY APPLE

Podophyllum peltatum

Other common names: American Mandrake, Wild Lemon, Wild Jalop, Raccoon Berry, Hog Apple.

Where to find it: In low moist woodlands from Quebec to Minnesota and southwards, especially in New England, but as far as Florida and Texas.

Parts used: Fruit, in summer.

How used: Fresh, frozen, or canned; in jam and jelly.

This woodland plant is a most striking one when seen growing in large colonies. The foot-wide shiny green umbrellas sway lightly in the breeze, often covering acres of ground. The leaves are deeply lobed, in six or more sections, and each is held aloft by a stiff stem attached to its center. When the waxy white flower is open, the perfume is both elusive and heady. The inch-wide flowers appear only on twin-leaved plants, and look as though they were produced in a plastics factory.

Here in the Ozarks the May-apple leaf pushes up through the ground just about when the redbud trees are beginning to tint the winter-grey forest with their dusky pink. The flowers appear in May and are followed by fruits shaped like fat lemons and colored like wild honey; they ripen in late July or in August. As the fruits ripen, the stems weaken and it is not unusual to find that the fruit has pulled the plant almost to the ground.

The fruit is said by many to taste like the semitropical guava, but to me it's unique. There was never a more beautiful jelly than that made from mandrakes (our favorite name for this fruit)—held up to the light, it looks as though sunbeams have been caught and preserved. Mandrake jam or marmalade is not so pretty to look at, but it is deeper in flavor.

Whenever I see mandrakes growing I have visions of pixies and elves waiting out a spring shower under the broad leaves, perhaps even inviting compatible earth creatures to join them. But whether you are looking for elves or fruit, May apples bear looking under at fruiting time. And when you have found the fruit, a slight warning: eat only the fruit. The roots were used as "strong medicine" in the past and, like the stems and leaves, are poisonous.

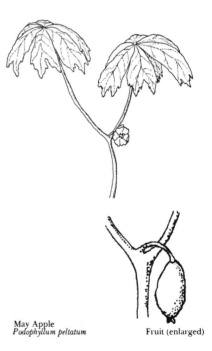

May Apple
Podophyllum peltatum

Fruit (enlarged)

MAYPOP

Passiflora incarnata

Other common names: Passion Flower, Passion Plant, Passion Fruit, Apricot Vine.

Where to find it: South to Florida and Texas from a line through Pennsylvania, Illinois, and Oklahoma; found in fence rows and along roadsides and in fields.

Parts used: Fruit, in late summer.

How used: Fresh, or in marmalade, punches, or frozen desserts.

Maypop flowers are unusual and lovely to look at. Often called passion flowers, they are showy, with white to pale-pink petals and sepals and with a crown or corona of purple or pink threadlike divisions that often extend beyond the edges of the petals. There are five erect stamens. The flower has a fragrance like that of carnations, very attractive to butterflies and bees.

The plant is climbing or trailing, with vigorous stems held by tendrils to any support they can find. The large leaves, up to 5 inches across, are three-lobed and their edges are finely serrated. Occasionally there will be a hint of pink in the veins of the leaves.

The flowers begin their glorious blooming period in June in the South and may bloom as late as September in colder climates. The fruit matures about a month after the plant flowers. Maypops are about the size and shape of a hen's egg, varying a bit in size. They ripen to a deep yellow with a brown tinge. The skin is thickish and slightly tough. When squeezed, the fruit pops open, exposing the seedy, flavorful pulp.

May-popping is a nostalgic delight of many rural Southerners. One of the diversions of long hot summer days was to find this vine and pick the fruit. At first we would pop open the skin and suck the juicy inside, but before long there would be a popping contest—this was to see who could jump on the fruit to make the loudest pop, the quickest pop, the longest pop, and usually ended up by each child trying to pop the other kid first without getting popped back.

Maypop
Passiflora incarnata

MILKWEED

Asclepias syriaca

Other common names: Common Milkweed, Antelope Horn, Silk-weed.

Where to find it: Along railroads and roads, in fields, pastures, woods, and in waste areas. The northern boundary of its range runs from New Brunswick to Saskatchewan and the southern boundary runs from Georgia west to Oklahoma; most common from Georgia north to southern New England and west to the Great Lakes. Other milkweed species are common throughout the United States.

Parts used: Young sprouts under 6 inches high and leaves from plants under 6 inches, in spring; flower buds in late spring and early summer; seed pods before maturity in summer.

How used: As vegetable, fresh or frozen.

The sprouts of the milkweed we're interested in, *Asclepias syriaca* or common milkweed, are downy as they push up in the late spring. The leaves at first clasp the stalk but soon open and continue to grow into an oblong oval shape with a heavy central rib. They grow opposite each other on the stem and remain downy underneath. The young sprouts, with their leaves still unfurled, may be used as a good substitute for asparagus when they are 6 inches or less in height. The young leaves may be added to the greens pot before the plant is 6 inches high.

The flowers of the 2- to 6-foot plant are at the tips and along the upper part of the stems. They appear from June to August, and the fragrant blooms, ranging in color from near-green to purplish-pink, appear for three or four weeks. The separate flowers in the umbels are beautifully shaped, each with 5 little "petals" turning down and 5 others turning up to create an effect of lacy loveliness. There are dozens of flowers in one head.

Before the flowers open, the buds are so tightly clustered that they look a little like a small head of broccoli. They are delicious, and it is often easy to pick a large amount and still leave enough for seed. Like all parts of the milkweed, they require special preparation—see the recipe section. The seed pods of all milkweeds are lance-shaped and are eventually filled with flat brown seeds, each topped by a fluffy wig of silken floss. The pod of *A. syriaca* is both hairy and warty but nevertheless it is unsurpassed as a wild food. Pick it before it matures, while it feels solid to the touch; if it feels like foam rubber, the silk is already forming and the pod won't be good to eat.

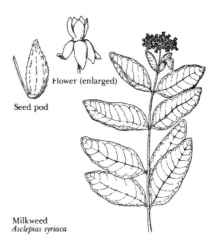

Flower (enlarged)

Seed pod

Milkweed
Asclepias syriaca

MINT

Species of the *Mentha* genus

Other names: Spearmint, Garden Mint, Lamb Mint, Spire Mint, all *Mentha spicata;* Peppermint, Candy Mint, Brandy Mint, all *M. piperita.*

Where to find it: Both these species are found in damp low ground and around springs throughout the United States.

Parts used: Leaves, at any season when in growth.

How used: Fresh as herbal seasoning, in salads, teas, jelly, and punches; dried, in tea and as seasoning.

Someone who knew absolutely nothing about wild plants—or any plants, for that matter—would be able to identify spearmint and peppermint. Out of all the innumerable members of the Mint family, these two have the flavors which, while different from each other, are the ones usually described as "minty."

Spearmint, a European native long established in the New World, grows to about 2 feet, arising from a creeping root stock. It has the square stems of virtually all mints, in this case reddish-tinged. The oval to lance-shaped leaves are a deep green, unevenly toothed on the edges, and almost stemless. The plant has slender spikes of pale pink to lavender blossoms which grow in crowded whorls or circles around the stem, appearing from about June through October. Spearmint-flavored chewing gum and mint jelly are your keys to identification here.

Peppermint also grows from a creeping root stock, but it has a purple tinge in its

Spearmint
Mentha spicata

stems; it can reach 3 feet or so in height. The leaf is a bit darker than that of spearmint and is veined more obviously; it is easy to distinguish from spearmint because each leaf has a stem. Peppermint is the flavor of the ever-popular pink-and-white-striped candy sticks. Peppermint blooms from June through September or October. The flower heads are shorter and fatter than those of spearmint but similar in color.

Mint leaves should be gathered before the plant blooms for the best flavor; if you want to use mint while in bloom, I suggest you use a larger quantity than usual.

To dry mint for tea is a fragrant and rewarding job. Clip the stems near the ground and wash them well through several waters, then shake off all possible moisture. Tie about 10 stems in a bunch and hang them in a high and dry place— we use the open-beamed kitchen at Wildflower—until they are fully dried. Then strip off the leaves and package them airtight for storage out of the light in a cool place.

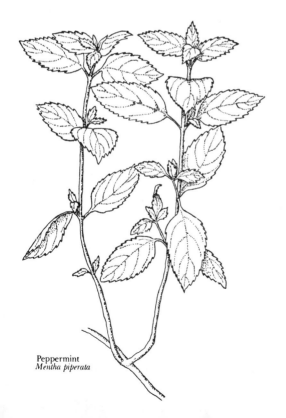

Peppermint
Mentha piperata

MULBERRY

Various species of the *Morus* genus

Other names: Red Mulberry, *Morus rubra;* White Mulberry, *M. alba.*

Where to find it: Red mulberry in fields and along roadsides from Vermont west to Minnesota and South Dakota, south to Florida and Texas. White mulberry in low, wet ground and in fence rows in most parts of the United States.

Parts used: Fruit, gathered in the summer.

How used: Fresh, frozen, or canned; dried.

Although most mulberry trees are under 25 feet in height and are often more like bushes than trees—hence the childhood ditty about the mulberry bush—they can grow much taller. They have rather thin greyish-brown bark that often flakes off the trunk. The leaves are alternate on the branches and are thin and bright green; they vary in shape, sometimes looking almost mittenlike. The flowers appear in catkins and are followed by fruits that look much like blackberries while they are unripe. The white mulberry, when ripe, is most usually white, but it may be pinkish or even purple. The red mulberry fruit is deep purple, or sometimes red.

Mulberries are a very juicy fruit and their seeds aren't the bother that those of blackberries sometimes are. The flavor is unique, and not only does it seem different to different persons, but it may vary from tree to tree. We find it delicious. For some reason Americans have gotten away from eating this berry to any great extent, although it is a staple in other places, Afghanistan for instance. I sometimes wonder why we will fight chiggers, heat, ticks, and briers to pick blackberries, when we could be sitting in the shade of a mulberry bush simply picking the ripe fruit from the ground, or climbing the tree to pluck the berries.

Mulberries are good in pies, cakes, jam, and syrup, and they make a good nibble when dried. Here's a simple way to dry them: Use a darning needle strung with carpet thread with a knot at the end: String first a large button, then the mulberries. Hang the strings outdoors in the warm shade, bringing them in at night; or, if it's rainy, hang them indoors to dry; they will be fully dry in 10 days to two weeks. Once dried, they may be placed in a little warm water to rehydrate, then used as you would use fresh berries.

Red Mulberry
Morus rubra

MUSHROOMS

This introduction to the eight entries in the mushroom section is meant to be an introduction to the identification of mushrooms in general. From this you should go on to use field guides and detailed reference works as you learn which kinds of mushrooms are safe to pick and good to eat. With these plants, more than any others, it is absolutely essential to be correct in your identification before even tasting them, as some mushrooms are harmful and a few species are deadly. You should always follow the rules of safety given here and in all good mushroom books.

Just like green plants, each mushroom has a botanical name, which I have included in each of the entries that follow. The two (or sometimes more) Latin words in each name identify the plant by indicating first its genus—its surname, so to speak—then its species. The naming system for plants is a long-established international one, more than 200 years old, that is brought up to date from time to time. Changes in names are necessary when the taxonomists' analysis of a plant, sometimes including chemical and microscopic tests, show that it belongs to another botanical category from the one to which it has been assigned. A number of such changes have been made for mushrooms, and so the names used in books can be confusing—some good sources may use one name, some the other. So, where there are two or more scientific names for a mushroom, I have given them both, in addition to the best-known common names. Using this scientific nomenclature makes it perfectly clear what plant is meant—when a common name only is used, it might mean one mushroom to one person, but another kind to another person.

The mushroom is a plant without chlorophyll and therefore it cannot manufacture its own food from water, air, and soil minerals, as other plants do. It depends on organic matter, either in the soil or in wood, living or dead, for sustenance. The fruiting body you see growing above the surface of the soil or on trees or stumps is comparable to the fruit of a tree. The "tree" itself—the actual fungus plant—is underneath the ground or within the wood. The plant, called mycelium, arises from a germinated mushroom spore and consists of a network of countless tiny branching filaments. This mycelium, or spawn, gives rise to the fruiting bodies—the mushrooms and other fungi—that produce the spores to start the cycle all over again. The plant, by digesting organic matter, obtains food to increase its own growth, in the process causing the decay of wood or other matter that supports the cycle.

Several common types of fruiting bodies are shown in the illustration (Fig. 1). The fungi discussed in this section are all one or another of these types.

Most common mushrooms have a stem and a cap; however, some, such as the puffball and the oyster mushroom, have little or no stem. Some common types of stem attachments are illustrated (Fig. 2). Some typical cap shapes are also shown (Fig. 3).

Most edible fungi have gills, pores, or teeth on the underside of the caps, with cells containing microscopic organs from which the spores emerge. (Sometimes, however, as in the puffballs, the spore-producing tissue is inside the fungus.) The gilled mushrooms include many kinds of

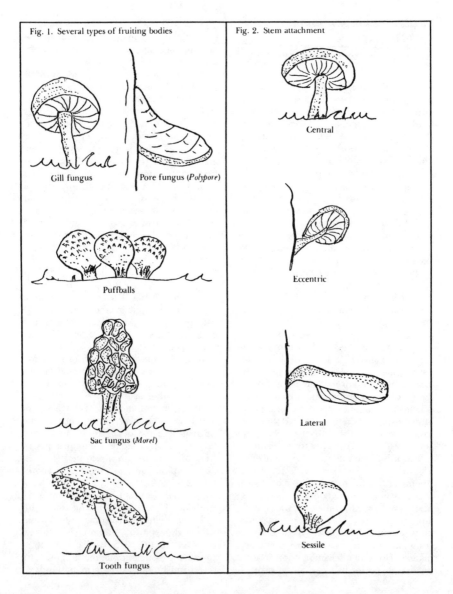

Fig. 1. Several types of fruiting bodies

Gill fungus   Pore fungus (*Polypore*)

Puffballs

Sac fungus (*Morel*)

Tooth fungus

Fig. 2. Stem attachment

Central

Eccentric

Lateral

Sessile

interest to the pot hunter. The gills are attached in various ways that can help in identification; some types of gill attachment are shown in Fig. 4.

One of the keys to identifying a mushroom is the color of the spores. To ascertain this, we make spore prints: Take a piece of black paper and a piece of white paper and lay them flat where they will be undisturbed. Cut the stems off the mushrooms near the cap and place the caps, gill or pore side down, on the paper, some on each color of paper. Cover the caps with a bowl or other protection and leave them for several hours or overnight. When you lift off the cover and remove the caps, there will be delicate prints formed by the microscopic spores.

Dark spores will be more apparent on white paper; light ones will show up best on the dark paper. Spore colors range in many shades from white to pink, brown, black, or even purple, depending on the species of mushroom. One of the loveliest gifts I have ever received was a delicate purple spore print that Toby had preserved by spraying it with the fixative used for pastel drawings.

Puffballs, of course, can't be spore-printed, but they are perhaps the safest mushrooms for the beginning pot hunter to eat. However, before eating *any* but very large puffballs, this precaution must be taken for each specimen: Slice it right down the middle, from top to base, and look at the flesh. It will appear solid if it is a

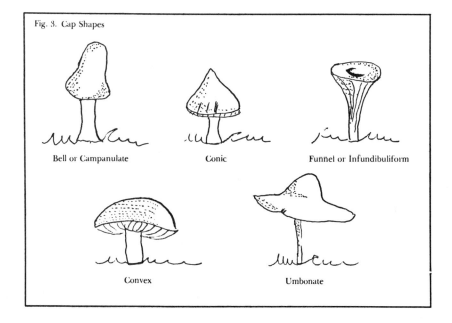

Fig. 3. Cap Shapes

Bell or Campanulate

Conic

Funnel or Infundibuliform

Convex

Umbonate

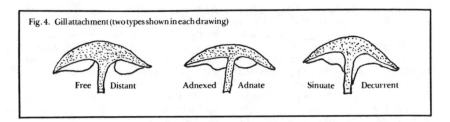

Fig. 4. Gill attachment (two types shown in each drawing)

Free   Distant   Adnexed   Adnate   Sinuate   Decurrent

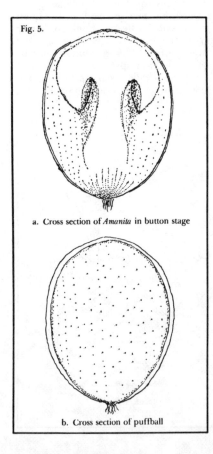

Fig. 5.

a. Cross section of *Amanita* in button stage

b. Cross section of puffball

puffball; if the fungus is the button stage of one of the deadly members of the *Amanita* genus, there will be the outline of a cap and stem (Fig. 5). Needless to say, discard any specimen showing the outline, and wash your hands, the knife, and anything that has touched the mushroom.

RULES. These rules should ALWAYS be observed when you hunt mushrooms for the table:

1. Know your mushroom: identify it positively before eating or even tasting it. In the beginning, repeatedly identify new specimens of the same kind until you know the mushroom in all its stages and can recognize it instantly.
2. To identify a mushroom, cross-check it in at least three reliable guides. Make a spore print. Repeat these steps with fresh specimens as you find them until you know the mushroom perfectly.
3. Eat only fresh specimens that are firm and sound, not at all decayed or worm- or insect-eaten. Spoiled mushrooms of a good species can be harmful.
4. Never mix different kinds of mush- rooms in the same container when collecting—separate them in paper or plastic bags. This is to prevent the contamination of edible species with those that may prove to be inedible or even poisonous.
5. When trying a new, fully identified

species of mushroom, eat only a small portion, well cooked, and don't mix it with any other kind of mushroom. This is to determine if the particular kind of mushroom agrees with you—a given kind may be one man's food and another man's poison.

It's simplest to learn to find and identify mushrooms in company with a seasoned hunter, one who knows the rules and who has eaten his finds safely, but this isn't always possible. Because I did not know anyone who gathered and ate wild mushrooms, I studied mushroom books for several years before I ventured into the kitchen to cook my first ones. Books are still essential (some good ones are listed below), but the rules set out here and the information in the separate mushroom articles should save you time. The eight species and their edible relatives that I discuss below are considered simple to identify, and all are completely safe for the table.

RECOMMENDED BOOKS:

The Mushroom Hunter's Field Guide, by Alexander H. Smith. The University of Michigan Press, Ann Arbor, Michigan, 1963.
Mushrooms of North America, by Orson K. Miller, Jr. E. P. Dutton & Co., New York, 1972.
Collins Guide to Mushrooms and Toadstools, by Morten Lange and Bayard Hora. William Collins Sons & Co., Ltd., London, 2nd edition, 1965.
Non-flowering Plants, by Floyd S. Shuttleworth and Herbert S. Zim. Golden Press, New York, 1967.
"Bizarre World of the Fungi," by Paul A. Zahl, *National Geographic,* October, 1965. (Back issues are available.)

CHANTERELLE

Species of the *Cantharellus* genus.

Other names: Chanterelle, Golden Chanterelle, Yellow Chanterelle, all *Cantharellus cibarius;* Vermilion Chanterelle, Red Chanterelle, both *C.cinnabarinus.*

Color of fruiting body: Vermilion chanterelle is vermilion red, sometimes fading to pink. Chanterelle or golden chanterelle is egg-yolk yellow, sometimes fading to a paler shade.

Shape of cap: Vermilion chanterelle is at first rounded, then funnel-shaped, sometimes with a wavy margin. Golden chanterelle is funnel-shaped, with a wavy margin.

Color of spores: Vermilion chanterelle, red; golden chanterelle, yellow.

Gill attachment: Decurrent.

Where to find it: Under both conifer and hardwood trees. In the Pacific Northwest and southwest Canada, in fall and winter; in the Midwest and East in spring and fall; in the South in spring, fall, and occasionally winter.

How used: Fresh, either raw or cooked; dried, canned, or pickled.

The chanterelles differ from most gill fungi in that the gills are always blunt rather than sharp-edged. They may appear like ridges and they always run down the stem of the mushroom. These two species of *Cantharellus* are small mushrooms, especially the vermilion chanterelle, with caps seldom more than about 3 inches across and with stems up to 3 inches long. They are often found growing thickly—I've seen patches covering an

Vermilion Chanterelle
Cantharellus cinnabarinus

entire hillside. It is a breathtaking sight to come suddenly upon a carpet of lush green moss covered with these brilliantly colored jewels of nature.

These beautiful funnel-shaped mushrooms have the texture of velveteen—there is no sheen on the surface of the caps. They can be differentiated from the poisonous *Clitocybe illudens*, the Jack-o'-Lantern, whose cap is of a similar color, because the latter mushroom has gills that are very sharp and crowded, unlike those of chanterelles, and it also glows in the dark.

I have found the vermilion chanterelle growing in fairy rings, those patterns that evoke thoughts of fairies and elves, fiddlers and flutes. These rings are formed by several kinds of mushrooms when the mycelium grows outward in a circle that widens year by year. They are fascinating, regardless of the kind of mushroom growing in the ring, which may be many feet across.

Other edible mushrooms of this genus: *Cantharellus clavatus, C. floccosus; C. subalbidus.*

JUDAS'S EAR

Auricularia auricula-judae. Also called *Hirneola auricula-judae.*

Other common names: Jew's Ear, Cloud Ear, Tree Ear, Little Ear.

Color of fruiting body: Beige, rust, or orange-tan.

Shape of fruiting body: Roughly spatulate or ear-shaped.

Color of spores: White.

Where to find it: In late fall and winter, on dead or dying wood; throughout temperate areas of the United States.

How used: Fresh or dried, as a vegetable.

The fungus called Judas's ear is translucent, cartilaginous, and shaped somewhat like the human ear. The surface is damp and velvety and often has veins. The under surface is lightly filmed with a white dusty coating. The size of this fungus may be anywhere between an inch long and twice the size of a human ear.

A fairly common fungus, the Judas's ear is found around Wildflower mostly on deciduous trees, although it is reported to grow on conifers too. It is not unusual to come upon a dead or dying tree limb covered with several pounds of "tree ears."

Judas's Ear
Auricularia auricula – judae

It produces especially abundantly in damp and cool-to-cold seasons; it is at its peak here in the fall and winter.

One of the things that appeal to me most about this fungus is that it is so easily preserved by drying. I simply place the fresh, fleshy specimens whole on a wire drying rack in a dry place (not in the sun) and let them remain until they are brittle; this usually takes about a week. They shrink to the size of cornflakes; when rehydrated in warm water they'll return to their original size and shape. I've kept them stored dry in sealed jars for years with no ill effect on their flavor.

Ear mushrooms—also called tree ears and cloud ears—are great favorites in the Orient, and were among the first Far Eastern foods to be exported. You can find them in stores selling Oriental specialties. If you can't find them wild, you may want to try a package of the imported ones. Use this fungus, fresh or dried, in dishes cooked with liquid—it becomes inedibly tough when fried.

The tree ear was once thought to grow primarily on elder trees. Because Judas hanged himself on an elder, so goes the legend, the fungus grows on that tree to remind us of his betrayal of Christ. Hence the name "Judas's ear," often corrupted to "Jew's ear."

MEADOW MUSHROOM

Agaricus campestris. Also called *Psalliota campestris.*

Other common names: Champignon, Pink Bottom.

Color of fruiting body: Creamy-white, sometimes flecked with brown.

Shape of cap: Convex to umbonate.

Color of spores: Purplish-brown.

Gill attachment: Free.

Where to find it: Throughout the United States, in open fields, meadows, lawns, and golf courses, from late spring to fall.

How used: Fresh or frozen, as a vegetable.

The meadow mushroom is similar in appearance to its relative, *Agaricus bisporus,* the most widely grown commercial mushroom. Its cap is dry and creamy white, and may be silky smooth to minutely hairy. Flecks of cinnamon brown often appear near the center of the cap. The cap is from 1 to 4 inches across.

The fibrous stem is seldom taller than the diameter of the cap. This stout stem is also dry-surfaced, and it has a ring around it; sometimes it is hairy below the ring, but

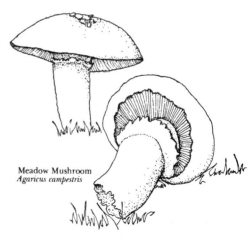

Meadow Mushroom
Agaricus campestris

never above it. There may be fragments of tissue on the edge of the cap and on the ring. These are the remains of the veil which covers the gills in the early, button stage of growth. During expansion of the cap the veil breaks and the pink gills become obvious and are a strong identifying factor. At this stage the mushroom is perfect for eating. The gills gradually darken to dusky rose and then to deep chocolate brown.

Meadow mushrooms are most often found in open sun in cleared areas, such as lawns and golf courses. If you decide to check out the local golf course, I suggest you inquire at the clubhouse first for permission—golfers are not ardent admirers of mushroomers on the course! Many parks, too, have good spots to look for meadow mushrooms.

The novice pot hunter who has followed the rules of identification need have no fear of this mushroom, which is a good one with which to begin. In the South and the Southwest begin looking for it in the late spring. Farther north and east it will begin to appear later. As long as the days continue to be warm and there is nightly dewy moisture, you can expect to find the meadow mushroom, even into the fall.

Other edible mushrooms of this genus: *Agaricus silvaticus, Agaricus rodmani, Agaricus arvensis, Agaricus augustus.*

MOREL

Morchella esculenta

Other common names: Common Morel, Sponge Mushroom, Dry-Land Fish (Ozarks), Landfish; Dowali (Cherokee).

Color of fruiting body: Beige, tan, or creamy white; ridges between pits are occasionally lighter.

Shape of cap: Conical.

Color of spores: Yellowish.

Where to find it: Throughout the United States in temperate-climate areas. Frequently in old orchards, lightly wooded areas, burned-over places. Season is about late February in the South, May farther north.

How used: Fresh and dried, as a vegetable.

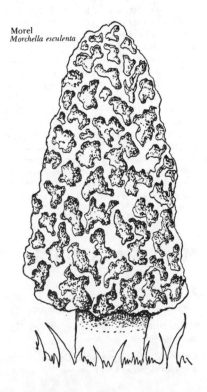

Morel
Morchella esculenta

This morel is one of the most sought-after fungi wherever it will grow. Its cap is an elongated cone and is distinctly pitted, much like a sea sponge or a weatherbeaten piece of honeycomb. The color of this species, the common morel, ranges from cream to tan. The caps of other edible morels may be cinnamon, rust, or even nearly black. The cap is joined firmly and continuously to the stalk, which, firm like the cap, is hollow. Morels are from 2 to 6 inches tall at maturity.

The morel season is short, seldom more than a month long. This fungus requires a near-perfect combination of temperature and moisture at just the right season if it is to produce abundantly. Morels are on the super-safe list for novice mushroomers. Only one other mushroom resembles them—*Gyromitra esculenta* (*Helvella esculenta*), and the resemblance is superficial. The cap of *G. esculenta*, the false morel, is wrinkled and lacks the pits of the true morel. Some people are sensitive to false morels, so I don't recommend them for eating.

Because morels are hollow they are a particular delight to the cook, as they lend themselves to stuffing—see some of our recipe ideas. Never eat morels raw—and before cooking always steep them in boiled, salted water as directed in the recipes.

If you are lucky enough to find more morels than can be eaten fresh, string them on heavy thread, using a darning needle. Hang your morel garland in a dry place until the pieces are brittle, then store airtight. When you use them, prepare them as you would fresh raw morels, soaking them first in salted hot water.

Other edible morels: *Morchella angusticeps*, *M. conica*, *M. hybrida*, *Verpa bohemica*.

OYSTER MUSHROOM

Pleurotus ostreatus

Other common name: Oyster Cap.

Color of fruiting body: Caps white through creamy to tan or brown, occasionally gray; white gills.

Shape of cap: Fan-shaped, or like the half-shell of an oyster. Many caps in each fruiting body.

Color of spores: White, with a tinge of pale lavender or lilac.

Gill attachment: Decurrent.

Where to find it: Throughout the United States; found on dead or dying trees, especially hardwoods. Most abundant in spring and fall; may appear in other seasons.

How used: Fresh or dried, as a vegetable.

The oyster mushroom is both a town and country dweller. It is found on dead and dying trees, especially hardwoods, but also on some conifers. It likes company, so it grows in dense clusters of caps, crowded and overlapping. These yield abundantly in successive growths.

Each cap may be like a shell or a fan, but they vary in form. The edges often curve down and are slightly fluted. The caps are smooth, but the stems may be slightly woolly at the base. The caps range from an inch to about 6 inches in diameter, although caps a foot or more across aren't unknown. The flesh is white, juicy, and dense. (Small, young specimens are best for the pot, naturally.) The white gills are branched and fan out toward the outer edge of the cap. Toward the stem the gills become crowded, practically fused to-

Oyster Mushroom
Pleurotus ostreatus

Oyster mushrooms can grow in incredible abundance. I was leading a Sierra Club group on a field trip one hot August day when we came upon a small river lined with dead and dying elms and sycamore trees that were covered with great beige oyster mushrooms. We gathered more than two bushels on the spot. Someone had come prepared with iron skillet, seasonings, and butter, and we built a campfire on a large flat rock in the river. We all took turns sautéing mushrooms, eating them, and wading in the water. It was one of the nicest hot summer afternoons I can remember.

Oyster mushrooms are distributed widely over the country and may be found in all seasons in parts of the South, Southwest, and West. Hereabouts they are often found in the winter and are still good even if frozen. Seasoned "oyster hunters" keep a lookout in the woods for a loose "oyster log," one they can take home, where it may be watered to keep the mycelium producing a continuous supply of mushrooms.

Other edible mushrooms of this genus: *Pleurotus sapidus, P. ulmarius, P. salignus, P. pulmonarius.*

PUFFBALL

Species of the *Calvatia* and *Lycoperdon* genera

Other names: Giant Puffball, Snuff Box, Devil's Snuff Box, all *Calvatia gigantea* (also called *Lycoperdon maximum*); Small Puffball, Jeweled Snuff Box, Studded Puffball, Gemmed Puffball, all *Lycoperdon perlatum.*

Color of fruiting body: White or creamy white, beige, or tan.

gether. The stems are stout and vary in length according to the position of the cap in a cluster. At first spongy, later woody, they are inedible, and should be cut away, together with any damaged parts of the cap.

Shape of fruiting body: Globular.

Color of spores: Olive, olive-brown, yellow ochre, brown to purplish-brown.

Where to find it: On the soil surface, sometimes on decayed wood, throughout the United States. Look in lawns, meadows, old pastures, and in waste spots. Fruiting season mainly summer, but varies according to locality and growing conditions.

How used: Fresh, as a vegetable.

Puffballs, large or small, are intriguing fungi. They fall into the classification of "stomach fungi" because of their pouchlike structure. Although puffballs vary from species to species in size, shape, color, and texture of skin, and the color of the spores, in general they look alike. A puffball is at first a firm fleshy globe covered by tough skin. There is little or no stem. Some species have smooth skin; others have a rough, cracked, patterned, studded, or hairy surface. The flesh of all edible

Giant Puffball
Calvatia gigantea

puffballs is white and firm, then it gradually turns a deeper and deeper yellow, then to a greenish-brown slime. Soon it becomes dry and powdery, resembling snuff. This powder consists of the spores, produced inside the fungus.

Puffballs are edible only while the flesh is snow-white; they become bitter with the first faint tinge of yellow. No true puffballs are known to be poisonous, though some are not good to eat. (All species listed here are edible.) Before using small or medium puffballs, always observe this rule of safety: Cut open each one from top to bottom to be sure that it doesn't contain the outline of a cap and stem, which could mean that it is the "button" stage of one of the deadly members of the *Amanita* genus.

Calvatia gigantea (*Lycoperdon maximum*) is the largest of the puffballs, quite often weighing 3 or 4 pounds and known to grow to many times that weight. The skin is white and smooth, and it may be tough enough to make it necessary to peel the puffball before cooking. *L. perlatum* is probably the most common small puffball. It is round to pear-shaped and usually has

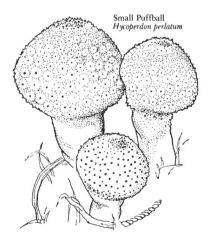

Small Puffball
Hycoperdon perlatum

a short stem. Its white skin is studded with cone-shaped spines that are easily brushed off. It may be as small as a pea or up to 2 inches across. It grows in clusters and is easy to collect in abundance.

Other edible puffballs: *Calvatia craniiformis*, *C. caelata*, *C. cyathiformis; Lycoperdon pyriform; Calbovista subsculpta.*

SHAGGY MANE

Coprinus comatus

Other common names: Shaggy Ink Cap, Shaggy Beard, Lawyer's Wig.

Color of fruiting body: White or greyish, with darker scales ranging in color from pinkish to brown.

Shape of cap: At first club-shaped or a long oval, later expanding to a bell shape with split edges.

Color of spores: Black.

Gill attachment: Free.

Where to find it: In rich or well-fertilized soil or compost piles, in lawns, gardens, along edges of roads, in most temperate regions of the country. Fruits in summer and fall, sometimes in spring.

How used: Fresh, or frozen after cooking.

This shaggy mushroom is a lovely sight to behold. As it first pushes from the ground its stem is entirely covered by the clublike cap. As the cap slowly expands and splits at the edges, it becomes so scaly that it looks much like a curling wig, with its strands turning up slightly at the ends. The cap is at first white to grey, and as the scales appear they gradually darken from

Shaggy Mane
Coprinus comatus

pinkish beige to brown. The color of the crowded, sharp-edged gills gradually changes to rosy pink, then to black as the mushroom passes the eating stage. After this point the edge of the cap begins to slough off and, with the gills, dissolves into an inky fluid in the process called autodigestion. This process is quick—the cap melts away into an inky-black blob within a two-day period after the shaggy mane reaches maturity. It is interesting to note that members of the *Coprinus* genus were once used to make writing ink; the blackish mature mushrooms were boiled in a little water and the fluid was then strained off to use as ink.

The cap of the shaggy mane may be from 2 to 6 inches long, and the hollow stalk is usually 5 to 7 inches long, sometimes more. The stalk has a movable ring that often slips off with maturity. These mushrooms occasionally grow singly, but more often I have found them in clusters. They grow tallest on fertilized lawns or on compost piles.

Shaggy manes are delicately flavored and should be picked for eating before any signs of inkiness appear, and they should be cooked promptly. As with all mushrooms, eating deteriorated specimens could cause an upset stomach. Some species of *Coprinus* may cause nausea when accompanied by alcoholic beverages at a meal, so I recommend abstinence from alcohol when eating mushrooms belonging to this genus.

Other edible mushrooms of this genus: *Coprinus atramentarius, Coprinus micaceus.*

SULPHUR SHELF

Polyporus sulphureus. Also called *Laetiporus sulphureus.*

Other common names: Sulphur Polypore, Sulphur Cap, Chicken of the Woods, Chicken Mushroom.

Color of fruiting body: Yellow and orange; sometimes creamy in part.

Shape of fruiting body: Spatulate and sessile.

Color of spores: White.

Gill attachment: Caps have a pore layer on the undersurface rather than gills.

Where to find it: On deciduous trees, usually dying or dead, in the late summer and autumn throughout temperate regions of the United States.

How used: Fresh or frozen, as vegetable.

This most showy of mushrooms is the beauty of the fall. Its fanlike caps, with yellow pores rather than gills on their lower surfaces, grow in large clusters or in layers, with the caps overlapping each other. The caps may measure 6 to 8 inches across and will be firm and fleshy, often an inch thick at the nearly stalkless base.

The colors of the caps add brilliance to the autumn woods. The fruiting body is usually multicolored, in shades of red and yellow ranging from reddish-orange to creamy near-white. It is attached to the tree by a tough base, which is inedibly hard. In preparing the sulphur shelf for cooking, discard any worm-eaten parts and check to be sure you're using only the tender parts of the caps, which are often only the edges. Discard any woody portions—they won't become tender no matter how long you cook them.

The sulphur shelf can be used interchangeably with oyster or meadow mushrooms or chanterelles. This fungus is different in character from the tree ears (Judas's ear), morels, and puffballs, but it is good in most recipes calling for mushrooms.

Other edible mushrooms of this genus: *Polyporus frondosus (Polypilus frondosus), Polyporus umbellatus (Polypilus umbellatus).*

Sulphur Shelf
Polyporus sulphureus

MUSTARD

Various species of the *Brassica* genus

Other names: Wild Mustard, all species. Brown Mustard, Indian Mustard, both *Brassica juncea;* Black Mustard, *B. nigra;* White Mustard,*B. hirta;* Charlock,*B. Kaber.*

Where to find it: Throughout North America, in fields, gardens, waste places, and along roadsides and railroads.

Parts used: Leaves in spring and summer; seeds in late summer and fall.

How used: Leaves fresh, frozen, or canned, as a vegetable; seeds dried and used as spice, or ground for use as condiment.

There is a superabundance of species and varieties of mustard, often growing in unbelievable copiousness. The genus *Brassica* is extravagant in the number of its members, many of which resemble each other. In addition it includes many vegetables of widely varying appearance, including turnips and broccoli and the rest of the tribe of cabbages.

All mustards have spikes of four-petaled yellow flowers, growing along the stems and at their tops. The flowers are followed by small beaked spear-shaped seed pods about half an inch long. These hold the seeds, which are pale to dark brown when they are ripe. Mustard seed is used in pickling and for making many kinds of prepared mustard. The plant grows from 2 to 6 feet high, according to the species and growing conditions, and branches widely. The leaves vary in shape—some are almost oval, some lobed, some coarsely cut, but all have a similar

flavor. Often the leaves will be a bit bristly to the touch, but when young they are a fine pot herb. If you keep plants cut back, there will be several crops of young leaves for the table.

Originally a European plant, mustard quickly became naturalized in the New World and was once used mainly for medicinal purposes. The crushed seed was mixed into a paste—mustard plaster—to spread over sore muscles or a congested chest.

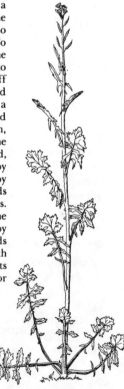

The wild seed is still worth gathering to be made into a condiment—see the recipe section—or to use in pickling. To harvest it, when the seed pods begin to turn yellow, clip off the seed stalks and hang them up in a cloth bag, or spread them out in a warm, dry place. When the pods are fully dried, remove the seeds by beating the bag or by rubbing the pods between the hands. Then winnow out the pods and trash by pouring the seeds back and forth between two baskets in a breezy place (or use an electric fan).

Brown Mustard
Brassica juncea

ONION

Allium stellatum

Other common name: Wild Onion.

Where to find it: This species is found in limestone bluff and glade areas from Ontario and Saskatchewan south to a line drawn from Ohio southwest to Texas. Related species are widely distributed over North America.

Parts used: Bulbs and tops, spring and summer.

How used: Fresh, as a vegetable or as seasoning.

This particular wild onion—there are many related species, all generally called "wild onion"—is similar to garden onions in that it has a definite bulb at the base. Its leaves are slender and grasslike rather than hollow like those of some of the other wild members of the *Allium* genus, such as chives and field garlic. The leaves are quite sparse. The round heads of flowers, greenish white to pinkish or lavender, appear in July and August atop the plants, which are usually a foot or so high. Often the foliage dries up at blossoming time, but the flower head remains to mark your spot for digging the bulbs right through to fall. Use this onion just as you would any tame sort, and see our recipes for using the small bulbs as a vegetable.

Onion plants grow all over the world where conditions are suitable, so I don't suppose it should be too surprising that onions should be widely used as a tonic. I have found that the folk of the Ozarks, Appalachians, and Rockies in the United States share a bit of onion lore with the people of the Sierra del Grados in Spain and the mountain people of Afghanistan. This is the use of onion tea or broth as a spring tonic. It's made by boiling fresh or dried chopped onion bulbs in a bit of salted water, then straining off the liquid to drink.

The *Allium* genus is quite large, and it's easy to mix up its members, which include chives, leeks, and garlic as well as onions. But in gathering all of these plants the aroma is the key. Does it look anything like any onion you ever saw, and does it smell like an onion? Your taste will be your real guide, and you will not go wrong.

Wild Onion
Allium Stellatum

PAPAW

Species of the *Asimina* genus

Other common names: Paw-Paw, False Banana, Custard Apple.

Where to find it: *Asimina triloba* grows from New York State west to Michigan and eastern Nebraska, and south to Florida and Texas; it is occasionally found in the Northwest. *A. parviflora* is found on the coastal plain from southern Virginia as far south and west as Florida and Mississippi. Look for papaw in moist, rich woods, on wooded slopes along streams, in ravines, under bluffs, and, on the coastal plain, in pine woods.

Parts used: Fruit, in the fall.

How used: Fresh or cooked, as dessert or snack.

This tall shrub or slender smallish tree from 8 to 30 feet tall looks as though it had escaped from a more tropical world than ours. Often growing in thickets, it has smooth bark splotched with grey and brown; old trees have a fissured texture. Commonly you'll find papaws growing in the shade of larger trees.

The leaves of a papaw tree are alternate on the branches and are narrow at the base, broadening past the middle of the leaf. The leaf of *Asimina triloba* tapers to a point, while that of *A. parviflora* is broader, almost oval, and smaller. Both are shiny deep green with well-marked veins; leaves of *A. triloba* may be 8 to 12 inches long. Each papaw branch has a leaf cluster at the end.

The flower is deep purplish or maroon, almost brown, and looks like one three-petaled flower placed inside another. The flowers appear singly or in pairs in April or May. Papaw fruits are at first green, then yellow, then yellowish-brown when ripe. They look very much like smallish baking potatoes misplaced in a tree. They are from 4 to 6 inches long, with yellow pulp that is custardlike in texture and with several large, rather oblong seeds that are easily extracted. The fruit has a very distinct fragrance and taste—it is quite unlike any other fruit I've ever eaten. It really tastes tropical, and that's understandable, as its genus is the only temperate-zone member of the Custard Apple family of plants, which includes many of the best tropical fruits, including the true custard apple from which the papaw has borrowed one of its common names.

Gather papaws green, to be ripened at home, or gather them ripe, then prepare for a treat. Many of us jumped rope as children to the little rhyme, "Picking up paw-paws/Putting them in a basket." To put this fruit in a basket and bring it home to eat raw or cooked is every bit as much fun as jumping rope to the old-time ditty.

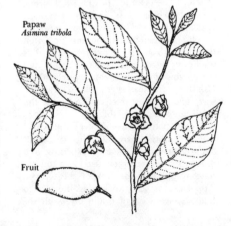

Papaw
Asimina tribola

Fruit

PECAN

Carya illinoensis

Other common names: None.

Where to find it: In moist river bottoms, prairies, woodlands, and open fields from Florida to Texas, and north to Ohio, Indiana, Illinois, and Iowa.

Parts used: Nuts, gathered in fall and early winter.

How used: Fresh or frozen.

The pecan is in the same genus as the hickory and, like the hickory tree, it is also large and branching, attaining a height of more than 100 feet under favorable growing conditions. Its leaves are compound and up to 20 inches long, with 11 to 17 leaflets, which are finely toothed and slightly sickle-shaped. They have a pungent odor if bruised. The bark of young trees is smooth, but with age it becomes deeply ridged. The tree is widely cultivated both for its nuts and its wood, which is used for making boxes and crates as well as fine furniture.

The brown-shelled nut is at first enclosed in a four-winged husk, which usually splits and falls away from the nut before harvest time. The long oval nut is from 1 to 2 inches long and has a sharp point at one end. The shell is thin and easily cracked with a conventional nutcracker. The kernel is sweet; and because it comes out of the shell so easily, it is simple to shell large quantities of pecans for making pies, cookies, and candies and for eating fresh.

Because the nut falls from the tree when it is ripe and the hull breaks away naturally, this is the easiest of all nuts to gather in abundance. Daddy Taylor says that if the hull remains on a nut that has fallen from the tree, it is because the kernel is defective; so you can count on the hulless nuts on the ground to be the good ones. I usually store the nuts in the shell for two weeks or more before cracking them; they tend to taste better after this drying period.

After the kernels are removed from the shells, it is wise to freeze them if you don't use them soon; they tend to turn rancid within a couple of months if not frozen. Look in the recipe section for some really delicious pecan recipes.

Nut in husk

Nut

Pecan
Carya illinoensis

PEPPER GRASS

Various species of the *Lepidium* genus

Other names: Field Pepper Grass, Pepperweed, Field Pepperweed, Field Cress, Cow Cress, all *Lepidium campestre;* Pepper Grass, Virginia Pepperweed, Poor Man's Pepper, all *L. virginicum.*

Where to find it: Various species in dry soils, on roadsides, waste grounds, in clearings and fields virtually throughout the United States and southern Canada.

Parts used: Leaves as salad or pot greens, in spring; seed pods as seasoning, fresh or dried.

How used: Leaves fresh; seeds fresh or dried.

Pepper Grass
Lepidium virginicum

The leaves of this member of the large Mustard family vary from species to species and even from habitat to habitat. The lower leaves of *Lepidium campestre* make a rosette pattern at ground level and are broadly lance-shaped above, while those of *L. virginicum*, which are more sharply lance-shaped on the flower stem, are more oval, somewhat pinnate, on the lower parts of the plant and don't form a rosette. Both species have flower stems that shoot up in the center of the plant to a height of from 6 to 36 inches and produce a cluster of tiny whitish-green flowers. As these fall off they are followed by equally tiny hot-tasting seeds in a papery covering. These little pouches have in them a spiciness that is really special in a salad, and they are great in a pot of soup. The young leaves give added zest to a pot of cooked greens. Pick the leaves before the seeds form to get them at their best.

It is not unusual to see acres of this plant growing and going to seed at once. While the flowers still surmount the stems is the time to pick the seed tops for the salad bowl and the soup or greens pot. To collect seed pods for use as a condiment, gather the stalks when they are fully seeded out but still green, perhaps with a small tuft of flowers still at the tip. Tie them in bunches of 10 to 15 stalks and hang them upside down in a warm, dry place. When they have dried for about two days the seeds can be removed from the stems by rubbing the heads between your hands several at a time. They need no winnowing—they seldom come out of their capsules. You can store the seeds in plastic bags until you want to use them. When they turn straw-colored they're too dry to be at their best. At that stage they are good bird feed.

Pepper Grass
Lepidium campestre

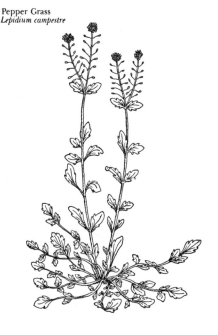

Seed pods
(enlarged)

PERSIMMON

Diospyros virginiana

Other common names: Sugar Plum, Wild Fig, Possum Wood.

Where to find it: In rocky, open woods, along streams, roadsides, and fence rows, and in fields from Florida to Texas, with its northern range along a line from New York to Kansas.

Parts used: Fruit, gathered in late fall and winter.

How used: Fresh, frozen, or dried, as a fruit; in breads, cakes, puddings, preserves.

Persimmon
Diospyros virginiana

At full size the persimmon tree may reach 50 feet, but it is often more shrublike, and it may grow in patches or thickets. The bark of old trees is nearly black, with an appearance like that of alligator leather. The leaves are about 2½ inches long and oval, with smooth margins which are often slightly wavy.

The fruit is shaped somewhat like a plum. At first hard and green and very astringent—"puckery," as we say—the fruit turns pulpy, sweet, and orange or yellowish-brown in color as the cold weather begins. The persimmon contains several flat, shiny little seeds. Only after a frost—and sometimes only quite a while after the first frost—will the fruit be truly ripe enough to gather in quantity. I've foraged for persimmons for years and I've found that the best ones to take are the intact ones on the ground; I never shake the tree to get more fruit, which may not be ripe.

A colander is a must for persimmon-

pulping (or, as a friend suggests, you might use a food mill). Simply put a handful of washed persimmons in the colander or food mill and push the pulp through; this gets rid of the seeds and most of the skin. If you have picked a lot of persimmons, you will want to put some of them up for later use. The easiest way is simply to freeze the pulp, or, if the fruits are on the dry side, to freeze them whole for later thawing and pulping.

Persimmon pulp substitutes well for dates if you spread the pulp out to dry overnight. Or you can hang whole persimmons in plastic mesh bags to dry near a heat vent or up on the beams; dried, they make a good nibble.

Perhaps the most exciting thing about a persimmon to me is the surprise inside the seed: the leaf embryo is in the shape of a tiny knife, fork, or spoon. There are more spoons than knives or forks, and I can't resist opening the seeds to see which of these tiny implements will be there, fit to grace the table of an elf.

PLANTAIN

Various species of the *Plantago* genus

Other common names: Common Plantain, Broad-leaved Plantain, Whiteman's Foot, English Plantain, Buckhorn, Ribgrass, Ripple Grass, Ribwort, Jack Straw, Lamb's Tongue, Hen Plant.

Where to find it: In lawns and fields, on roadsides, and in waste places throughout southern Canada and most of the United States, especially in the east-central states.

Parts used: Leaves in spring; seed (for bird feed) in late spring and summer.

How used: Fresh or canned, as a vegetable.

The leaves of all the several species of plantains are heavily veined, with conspicuous ribs that enclose a tough stringlike fiber that must be removed before cooking. The common or broad-leaved plantain, *Plantago major*, has ovate leaves up to about 6 or 8 inches long and half that wide. Pick this one when about 2 inches long and still tender. English or buckhorn plantain, *P. lanceolata*, has very slender, lance-shaped leaves that can grow up to 10 inches or so; these, too, should be picked while young, before they're more than 2 or 3 inches long.

This is such a common dooryard and lawn weed that it's easy to get enough for the pot. The leaves add distinct flavor to mixed greens and are worth the bother of preparation (see recipe section). Begin looking for plantains just as the forsythias begin to show color and the weeping-willow buds have begun to swell and open. When you find them, pick plenty; they lose bulk in preparation and in cooking.

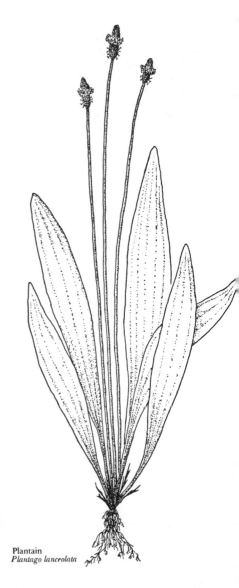

Plantain
Plantago lanceolata

Both the plantains discussed here have spiky flower heads with just a whisper of blossom. From late spring through the summer you can gather the spikes for birdseed. At Wildflower we often gather enough to augment the winter feed of our small flock of laying hens. If space for storage is limited, strip off the seeds and dry them for a few days in the sun; or, if you have the room, hang the clusters of seed stalks in a dry spot, such as an attic, and strip the seeds off as you need them for your birds, whether wild or tame. In the bird market in Seville, Spain, it is a common sight to see young vendors hawking their tightly tied clusters of plantain seed for just this use.

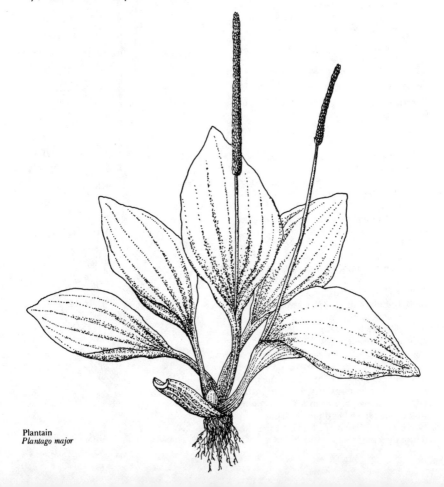

Plantain
Plantago major

POKEWEED

Phytolacca americana

Other common names: Poke Salad, Poke, Pokeberry, Scoke, Garget, Pigeonberry.

Where to find it: In rich soil around farm buildings and lots, along railroads and roadsides, along the edges of pastures, gardens, fields, and woods. Ranges south of a line running from Maine across Quebec and Ontario to Minnesota, to a southern boundary from Florida west to Arizona and into Mexico.

Parts used: Shoots in spring, stalks and leaves in spring and summer.

How used: Fresh or frozen as a vegetable, and preserved as a pickle.

After the dandelion, this truly native plant is perhaps our best-known edible wild plant and, like the dandelion, it is one of the first to appear in spring. When the poke shoot first pushes up it has its leaves folded closely around it. These gradually open and grow into large ovate-lanceolate leaves—that is, leaves shaped somewhat like an egg and somewhat like a lance head. At maturity an old plant may be 10 to 12 feet tall.

The spray of small green-to-white poke flowers slowly turns into a head of grapelike green, then purple-red berries. These berries are relished by birds but are considered poisonous to humans. In fact, the poke plant contains phytolaccic acid in the leaves, roots, and stalks as well as the berries; there is more in the roots and the red outer skin of the mature stalks than in the mature leaves. Until the flower head forms, the young shoots and the leaves are a fine pot green. The acid is easily removed from the greens by parboiling them, then cooking them in fresh water (see the recipe section). I also prefer to parboil the young shoots. If all the colored skin is peeled off—an easy operation, as it strips off readily—it is not necessary to parboil poke stalks.

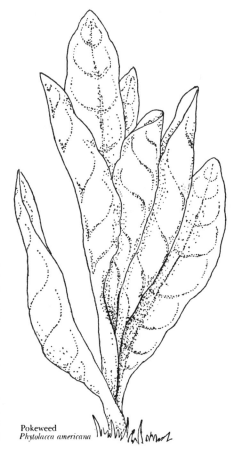

Pokeweed
Phytolacca americana

Poke is not only a widely distributed plant but a large one, so there is no shortage of green vegetables when it can be located. If you are new to foraging for poke, look for last year's stiff and broken stalks, then watch for the new young sprouts to appear at their bases. If you pick often and break back the fast-growing plant, you can assure yourself of a crop that often continues into the summer. It's not unusual to have another fresh crop of sprouts in the fall, too.

Pokeweed
Flowers and berries

PRICKLY PEAR

Various species of the *Opuntia* genus

Other names: Indian Fig, Prickly Pear Cactus, Tuna. Common or Eastern Prickly Pear, *Opuntia compressa*, is also called *O. vulgaris* and *O. humifusa*.

Where to find it: Several species, widely distributed throughout the country; found in sandy ground, including seashores; in open, dry fields and rocky slopes, including mountains, and in deserts.

Parts used: The pads (fleshy stems), gathered at any season; the fruits (prickly pears) gathered after ripening in the fall.

How used: Pads, cooked as a vegetable. Fruits, eaten fresh or cooked in syrup or candied.

This common yellow-flowered cactus is found in a surprising number of regions, although we tend to think of it as a desert plant. It even thrives at the seashore on both coasts.

The fruit is what we're most interested in, although the pads are a palatable food if one is quite hungry. The thick but flattened oval pads or joints, which are stems, not leaves, are covered with clusters of long or short thorns growing from pore-like areas; *Opuntia tortispina*, found especially in the Midwest, West, and Southwest, has especially long prickles. The pads, about 3 to 6 inches long, are jointed together and are often found in large, low clumps. The true leaves are usually not to be seen—they're tiny and drop from the plants at an early stage. See the recipe section for cooking suggestions for the pads.

The bright-yellow flowers, sometimes with red centers, are held to the pads by the "prickly pears," the green, immature fruit. (The fruits are called pears because of their flavor, I suppose—but I think the flavor is slightly suggestive of a very mellow pear.) The pears turn deep red when ripe and ready for picking. The plant blooms over a long period, from early to late summer, and the fruits therefore ripen over a similarly long period. I find that it is often after they have turned dark red and shriveled up a bit that they are best for eating. I have even picked them in the dead of winter, when they have frozen, and made syrup and candied fruit from them.

If you want to remove the prickles from the fruit before peeling it, try rubbing them off with heavy gloves, or scrape them with a blunt knife; or do as one book suggests and singe the fruits over a flame for a moment.

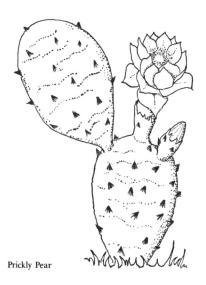

Prickly Pear

PURSLANE

Portulaca oleracea

Other common names: Pursley, Pussley, Pigweed.

Where to find it: Along roadsides, in old pastures and garden spots, as a garden weed, and occasionally on rocky bluffs, throughout southern Canada and the United States; most common in the eastern half.

Parts used: Stems and leaves, from spring through early fall.

How used: Fresh as a vegetable, or pickled as a condiment.

Portulaca is a common garden flower, especially in the South and West. The ornamental portulaca is sown in flower gardens and is grown in some places to prevent erosion on superhighway borders. It is a creeping plant with vivid white, red, yellow, or orange blooms.

The portulaca we are considering here is an edible annual member of the genus, although it is often a hated weed in vegetable gardens—interestingly enough, in the past it was often sown as a crop in just such gardens, whereas today we are inclined to weed it out.

Purslane has reddish-green or purple-tinted stems that are very fleshy—squeeze one, and fluid oozes from it. The leaves are from half an inch to 1½ inches long and roughly wedge-shaped in cross-section. The plant is usually only a few inches high, but it spreads its jointed stems widely, so the greenish-purple leaves can cover a lot of ground. The small bright-yellow flowers are inconspicuous.

This plant can be important to the cooking pot. It is usually abundant enough in our area to be picked by mid-June, but farther north the harvest begins later. If you clip only the succulent stem tips, the plant will produce a continuing crop; to keep the supply coming, don't let the flowers develop.

Purslane is somewhat mucilaginous—like okra—and some find this objectionable. I rather like this quality myself and often use the leaves in a salad because of it. The leaves and stems are a good addition to any pot of greens, and when added to soup, their flavor, as well as their thickening power, are welcome.

If you like purslane a lot, it's simple to let some of the plants blossom and then gather the ripe seeds. Sow a row in your garden after the danger of frost is over in the spring.

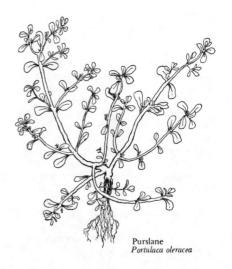

Purslane
Portulaca oleracea

SASSAFRAS

Sassafras albidum

Other common names: Mitten Tree, Cinnamon Wood, Tea Tree, Ague Tree.

Where to find it: In light woods and overgrown fields, along roads and railroads in acid soil from Florida to Texas and north to Maine and Michigan.

Parts used: Leaves, in spring; rootlets and bark of roots, late fall, winter, and early spring.

How used: Leaves dried and ground for seasoning; root bark and rootlets dried for tea and candy flavoring.

The sassafras is usually a small shrubby tree, often growing in large patches, but in favorable spots it may reach 80 to 90 feet in height. It is easily identified by its leaves, some of which will always be mitten-shaped, while others on the same tree will either be oval or have two "thumbs," one on either side of the dark-green leaf. Immature leaves are silky underneath. On young trees the bark seems reddish but later it is grey, with a touch of reddish-brown showing in its deep furrows. The greenish-yellow flowers appear as the tree leafs out. In autumn sassafras leaves turn rose and yellow and scarlet and deep orange. The fruit is a blue-black berry; birds love it.

The usable parts of the sassafras are the rootlets, the bark of large roots, and the young leaves. The roots and root bark make a marvelous deep-flavored tea, and the dried leaves make filé powder, a famous ingredient of Louisiana gumbos.

To make filé, dry the young leaves as you would any other herb. When they are crisp, pound them in a mortar or grind them in a blender until you have a fine powder. Store it airtight. Stir a table-spoonful of filé into a quart of finished gumbo to thicken and flavor it—don't boil after adding the filé.

When the trees are dormant, dig up a sapling and take its roots for tea. (Roots in active growth tend to be bitter.) Scrub the roots clean, then peel off the fleshy bark. Break or snip the rootlets into bits. Dry thoroughly—I place the roots on a wire-mesh rack above my fireplace—until they are brittle; a warm, dry attic or closet is a good place for drying, or you can spread the roots on a cookie sheet and bake them at 200° for 2 or 3 hours. Store airtight.

Sassafras tea (see the recipe section) is pink to deep red, fragrant, and very easily made; you can even re-use the bark several times. Our ancestors used it medicinally, drinking the tea in the spring to "thin the blood." Recently this plant has been among those being laboratory-tested for the presence of carcinogens. An abundance of super-strong doses given to laboratory animals was found to be carcinogenic under those circumstances. However, I think it is doubtful that any ill effects would turn up in a person who drinks a few quarts of sassafras tea a year.

Sassafras
Sassafras albidum

SORREL

Various species of the *Rumex* genus

Other names: Red Sorrel, Common Sorrel, both *Rumex Acetosella;* Green Sorrel, Garden Sorrel, French Sorrel, both *R. Acetosa.* Both species sometimes called "sour grass" or "sheep sorrel."

Where to find it: Various species throughout the United States, especially from the mid-Atlantic states to midcontinent, and also in the Northwest.

Parts used: Leaves, spring and summer.

How used: In salads; cooked as greens.

The sorrels are, like the docks, members of the *Rumex* genus. The two I will describe are both perennials and are similar in many ways, their size and coloration being their chief differences.

Red sorrel, *Rumex Acetosella*, is much the commoner plant; it produces a low rosette of rather arrowhead-shaped leaves and has slender flower stalks that reach 4 to 16 inches in height. The juicy bright-green leaves have two lobes near the leaf stem that point outward and a slender, lance-shaped center lobe. The plant often shows a pink tinge, and its flowers are yellow to red. The seeds are reddish-brown.

Green sorrel, *R. Acetosa*, is found growing wild as well as in gardens. It is from 12 to 36 inches tall and has leaves like stout arrowheads, without the pronounced lobes of red-sorrel leaves.

Both plants are quite acid to the taste, and because of this they have been welcome additions to the salad bowl for centuries. Green or garden or French sorrel has long been cultivated as a pot herb and salad plant, and seed is offered in American seed catalogues. Both plants are used in soups, as cooked greens, and as a vegetable purée.

In the South it is not unusual for sorrel to be found in growth throughout the year. If it has shade and moisture and the leaves are kept picked back and no flowers are allowed to form, it continues to send up new crops of greens for months. At Tameweed next door the conditions are so good that there's not a time during the year that I can't pick a handful of the sour, succulent leaves to add zest to a salad. These sorrels are no kin to the oxalis or wood sorrel, but because both are acid in flavor I often interchange them in the salad bowl.

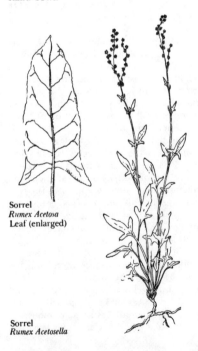

Sorrel
Rumex Acetosa
Leaf (enlarged)

Sorrel
Rumex Acetosella

SOW THISTLE

Various species of the *Sonchus* genus

Other names: Field Sow Thistle, Perennial Sow Thistle, both *Sonchus arvensis;* Common Sow Thistle, Annual Sow Thistle, both *S. oleraceus;* Spiny Sow Thistle, *S. asper.*

Where to find it: Field sow thistle, especially in north-central states but throughout the northern half of the country and spottily elsewhere. Common sow thistle, all of the United States but especially from Pennsylvania south to Florida and along the entire West Coast. Spiny sow thistle is common in the Southeast as well as along the West Coast and southeast into New Mexico. All species grow in fields, gardens, waste places, and along roadsides and railroads.

Parts used: Leaves, from early spring until midsummer.

How used: Fresh, frozen, or canned, as a vegetable.

This thistle is not the tall prickly plant that sports large purple flower globes, nor is it the nodding musk thistle, nor the Scotch thistle that is Scotland's national flower, although it is in the same large plant family as these others.

The leaves of the sow thistles are shaped like those of the dandelion, many times enlarged. Some are deeply lobed, others are not, but all are edged with harmless prickles. The bases of the leaves clasp the stems. The species we're describing here grow from a few inches to as much as 8 feet tall, and some have leaves that can be as much as 10 inches long.

The field sow thistle, 1½ to 8 feet tall, has orange-yellow flowers that, like those of all its relatives, resemble dandelions. They appear—again, like all sow-thistle blooms—after the leaves have passed their prime for eating. The common or annual sow thistle, up to 3 or 4 feet tall, has pale-yellow flowers. Spiny sow thistle also has pale-yellow flowers and grows to about the same height.

When the tender young leaves are picked off the stems, milky sap appears; this is gummy and tends to be bitter. If you want to parboil sow thistle to make the flavor milder, see the directions in the recipe section. All species are good pot herbs, and all are equally welcome to dinner.

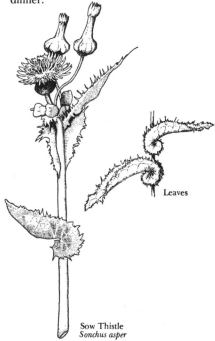

Leaves

Sow Thistle
Sonchus asper

SPRING BEAUTY

Species of the *Claytonia genus*

Other common names: Claytonia, Fairy Spuds.

Where to find it: From southeastern Canada westward to Minnesota and south to a line from Georgia to Texas. Related forms are also found to the westward of this range. Found in moist woods and fields and often in lawns.

Parts used: Corms or tubers, in spring and summer.

How used: As a vegetable.

Spring beauty or claytonia is often the first little pink or white flower seen blowing in the early spring breezes. The dull olive-green leaves of *Claytonia virginica* are lance-shaped, resembling blades of grass, but are thicker and juicier than grass. The leaves of *C. caroliniana* are much wider.

The tiny pink or white flowers of both species bloom in a loose spray emerging above the leaves and have distinctive crimson veins in their five petals. They appear from March onward, depending upon local conditions.

The corms or tubers of spring beauty are the food offering it has for us, although the leaves can be added to the greens pot. The corm ranges from the size of a small pea to that of a marble and has a most surprising nutlike flavor; it tastes much like a chestnut or a chinquapin, although it has the texture of a potato.

Spring-beauty corms are difficult to dig because they grow deep. Pick a spot heavily covered with flowers (although this isn't necessarily a guarantee of many corms, because many flowers appear on each plant). The long-bladed sharpshooter spade or shovel is the best tool. Dig deep and turn over a spadeful of soil: if the patch is a good one, you will have a handful of the sought-for treat.

If your hunting ground is well covered with flowers and you space out your holes, you needn't worry about endangering the species—removing a few cupfuls of corms seems only to give more room for the others to multiply. This is much like thinning iris in the flower garden. Be sure to replace the plug of soil you've taken the corms from, as it will be needed if the remaining plants are to spread. In some areas spring beauty is a protected wild flower and should not be dug. Be sure to look into that aspect in your state or locality before foraging for the fairy spud.

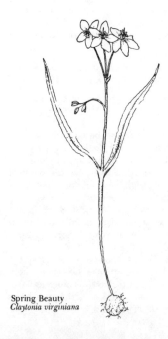

Spring Beauty
Claytonia virginiana

SUMAC

Species of the *Rhus* genus

Other names: Shoemake, Indian Lemonade, Lemonade Tree, all species. Smooth Sumac, *Rhus glabra;* Staghorn Sumac, *R. typhina;* Dwarf Sumac, Winged Sumac, Shining Sumac, all *R. Copallinum;* Fragrant Sumac, *R. trilobata* (also *R. aromatica*).

Where to find it: Throughout most of the United States and southern Canada and into Mexico, in various habitats according to species. Sumac likes roadsides, edges of woods and fields, old clearings, open rocky woods. It often grows in thickets.

Parts used: Berries, in late summer and fall.

How used: Dried or fresh, in a beverage or in an infusion for jelly.

Sumacs may be shrubby and as low as 4 to 5 feet *(Rhus trilobata)* or treelike and as tall as 60 feet *(R. typhina),* but all species are alike in having a fernlike leaf pattern and in producing tart red berries that are good for making beverages. None of these "good" sumacs resemble the poisonous members of the *Rhus* genus—poison ivy, poison oak, and poison sumac. The closest to being a "look-alike" to harmless sumacs is *R. Vernix,* the poison sumac, which has white berries in drooping clusters that can't possibly be mistaken for the pyramidal heads of red berries of the sumacs we're interested in.

The sumacs have compound leaves with as many as 15 pairs of leaflets opposite each other on a stem ending in a single terminal leaflet. They have a tropical look and often grow in thickets. They are among the first plants to show autumn color, changing to bright red and orange as early as August in the South. The clusters of hairy red berries are always velvety to the touch and vary in color from bright red to russet.

When the berries are ready for picking the stiff stem begins to wilt, making it easy to snap off. Place the heads in a cloth bag, such as a pillowcase, and hang them in a dry place for a couple of weeks. Then remove the fruits by rubbing the clusters between your palms, wearing garden gloves to protect your hands. The dried berries can be stored airtight until you need them.

After making your infusion for tea or jelly (Index), strain it through two or three layers of cloth to remove the tiny hairs. The extract will be a perky pink color when the berries are picked early; if picked later, when they have turned brownish, the infusion will be somewhat duller in color.

Smooth Sumac
Rhus glabra

SWEET GOLDENROD

Solidago odora

Other common names: Fragrant Goldenrod.

Where to find it: Grows in open woodlands and on rocky bluffs and slopes from New Hampshire west to Ohio, then to Kentucky, Missouri, and Oklahoma and south to Florida and Texas.

Parts used: Leaves and flowers, midsummer to late fall.

How used: Fresh or dried, for tea.

Goldenrods grow like gay yellow plumes. A field in flower, undulating in the breeze, makes me think of a deep ocean frosted with golden foam. Most goldenrods are a sign of the harvest season, but this particular one is almost a summer flower, a transitional plant.

The leaves of sweet goldenrod, unlike those of most of the ninety or so other species in the *Solidago* genus, are smooth on the edges, without any of the usual toothy jags or ripples. They are slender and lance-shaped, up to 2 inches long. They are smooth, almost glossy, and show transparent dots when held up to the light; people with a sensitive touch can feel the dots on the surface of the leaf.

The silhouette of the flower panicle of sweet goldenrod is distinctive; the tiny yellow flowers are piled at the top of the plant and more or less on one side of it, like a plumy ostrich feather in egg-yolk yellow.

The easiest identifying point of this plant is the anise odor of the crushed leaf; this fragrance is what makes sweet gol-

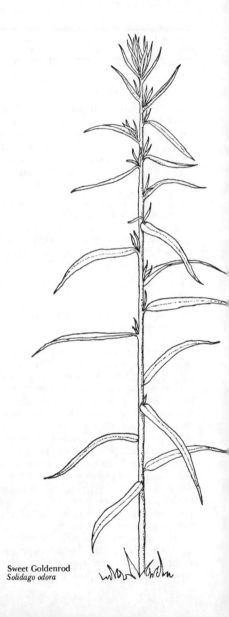

Sweet Goldenrod
Solidago odora

denrod an important tea plant for us. Tea can be made from either fresh or dried leaves. I usually gather the leaves in late July and August, when the fragrant oils are at their peak, although I have picked it as late as November.

To prepare this tea plant, pick the stems at about 4 to 6 inches from the ground. Tie 12 to 20 or so of them together and hang the bunches upside down from the rafters of a kitchen or attic or other warm, dry place. When the leaves and flowers are thoroughly dry, strip them off and store them in an airtight container.

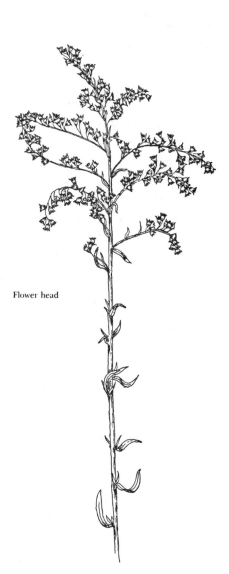

Flower head

VIOLET

Various species of the *Viola* genus

Other names: Bird-Foot Violet, Johnny-Jump-Up, Pansy Violet, Hens and Roosters, all *Viola pedata;* Meadow Violet, Common Blue Violet, Butterfly Violet, all *V. papilionacea.*

Where to find it: Bird-foot violet, in dry fields and open woods, nearly always in acid soil, from New Hampshire west to Ontario and Minnesota, south to Florida and Texas. The common blue violet is found in moist ground near streams and ponds, in damp woods and along roadsides from Maine and southern Canada west to Wyoming and south to Georgia and Oklahoma. Many other *Viola* species are found throughout North America.

Parts used: Bird-foot violet: flowers, in the spring. Common blue violet: flowers, March through June, frequently again in the fall; leaves in the spring.

How used: Flowers, candied or in syrup or desserts or added to salads; leaves in salads or soups or as greens, fresh, frozen, or canned.

Violets of innumerable kinds grow in North America, among them those we're discussing here. The many others include the wood violet, prairie violet, sweet violet (escaped from gardens), and the marsh violet.

The two I know the best are the bird-foot violet, *Viola pedata,* and the common blue or meadow violet, *V. papilionacea.* The bird-foot violet is the most striking of all our violets. The leaf, instead of being more or less heart-shaped like those of all other violets, is somewhat like that of a palm, cut into several blades. Though they are distinctive in shape, the leaves are inconspicuous because the blossoms are so lovely: the plant is often called pansy violet because the flowers closely resemble the pansy members of the *Viola* genus. The flowers are the edible part. They are often bicolored, with purple top petals and lilac lower petals that are sometimes streaked with purple. Some plants have petals of solid pale lavender or deep purple.

The common blue violet has a heart-shaped leaf and, like all violets, five-petaled flowers. The blooms are light to deep violet-blue in color. The plant much resembles many of the other violets, which may have blooms of stark white, or white veined with blue, or lavender, purple, or even yellow.

All violet flowers are edible, and the leaves are delicious in a mixed salad or in the greens pot. If you want to freeze violet blossoms to use out of season in syrup (see Index), rinse them, shake off the water, and store them in the freezer in a plastic carton.

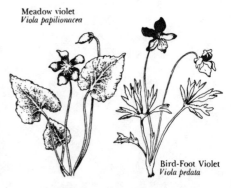

Meadow violet
Viola papilionacea

Bird-Foot Violet
Viola pedata

WATERCRESS

Nasturtium officinale

Other common name: Cress.

Where to find it: In or near springs and spring-fed streams and ponds throughout the United States.

Parts used: Leaves and stems, all seasons of the year.

How used: Raw, in salads and sandwiches; cooked, as a vegetable or in soups.

The many-segmented leaves of watercress have large, rounded terminal lobes and 1 to 6 pairs of smaller lateral lobes. This is a creeping and floating herb with many tiny root hairs growing along its fleshy stems and many branches that make it appear to grow in clumps. The flowers are white and insignificant, clustered at the tips of the stems. The cress is stronger and more pungent when in bloom, but it is edible at every stage of growth.

Watercress is found in virtually every country of the world. Here it is seen everywhere on vegetable counters, tied in small bunches or bagged in plastic, with healthy price tags attached. It has been cultivated for many years, beginning with an early plantation near London. Now watercress growing is a mammoth commercial enterprise involving many water farms of many acres apiece, supplying an ever-demanding market.

Whether you pick watercress wild or get it at the market, it is a great food plant. It is a master salad maker, but it can be made into many delightful prepared dishes—try one of our watercress soups, or cook it as greens, or make rolled watercress sandwiches.

No special treatment is necessary in preparing watercress for the table. Make sure you pick it where pollution has not affected its wholesomeness or flavor, and rinse it through several waters to get off any grit, silt, or tiny water creatures' larvae which may be attached to the stems.

This plant is to be found in all seasons, growing the year round in mild-climate areas. This alone makes it an important food plant to look for.

Watercress
Nasturtium officinale

WILD GINGER

Asarum canadense

Other common names: Asarabacca, Canada Snakeroot, Indian Ginger.

Where to find it: In moist woods, frequently on slopes, at the base of bluffs, or in ravines. From New Brunswick across southern Canada to Minnesota and south to North Carolina, Alabama, Arkansas, and Kansas.

Parts used: Rhizomes (roots) in the fall; also in spring and summer.

How used: Fresh as seasoning, or for candy, syrup, and beverages; dried as seasoning or in beverages.

Wild ginger, no kin to the better-known tropical ginger, is an elusive plant, shy about showing off its lovely three-petaled, bell-shaped flower. The two large heart-shaped leaves are thin and dark green, with distinct veins. They are borne on slender hairy stems up to 6 inches long. The odd purple-brown flower appears between the leaves on a short stem and droops its head toward the ground. Once you find the plant, note its location and come back in the fall for the roots when they are at their best. The roots, yellowish in color, are just under the surface. They may spread for a considerable distance from the base of the plant, and it is a simple matter to dig them with your fingers or a bit of thin rock. Always leave pieces of the root where you find it so the planting will survive—ginger multiplies profusely, and even a broken piece of root will continue to grow and help the patch to increase. Now that you have the roots, wash them

well but gently in several waters; they seldom have to be scrubbed, and no peeling is necessary. The roots are small compared to those of tropical ginger, and they may be snipped into small pieces to dry. I usually dry mine in a nylon stocking hung up near a heat register for 3 to 4 days, or until they are brittle. Or you can spread the roots on a baking sheet and place them in a 200° oven for 2 or 3 hours, or until crisp. Store dried ginger airtight and it will keep indefinitely.

Your dried roots may be large enough to be grated on a small grater; however, it is easy to crush them in a mortar. I use the roots fresh, too, using twice as much of fresh as of dry roots and crushing them with a pestle or a hammer, or snipping them fine with kitchen shears. If you use wild ginger in a recipe calling for the tropical spice, use double or triple the amount called for.

Wild Ginger
Asarum canadense

WILD PLUM

Various species of the *Prunus* genus

Other names: Wild Plum, *Prunus americana, P. hortulana;* Chickasaw Plum, *P. angustifolia;* Big-Tree Plum, *P. mexicana.* Many other species are given descriptive common names—Small Red Plum, Red Plum, Yellow Plum, Big Red Plum, etc.

Where to find it: Various plum species are found in thickets, pastures, prairies, and woodlands, some in sandy coastal regions, throughout the United States.

Parts used: Fruit, in summer and fall.

How used: Fresh, canned, frozen, and dried; in beverages, desserts, jams, jellies, sauces, and as a nibble.

The *Prunus* genus includes cherries and peaches as well as the almost countless kinds of wild plums found in various parts of the country. All wild plums are edible and may be used interchangeably. Some are shrubby, some are trees up to 25 feet tall; they are commonly seen in thickets along roadsides and the edges of woods and fields. Their masses of white to pinkish blossoms are a welcome sight in April or May after a long winter. The leaves are ovate to oblong and have a pointed end and a glossy surface; they are evenly toothed along the edges. The fruits ripen from late summer through early fall, depending upon the species and the locality. *Prunus americana*, the most commonly found wild plum, has red fruits, while others, such as *P. hortulana*, may have fruits ranging from yellow to red. Other kinds may have bluish or blue-black fruits, sometimes with a powdery bloom.

Besides canning plums and making juice and jelly, I like to dry them. If you want to oven-dry them, wash and stone the plums, cutting them in half. Pour boiling water over them and let them stand for 20 minutes, then drain them in a colander for half an hour. Cover a baking sheet with waxed paper, spread out the plums in a single layer, and dry them in an oven set at 150° until the pieces are dry but still flexible. Store them airtight. To sun-dry the plums, spread the drained fruit on a wire drying rack in the sun, and bring in the rack at night or in damp weather. Drying will take from three days to three weeks, depending on the weather. Haroldj, over at Tameweed, sometimes strings pitted plums in the same way as mulberries and air-dries them in strings with great success.

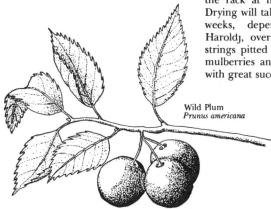

Wild Plum
Prunus americana

WILD RICE

Zizania aquatica

Other common names: Water Rice, Indian Rice, Water Oats. Southern Wild Rice, *Zizianopsis miliacea*, belongs to another genus. It is sometimes called Water Millet.

Where to find it: In swamps and shallow lake and pond borders from eastern Canada to Manitoba, from Maine to North Dakota and south to Florida, Louisiana, and Texas.

Parts used: Seed, gathered from midsummer into fall.

How used: As a vegetable or cereal.

Wild rice is not a member of the botanical genus that includes our everyday white or brown rice, *Oryza sativa*. It is an aquatic grass, found growing in dense clumps in marshy places or in shallow water where there is a mucky bottom. It has been successfully introduced into many areas of the country to which it is not native.

This is a very tall grass, from 6 to 12 feet tall, with stems as big around as a pencil at their bases. The leaves are lance-shaped and grow alternately on the stem; they have very rough edges. The flower stalk, bearing both male and female spikelets, is so showy that it would not be out of place in a florist's dried arrangement. The seed heads are as much as two feet long; the seed is purplish when mature and is tightly encased in a husk.

Like the Indians before us, we have found that the only really effective way to gather wild rice is from a canoe or a paddle boat. When the seeds have formed but are still green, we canoe out into a patch of wild rice and twist the seed heads into loose clusters, then tie them. When the seeds are ripe we go out again and pull each cluster over the side of the canoe and hit it with a short paddle or a stick, knocking the seeds onto a sheet in the bottom of the canoe.

Wild rice must be dried before it can be winnowed. Spread it on pans in an oven set at 200° and leave it for two or three hours, stirring it occasionally, or spread it out in a warm place to dry for two or three days. Rub the dry grains between your hands to loosen the husks, then pour them from one basket into another in a stiff breeze or in front of an electric fan; the husks will blow away, leaving the seeds. Then parch the grains for an hour in an oven set at 250°. The rice is then ready for storage.

Wash wild rice well in cold water to remove some of its smoky taste before cooking it. Use it in any way you'd use cultivated rice, and enjoy not having to pay the enormous prices marked on boxes of wild rice in fine food stores.

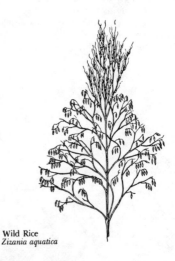

Wild Rice
Zizania aquatica

WILD ROSE

Various species of the *Rosa* genus

Other common names: None.

Where to find it: In fields, fence rows, and along roadsides throughout the United States and much of Canada.

Parts used: Fruit (hips) in late summer and fall; petals, spring and summer.

How used: Fruit used fresh, frozen, or dried for tea, jelly, or in desserts; petals made into preserves.

From early summer onward we are treated to the pink, white, and yellow blooms of roses growing wild in vast array. Although there are several native American rose species, many of the roses we see growing wild originally escaped from cultivation. According to the late great botanist M. L. Fernald, of Harvard, the Japanese rose, *Rosa rugosa*, is possibly the most commonly found of the naturalized roses. Its shrubby plants bloom so abundantly that it is often a solid splash of pale to dark pink. This particular rose has 5 single petals, and its stiff stems are covered with stickers. Other wild growers among the roses are double, some of them almost resembling the tame roses grown in gardens. Rose leaves are compound, with from 3 to 11 broad oval leaflets apiece. The leaflet edges are serrated or toothed, and the leaf stalk and the stems will more often than not have hairy prickles and thorns.

All roses produce fruits called hips. The hips are the edible part we seek; the other edible part is the petal, which can be candied or made into preserves. Rose hips are like small smooth berries with green-tinged or brown bracts remaining at the blossom end. As the hips ripen they turn pale to deep orange or to one or another shade of red.

Rose hips vary in size and flavor as well as color. One kind I pick is as small as a green pea, pale orange and tart-flavored; another is as large as a pecan, bright red and quite sweet. Many tame roses produce large hips, which seem to be a bit sweeter than those of most wild roses. I have found that for making tea it is good to mix several types together. A bright-red hip may be less flavorful and a light-colored one more so, so by mixing them I get a tea that not only tastes fine but has a pleasant color. If the color of your jelly doesn't suit you, simply add a drop or two of food coloring; here the flavor of the hips is the important point.

Wild Rose
Rosa rugosa

WILD STRAWBERRY

Various species of the *Fragaria* genus

Other names: Common Wild Strawberry; Wood Strawberry (*Fragaria vesca*).

Where to find it: In woods and clearings, on open slopes, prairies, and along roadsides and railroads, sometimes near streams. *Fragaria virginiana* (illustrated) ranges from Newfoundland to Alberta in the North and in the South from Georgia to Oklahoma. *F. vesca* can be found from Newfoundland to Manitoba, then south to Virginia and west to New Mexico. Many related species and varieties are found over much of the United States.

Parts used: Fruit, in late spring and early summer.

How used: Fresh, frozen, or canned. In desserts, preserves, and jellies; dried as a nibble.

I know few people who don't look forward with great anticipation to the first strawberries to appear in the market, in baskets piled high with fruit of ethereal fragrance and tantalizing taste. Of course "tame" berries are good, but wild ones are superlative.

Fragaria virginiana, the common wild strawberry, is hairy-stemmed and bears three coarsely toothed leaflets to a stem. The five-petaled white blossoms are borne in clusters on the flower stems, which are usually lower than the leaves. The fruit is variable in size, color, and flavor but is quite like commercially grown berries; the seeds are small and are embedded in pits on the skin. *F. vesca* is similar in form but has smaller flowers and fruit that are most usually held erect above the leaves in loose clusters. The seeds are on the surface of the berries, not in pits.

The wild strawberry is the same deep red you see on the male cardinal bird, but to me these fruits look like shimmering rubies sprinkled over with seeds like tiny chips of emeralds. It is an unforgettable sight to come upon a patch in the early hours of the day while they literally glitter with dew standing on the berries like crystal beads. The fact that these fruits will soon fill our baskets and then fill the kitchen with their tantalizing aroma seems at the moment to be almost unimportant, although nothing can surpass this luxury for dessert or for preserves.

Wild Strawberry
Fragaria virginiana

WINTER CRESS

Species of the *Barbarea* genus

Other common names: Yellow Rocket, Spring Cress, Upland Cress.

Where to find it: Along streams and in swamps and other damp places, along roadsides and in gardens and fields. Widely distributed, but grows especially from New England southwest to Arkansas and also in the north-central states, the Northwest, and in Canada from Newfoundland to Ontario.

Parts used: Leaves, in winter and spring.

How used: In salads; cooked as greens.

The plant illustrated is *Barbarea verna*, but *B. vulgaris* is similar. Both are members of the huge Mustard family and both have the typical flavor and bite of mustard leaves. They both grow in a rosette pattern, have smooth dark-green leaves, and reach a height of from about 8 to 30 inches, depending upon conditions. *B. vulgaris* has between 1 and 4 pairs of lobes per leaf and a single large, rounded terminal lobe; the terminal lobe of *B. verna* may follow 5 to 10 pairs of lateral lobes.

The flower stalk of winter cress rises from the center of the rosette of leaves and is crested with a loose cluster of golden-yellow four-petaled flowers, often showing the first color of spring. The seed pods that follow the flowers are slender and stand up at an angle along the stem. These can easily be clipped to dry for birdseed or to sow broadcast in a garden bed to produce a home-grown crop for the table.

Barbarea, the Latin name of this genus, comes from the belief that it is a good omen to eat this green on December 4, St. Barbara's Day. This indicates that the plant is a winter grower, and so it is. In winter we often cook a cupful or two to add to any greens we have canned in the summer. It's also a great addition, raw, to the winter salads we make with iceberg lettuce or cabbage from the market; I also add it to watercress to make a two-cress salad.

When used as a pot herb winter cress is quite strong, so it is best to parboil it for 2 or 3 minutes, drain it, and cook it again in fresh water. It loses a lot of bulk in cooking, so gather at least twice as much as you think you'll need. When parboiled the older leaves may be eaten; however, the young, tender ones are the best.

Winter cress is one of those plants once known as scurvy grass that were used to prevent scurvy, that dread disease of long voyages. The greens were dried and rehydrated in a soup for the sailors.

Winter Cress
Barbarea verna

WOOD SORREL

Various species of the *Oxalis* genus

Other names: Three-leaved Grass, Oxalis, all species. Violet Wood Sorrel, *Oxalis violacea;* Yellow Wood Sorrel, Common Yellow Wood Sorrel, Lady's Sorrel, Sheep Sorrel, *O. stricta.*

Where to find it: Violet wood sorrel, in dry upland woods and on prairies and roadsides, ranging north from a line from Florida to New Mexico to a line from North Dakota to Vermont. Yellow wood sorrel, all over the United States and north into Canada, south into Mexico, in dry, open areas, including lawns.

Parts used: Leaves, tender stems, and flowers, from early spring until frost; seed pods in the spring.

How used: As a vegetable and in salads. Seed pods used fresh in salads.

Spring has surely arrived when these delicate perennial beauties can be found. The leaves of all wood sorrels have three heart-shaped lobes. Those of violet wood sorrel are dark green splotched with purple, and the undersides are purplish. In maturity the leaves are often as large as a twenty-five-cent piece, and they are attached to the bulb by a spindly purple stem. They close up at night and on gloomy, sunless days. The fragile five-petaled flower is almost translucent and may be rose-violet, veined with lavender, or deep violet. The seed pod that follows the flower looks much like an okra pod and is seldom half an inch long; when young it's a good addition to a salad.

Yellow wood sorrel is a smaller-leaved

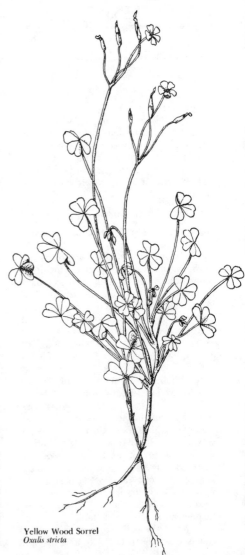

Yellow Wood Sorrel
Oxalis stricta

plant, with pale-green leaves smaller than a dime. The flowers are pale yellow and the plant itself is very spreading. The plant isn't as fleshy as violet wood sorrel, and the stems, though tasty, are almost too wiry to eat. The seed pods, too, are edible.

Wood sorrel can make a masterpiece of the salad bowl—it is juicy and piquant, with a lemony acid taste. Snip the stems up small, and be sure to use the flowers as well as the leaves. See the recipe section for ways of serving wood sorrel as a vegetable.

One word of caution: wood sorrel contains oxalic acid, which gives it its botanical name, *Oxalis,* as well as its acid flavor. This acid can be harmful if taken in large quantities, but is harmless if you eat no more than a normal serving at a time.

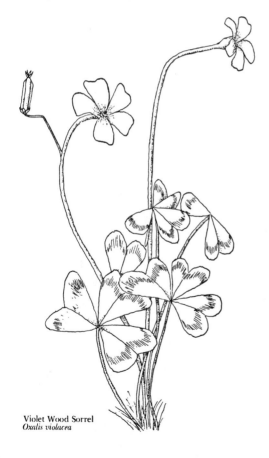

Violet Wood Sorrel
Oxalis violacea

YUCCA

Various species of the *Yucca* genus

Other names: Spanish Bayonet, Adam's Needle, both *Yucca filamentosa;* Bear Grass, Soapweed.

Where to find it: Although this plant is commonly associated with the West and the Southwest, various species are found throughout the United States. Open or sandy areas, dry prairies and plains, and dry, rocky woodlands are places to find it. It is often grown in gardens.

Parts used: Flower petals, in late spring and in summer; seeds, in late summer and fall.

How used: Flower petals in salads, or in fritters, or candied; seeds cooked as a vegetable.

The yuccas are large plants growing in the form of a rosette of stiff, spiky leaves, tightly clustered; they look like a bouquet of narrow or wide swords, the width of the blades varying with the species. The leaves of some kinds have small threads trailing from their edges, while others have edges with thornlike "teeth." The whole appearance of the plant is cactuslike.

The tall, woody flower stalk that appears from late spring onwards produces many white or cream-colored bell-shaped flowers, usually toward the top of the 2- to 4-foot stalk. Each flower may be 3 inches across. The waxy petals can be a welcome addition to summer meals. After the flowers drop off, pick the seed pods while they are still green, with tender white seeds inside—the seeds turn black when mature. We simply split the pods along the seam line with a knife, then remove the tightly stacked flat seeds. Enough yucca seeds for a vegetable course can usually be obtained from one stalk.

Food isn't all that yuccas supply. One species, *Y. filamentosa,* is still gathered by American Indians in the West for its threadlike fibers, used in making useful and decorative objects. *Y. glauca* has roots that yield a fair substitute for soap. I have crushed the well-washed roots with a hammer, then swished them around in warm water to obtain mild suds which will indeed get dishes clean, or even serve as a fair shampoo.

Spanish Bayonet
Yucca filamentosa

PART TWO
COOKING THE FORAGER'S HARVEST:
RECIPES FOR WILD FOODS

*The chief pleasure in eating
does not consist in costly
seasoning or exquisite flavor,
but in yourself. Seek your
sauce by labor.*

—HORACE

Cooking can be drudgery or it can be a joy, and the same goes for eating—and we who do the cooking can make dining a pleasure or a bore for our families and guests. Perhaps food does not literally make us what we are—surely we aren't actually "what we eat"—but our outlook on life is influenced by food more than we realize. We should not, perhaps, live to eat, but neither should we just eat to live.

It is easy to be taken in by the convenience of foods found in supermarkets. Too often we'll buy a certain food because it's so little trouble to fix, not because it's delightful to eat. For the same reason—convenience—we may serve the same familiar foods too often, instead of trying others which might turn out to be at least as good, or even better. And it is surely more interesting, both for the cook and for the family, to try out new foods and learn something of their background than it is to routinely throw a steak on the grill and put a potato in the oven to bake and eat with a dab of sour cream or butter.

Wild foods will, if you gather them yourself, add more to making life a "happening" than any other hobby I can think of. While you are learning new ways of cooking and presenting your wild-food finds, you will see, perhaps, why our progenitors were so fascinated by their fertile new land and what it produced. Also, you'll find that really interesting dinner conversation can arise when you've put an entirely new meal or a single innovative dish on the table, especially if the meal or the dish includes a delectable wild food you have gathered yourself.

Some of the recipes in the chapters that follow have come straight down through several generations of folk descended from early settlers. Others are borrowings from the "old countries" that have been reworked to use our American wild foods from the fields, roadsides, wetlands, and woods. All of them have been tested with ingredients gathered by myself, my family, and my friends, and all have been served to live, happy, and interested people who consider eating an experience rather than just a way to fill their stomachs.

A word about the recipes: Only insofar as the special preparation required by some wild foods is concerned is this a "basic" cookbook. I am assuming that my readers are familiar with the common terminology and methods of cooking, and so I haven't spelled out directions in kitchen-primer style; but anyone who can cook at all can cook wild foods with the help of these recipes. When I refer to a recipe to be found elsewhere in the book, the recipe title is followed by an asterisk; see the Index to find its page number.

APPETIZERS, SPREADS, AND SNACKS

BLACK WALNUT OR HICKORY NUT AND CHEESE STICKS

These nutted pastry sticks are great served warm from the oven, or they may be stored in an airtight container for later use.

Ingredients for Standard Pie Crust*
1   *cup sharp cheddar-type cheese, shredded*
1   *egg white, beaten until frothy with 1 tablespoon water*
¾   *cup finely chopped black walnuts or hickory nuts*

1. Preheat oven to 350°.
2. Make pie crust according to recipe,

but add the shredded cheese before mixing in the water.

3. Roll out dough ¼ inch thick and cut into finger-size sticks.

4. Brush all surfaces of sticks with egg-white mixture.

5. Roll in chopped nuts and place 1 inch apart on ungreased cookie sheets.

6. Bake 12 minutes, or until golden and firm to the touch.

7. Transfer to racks to become firm before serving. Serve warm or at room temperature.

Makes about 3 dozen.

WATERCRESS TURNOVERS

Cream Cheese Pastry:
¼   *cup (½ stick) butter, softened at room temperature*
1   *8-ounce package cream cheese, softened at room temperature*
2   *cups flour*
¼   *teaspoon freshly ground pepper*
½   *teaspoon salt*
4   *tablespoons water*

Filling:
3   *tablespoons butter*
½   *cup wild leeks (white parts only) or chives, finely chopped*
     Enough watercress, cooked (page 170) and drained, to make 1 cup when puréed through a colander or in electric blender
     Salt and freshly ground pepper to taste
½   *teaspoon crumbled dried basil or 1 ½ teaspoons fresh basil, minced*
½   *cup dry bread crumbs*

Garnish: 1   *lemon, thinly sliced*

1. Make pastry: Cream together butter and cream cheese.

2. Sift together flour, pepper, and salt.

3. Blend the two mixtures, using a

pastry blender or a large fork, then sprinkle in water and mix just until dough holds together in a ball.

4. Wrap in plastic and chill very thoroughly, for at least 1 hour, so it will be firm enough to roll out.

5. Preheat oven to 350°.

6. Make filling: Melt butter in a skillet over low heat and cook leeks or chives until tender but not browned.

7. Combine with puréed watercress, salt, pepper, and basil, then mix in bread crumbs.

8. Roll out pastry ⅛ inch thick and cut into 20 4-inch rounds.

9. Place about 2 tablespoonfuls of filling near the center of each round and fold in half.

10. Seal around the curved edges with the tines of a fork and place 2 inches apart on a baking sheet. Bake for 15 minutes, or till golden brown.

11. Serve hot, garnished with lemon slices.

Makes 20 turnovers.

ROLLED WATERCRESS SANDWICHES

1 *8-ounce package cream cheese, softened at room temperature*
1 *cup watercress leaves, chopped and moderately packed*
2 *loaves thin-sliced bread, 1-pound size, crusts cut off*
½ *pound (2 sticks) butter, softened at room temperature*
Watercress sprigs for garnishing

1. Beat together cream cheese and chopped watercress.

2. Spread bread slices with butter, then spread with cream cheese–watercress mixture.

3. Roll each slice firmly, holding roll with a toothpick if necessary.

4. Place in large shallow pan and cover with slightly damp towel until serving time; refrigerate if not served immediately.

5. Serve on a silver or glass tray, garnished with sprigs of watercress.

Makes about 40 sandwiches.

MARINATED MUSHROOMS

On an appetizer tray, these mushrooms are always popular. We always serve them chilled. They'll keep in the refrigerator for up to two weeks.

½ *cup white vinegar*
½ *cup oil, preferably olive*
1 *bay leaf*
6 *peppercorns, slightly crushed*
1 *tablespoon chopped parsley*
2 to 3 *cups of small whole meadow mushrooms or chanterelles, or the same amount of oyster mushrooms, sulphur shelf, or puffballs, diced*
Boiling water, as needed
1 *teaspoon salt*

1. In a saucepan boil together the vinegar, oil, bay leaf, peppercorns, and parsley for 5 minutes; cover and keep hot.

2. Place mushrooms in a pot, add boiling water to cover, and add salt. Simmer until tender, for 8 to 10 minutes, depending on size and kind.

3. Drain mushrooms (keep the liquid for another use), pat them dry on paper towels, and place them in a bowl.

4. Pour hot marinade over mushrooms and let them cool.

5. Transfer mushrooms and liquid to a glass jar, cover, and store in the refrigerator for 5 days or more before using. Serve chilled.

Makes about 1½ pints.

HICKORY NUT–STUFFED EGGS

6   *hard-cooked eggs, cooled, shelled, and*
       halved lengthwise
2   *tablespoons softened butter*
2   *tablespoons light cream*
2   *tablespoons prepared mustard, prefera-*
       bly Dijon
⅓   *cup hickory nuts, finely chopped*
       Salt to taste
       Freshly ground pepper, if desired
       Watercress for garnishing

1. Remove egg yolks, mash them, and blend well with butter and cream.

2. Add mustard, nuts, salt to taste, and pepper, if you like. Mix thoroughly.

3. Spoon mixture back into egg whites.

4. Arrange on a platter and garnish with sprigs of watercress.

Makes 12 stuffed egg halves.

DITTANY–SOUR CREAM DIP

We serve this as a snack or appetizer, with crackers or potato chips for dipping.

1   *tablespoon butter*
¼   *cup fresh dittany leaves, finely chopped*
2   *tablespoons chopped chives*
½   *cup commercial sour cream*
½   *cup cottage cheese, any kind*
       Salt (optional)

1. In a small skillet, melt butter over medium heat. Add dittany and chives and cook, stirring, for about 3 to 5 minutes, or until well wilted. Cool the mixture.

2. Place sour cream and cottage cheese in jar of an electric blender and blend until smooth.

3. Stir herbs into cream mixture. Taste and add salt, if needed.

Makes about 1 cup.

PALESTINIAN DITTANY DIP

This is an unusal dip, especially good on thin crisp toast.

½   *cup olive oil*
¼   *cup chopped fresh chives*
1   *cup chopped fresh dittany leaves*
¼   *teaspoon minced wild garlic*
½   *teaspoon salt, or to taste*
3   *slices thin white bread, cut into quarters*
       and toasted until crisp

1. Pour olive oil into a small skillet and set over low heat. Add the chives, dittany, and garlic and cook, stirring, for 5 minutes, or until herbs are well wilted.

2. Add salt to taste and serve warm, with the thin toast for dipping.

Makes about 1 cup.

JELLY-NUT SPREAD

½   *cup wild fruit jelly, any flavor that*
       pleases you, or wild-fruit jam
       or marmalade
½   *cup chopped pecans, black walnuts,*
       butternuts, or hickory nuts

Mix jelly and nuts well and use as a sweet spread or sandwich filling.

Makes about 1 cup.

MUSHROOM SPREAD OR RELISH

This canapé spread is also good as a relish to accompany wildfowl or rabbit.

  1½ *cups meadow mushrooms, sliced, or chanterelles*
      Boiling water
  ½ *teaspoon salt*
  ½ *cup stuffed olives, finely chopped*
  ½ *cup sweet pickles, finely chopped*
  1 *hard-cooked egg, finely chopped*
  2 to 3 *tablespoons Mayonnaise**
      Salt, if needed

1. Cover mushrooms with boiling water in a saucepan, add salt, and simmer for 8 to 10 minutes, or until tender. Drain (save the juice for another use) and cool.

2. Mix with remaining ingredients.
Makes about 2 cups.

MUSHROOM AND RADISH SPREAD

  1½ *cups chanterelles or sliced meadow mushrooms*
      Boiling water, as needed
  ½ *teaspoon salt*

  ½ *cup radishes, finely diced*
  1 *small cucumber, peeled and finely diced*
  2 *tablespoons chopped chives*
  1 *tablespoon Mayonnaise**
  1 *teaspoon Prepared Mustard* or mild-flavored prepared mustard*
  ½ *teaspoon paprika*
  ½ *teaspoon salt, or to taste*

1. Cover mushrooms with boiling water, add salt, and simmer for 8 to 10 minutes, or until tender. Drain (save the liquid for soup or gravy) and cool.

2. Combine mushrooms with remaining ingredients and chill in refrigerator for at least one hour before serving as a spread for canapés.
Makes about 2 cups.

FRUIT AND CREAM CHEESE SPREAD

This is a lovely sweet spread for sugar cookies, crackers, plain bread, or thin toast.

  1 *4-ounce package cream cheese, softened at room temperature*
  2 *tablespoons light cream*
  4 *tablespoons sugar*
  ½ *cup wild strawberries, blackberries, or mulberries, rinsed, hulled if necessary, and drained; or peeled, seeded, and mashed papaws; or chopped May apples*

1. Mix cream cheese and light cream, beating until fluffy.

2. Stir sugar into the fruit.

3. With a two-tined fork, combine the fruit with the cream cheese, mixing thoroughly.
Makes about 1 cup.

MINT AND APPLESAUCE SPREAD

Spread on sugar cookies or crackers for a sweet snack, or served with hot muffins and butter, this is unusual and delicious. It's also good as a relish, especially with pork or lamb.

1   *cup seedless raisins, soaked in warm*
        water for 30 minutes and drained
1   *cup chopped fresh spearmint leaves,*
        moderately packed
2   *tablespoons applesauce*
1   *tablespoon sugar*

1. Chop raisins fine, or run through food grinder.
2. Add chopped mint, applesauce, and sugar and stir well.
3. Serve at once or store, refrigerated, for up to 12 hours before use.
Makes about 2 cups.

NUTTED CREAM CHEESE SPREAD

½   *cup (1 stick) softened butter, at room*
        temperature
1   *4-ounce package cream cheese, softened*
        at room temperature
1   *cup nutmeats, finely chopped*
        (pecans, hickory nuts, but-
        ternuts, or black walnuts)
¼   *teaspoon salt, or to taste*
½   *cup celery, finely chopped*

1. Cream butter and cheese together.
2. Add nuts, salt, and celery and cream well.

3. Serve as a spread for halves of biscuits, or on crackers or crisp toast rounds.
Makes about 2 cups.

STRAWBERRY BUTTER

1   *cup butter (2 sticks), cut into pieces*
½   *teaspoon salt*
2   *teaspoons confectioners' sugar*
¾   *cup wild strawberries, hulled, rinsed,*
        and drained

1. Put butter and salt into the jar of an electric blender and whip until light.
2. Add sugar and berries and run blender at high speed for 2 minutes, or until spread is very fluffy.
3. Refrigerate in covered container. Use in tea sandwiches or on pancakes or toast. The spread will keep for a day or two when refrigerated.
Makes about 2 cups.

ORANGE AND ONION SPREAD

We like to spread this unusual combination on crackers as a canapé, and we also use it in sandwiches made with sliced turkey, duck, or goose.

1   *medium-sized seedless orange,*
        pulverized in an electric
        blender, peel and all
½   *cup wild onion bulbs, finely chopped*
¼   *cup wild leeks, including 3 inches of the*
        tops, finely chopped
2   *tablespoons chopped chives*
3   *tablespoons Vinaigrette Dressing**

Mix all ingredients well and chill before serving.
Makes about 1 cup.

PEPPER GRASS–RADISH SPREAD

A good spread for melba toast or crackers, and a good relish for cold duck or rabbit sandwiches. My nephew Haroldj also likes it as a dip for potato chips.

1   cup pepper grass seeds (page 85)
2   tablespoons Mayonnaise*
¼   teaspoon curry powder
½   package (4-ounce size) cream cheese
6   large radishes, coarsely chopped
    Small amount of water, if needed

Combine all ingredients except water in the jar of an electric blender and blend to a fairly smooth paste; add a little water if spread seems too thick to blend easily.
Makes about 1 ½ cups.

SPICED NUT NIBBLE

1   egg white
1½   tablespoons water
½   cup sugar
1   teaspoon salt
¼   teaspoon ground allspice
¼   teaspoon ground cloves
¼   teaspoon ground ginger
¼   teaspoon grated nutmeg
1   teaspoon ground cinnamon
½   cup black walnuts, coarsely chopped
½   cup hickory nuts, coarsely chopped
1   cup pecans, coarsely chopped

1. Preheat oven to 275°.
2. Beat egg white, water, and sugar together until frothy. Beat in salt, allspice, cloves, ginger, nutmeg, and cinnamon.
3. Mix black walnuts, hickory nuts, and pecans together.

4. Put nuts ½ cup at a time into the spiced syrup, lift them out with a slotted spoon, and place them on a greased cookie sheet.
5. Bake 45 minutes, stirring occasionally.
Makes about 2 cups.

PECANS TOASTED WITH CHIVES

4   cups shelled pecan halves
4   beef bouillon cubes, crumbled
½   cup dried chopped chives
¼   cup (½ stick) butter
    Salt and freshly ground pepper, if desired

1. Preheat oven to 300°.
2. Toast pecans in shallow pan in oven for 30 minutes, stirring occasionally.
3. Add crumbled bouillon cubes, chives, and butter, mixing well.
4. Return to oven for 15 minutes and continue to toast, again stirring often.
5. Add salt and pepper, if desired.
6. The nuts may be served immediately, warm or cool, or stored in an airtight container for future use. They will keep for a month in the cupboard, or indefinitely if frozen.
Makes about 1 quart.

SWEET ONIONS

I doubt that this is actually a "pickle," but the onions are sweet, crispy, and nippy when prepared this way. An unusual snack, they will keep for two days or so if refrigerated.

   2   *cups wild onion bulbs, peeled*
   ½   *cup sugar*
       Water

1. Place one layer of onions in a large-mouthed jar or a small crock.
2. Sprinkle with part of the sugar.
3. Repeat layers until jar is filled.
4. Add water to cover. Place a saucer or plate on top of onions and weight it down (I use a rock) to hold onions under the surface.
5. Refrigerate onions and allow them to stand overnight before serving.
   Makes about 2 cups.

SOUPS

ALLIUM BROTH

6 *cups water*
1 *cup of any finely chopped member of the Allium genus—wild garlic, leeks, or onions (white parts only), or chives*
2 *tablespoons wine vinegar*
Salt and freshly ground pepper to taste
1 *slice bacon, fried until crisp, drained, and crumbled*

1. Bring the water to a boil, add garlic, leeks, onions, or chives, lower the heat, and simmer, covered, for 30 to 40 minutes, or until the flavor suits you.
2. Add vinegar and let broth stand 5 minutes.

3. Strain off broth, add salt and pepper to taste, and serve steaming hot in mugs, topped with crumbled bacon and with rye toast on the side.
Serves 8.

ASPARAGUS SOUP À LA WILDFLOWER

This pale-green soup is nourishing and warming. I like to serve it on a crisp spring evening in crockery mugs, accompanied by melba toast rounds and tall glasses of milk.

2 *cups cut-up asparagus (stringy pieces and broken tips can be used)*
2 *cups strong chicken broth*
2 *tablespoons butter*
2 *tablespoons flour*
1 *teaspoon lemon juice*
1 *teaspoon sugar*

Garnish: *1 tablespoon chopped fresh or dried parsley*

1. Simmer the asparagus pieces for 15 minutes in the chicken broth. Drain, reserving cooking liquid.
2. In a 2-quart saucepan, melt butter over low heat and stir in flour. Remove from heat.
3. Gradually whisk the asparagus liquid into the butter-flour mixture and return pan to medium heat.
4. Stir until the soup base has thickened, then cook for a minute or two more. Set off heat.
5. Purée the asparagus, using a sieve, food mill, or electric blender.
6. Combine purée with the soup base. Add lemon juice and sugar.
7. Reheat soup and serve hot, garnished with parsley.
Serves 4.

CHILLED CREAM OF ASPARAGUS SOUP

½   cup water
25   spears of asparagus, thinly sliced
1   cup White Sauce*
1½   cups milk
¼   cup commercial sour cream
½   teaspoon salt
⅛   teaspoon freshly ground pepper, or to
     taste
1   teaspoon minced fresh basil leaves, or
     ½ teaspoon crumbled dried basil

Garnish: *Additional sour cream, or cooked asparagus tips*

1. In a saucepan, bring water to a boil. Add asparagus; simmer, covered, for 5 minutes.
2. In container of an electric blender, combine white sauce, milk, sour cream, salt, pepper, basil, asparagus, and cooking liquid. Blend at high speed for 2 minutes, or until smooth.
3. Refrigerate, covered, until very cold—several hours or overnight. At serving time, taste and add more seasoning, if needed.
4. Garnish each helping with additional sour cream or cooked asparagus tips.
Serves 4.

CREAM OF BLACK WALNUT SOUP

2   cups black walnuts, chopped
3   tablespoons chopped celery
1   tablespoon chopped chives
5   cups chicken stock
2   tablespoons cream sherry

2   teaspoons butter
1   cup heavy cream
     Salt to taste
     Grated nutmeg for topping

1. Combine black walnuts, celery, and chives with chicken stock in a saucepan, bring to a boil, then cook for 20 minutes over medium heat.
2. Stir in sherry, butter, cream, and salt to taste.
3. Reheat and serve in individual bowls, being sure to ladle some walnuts into each.
Top each helping with a sprinkle of nutmeg.
Serves 8.

BLUEBERRY OR HUCKLEBERRY SLUSH

This icy soup can be served as a first course, with or without the whipped cream, and it is also a delicious dessert, either for an afternoon tea party or following a light supper. Its color is a beautiful pale blue.

4   cups ripe blueberries or huckleberries,
     washed and drained
1   cup sugar
1   teaspoon ground cinnamon
¼   teaspoon grated nutmeg
6 to 8 cardamom seeds, tied in cheesecloth
     About 3 cups water
1   cup heavy cream
     Whipped cream for garnishing
     (optional)

1. Put berries, sugar, cinnamon, nutmeg, and cardamom seeds in a saucepan. Add water to cover.
2. Bring to a boil, reduce heat, cover, and simmer for 15 minutes.
3. Remove cardamom seeds and strain

off juice, using a colander; reserve berries and juice.

4. Freeze juice until slushy.

5. Meanwhile, mix cream with the cooked berries and chill.

6. At serving time, gently fold berry mixture into frozen juice.

7. Ladle into crystal punch cups and garnish each, if you like, with a blob of whipped cream. Serve immediately.

Serves 8.

JUDAS'S-EAR MUSHROOM SOUP

This soup can be made with fresh Judas's-ear mushrooms as well as the dried ones. It will require about 2 cups of fresh mushrooms, cleaned, then cut into tiny pieces with kitchen shears. Add them to the hot broth and continue with recipe as given. Tasty but not too filling, this soup is a great first course for a dinner of meat pie or roasted meat. I often add sliced fresh Jerusalem artichokes to the soup just before serving, if it is the season to obtain them. Sliced canned water chestnuts add an interesting texture also.

4   *cups chicken broth*
½   *cup dried Judas's-ear mushrooms (page 73), crumbled*
2   *tablespoons vegetable oil*
1 *or* 2 *wild garlic or leek plants (white parts only), chopped, or ¼ cup chopped chives*
1   *tablespoon fresh ginger root, ground or finely minced*
2   *tablespoons soy sauce, preferably imported*
½   *cup fresh or canned mung bean sprouts*

1. Heat broth just to boiling point. Add mushrooms and set aside, covered.

2. Pour oil into a small skillet and cook

garlic, leeks, or chives with the ginger root over low heat until softened, about 10 minutes. Add soy sauce.

3. Add contents of the skillet to soup, return to heat, cover, and simmer for 45 minutes.

4. Five minutes before serving, add bean sprouts and reheat.

Serves 6.

DANDELION BROTH

In the North a lawn covered with yellow dandelions is a reason to celebrate the coming of spring. This is not the case in the South, for here it is not at all unusual to find a few flowers blooming at any time of the year. When I notice the flowers I also start really looking for the tender, very young leaves of the plant. It is well worth the search to serve a pot of this broth. It's green and light and clear and particularly tasty on cool evenings in front of the fireplace. The chives give just a hint of onion flavor.

2   *cups very young dandelion leaves*
    Boiling water for blanching
6   *cups water*
½   *cup finely chopped chives*
    Salt to taste
    Lemon-peel twists for garnishing

1. Wash dandelion leaves, put in a pot, cover with boiling water, bring again to a boil, and boil for 1 minute. Drain.

2. Bring 6 cups of water to a boil; add chives and lower heat until liquid is just simmering.

3. Add blanched dandelion leaves and simmer, covered, for 15 minutes.

4. Strain, add salt, and serve broth hot in mugs with a twist of lemon peel in each.

Serves 8.

A BROTH OF GREENS

6   cups water
1   cup chopped mustard leaves, packed
    down
1   cup chopped dock leaves, any variety,
    packed
1   clove of garlic, slightly crushed
2   slices bacon, chopped
1   teaspoon salt, or to taste
½   cup Pernod or anise liqueur

1. Bring water to a boil in a large saucepan.
2. Add mustard, dock, garlic, bacon, and salt.
3. Turn heat low and simmer, covered, for 30 minutes.
4. Strain out solids and add Pernod or liqueur.
5. Serve hot in crockery mugs with thin toast or melba toast spread with Watercress Butter.*

Serves 6 to 8.

GARLIC AND HERB SOUP

Don't let the quantity of garlic scare you off—it is considerably less potent cooked than it is raw. This meal-in-a-bowl makes a filling light supper. Serve with a tossed salad and your favorite bread.

6   wild garlic plants, bulbs as well as leaves
    Boiling water for blanching garlic
2   quarts water
2   teaspoons salt
    Freshly ground pepper to taste
4   whole cloves
¼   teaspoon crumbled dried sage, or ¾
    teaspoon chopped fresh sage
¼   teaspoon crumbled dried thyme, or ¾
    teaspoon chopped fresh thyme

1   tablespoon dried parsley, or 3 tablespoons
    fresh parsley
1   bay leaf
4   egg yolks
¼   cup butter, softened

Garnish: ½ cup grated Swiss-type cheese

1. Cut tops off garlic, chop greens, and set them aside.
2. Pour boiling water over garlic bulbs; let stand a minute or two, then drain.
3. Strip off skins from bulbs and slice bulbs thin.
4. Put 2 quarts of water in a large saucepan and add garlic slices and tops, salt, pepper, cloves, sage, thyme, parsley, and bay leaf. Bring to a boil, lower heat, and simmer for 15 minutes. Remove bay leaf and cloves.
5. Beat egg yolks and butter together till thick and put into large saucepan.
6. Gradually pour the soup into the egg mixture, stirring continually.
7. Return soup to low heat and simmer for 5 minutes, stirring occasionally; don't boil.
8. Serve hot, sprinkled with the grated cheese.

Serves 6 to 8.

MUSHROOM BROTH

½   cup (1 stick) butter
2   cups cleaned and coarsely chopped
    Judas's-ear mushrooms, oyster
    mushrooms, or sulphur shelf
¼   cup finely chopped wild onions, white
    parts only
2   tablespoons lemon juice
6   cups strong beef bouillon
3   tablespoons dry red wine, or amount
    desired

1. Melt butter in a large heavy saucepan and add mushrooms, onions, and lemon juice.

2. Cover tightly and cook over low heat, stirring occasionally, for 10 to 15 minutes, or until mushrooms are tender.

3. Add beef bouillon and wine, bring to a boil, turn heat to low, and simmer soup for 10 minutes.

4. Strain soup, discarding vegetables, and serve broth hot in cups.

Serves 8.

BRAISED MUSHROOM SOUP

¼   cup (½ stick) butter
2   tablespoons finely chopped wild onions or leeks, white parts only
2   cups cleaned and coarsely chopped meadow mushrooms, sulphur shelf, or oyster mushrooms
1   teaspoon lemon juice
½   teaspoon salt, or to taste
¼   teaspoon freshly ground black pepper, or to taste
¼   teaspoon paprika
5   cups water
1   cup heavy cream

Garnish: *Croutons*

1. Melt butter in a large heavy skillet. Add onions or leeks and cook over low heat until tender but not browned.

2. Add chopped mushrooms and cook, covered, for 10 minutes, or until tender. Set off heat for about 10 minutes to allow mushrooms to absorb pan juices.

3. Add lemon juice, salt, pepper, and paprika, stirring gently to mix.

4. Return to low heat and add water gradually, stirring; bring to a boil, then simmer for a few minutes to blend flavors.

5. Stir in cream and reheat just to simmering. Serve hot, topped with croutons on each serving.

Serves 8.

MOCK VICHYSSOISE

This soup is a good luncheon main course. Hard rolls or saltines go well with it, or serve Whitehouse Acorn Griddle Bread* toasted and buttered. Finish off the meal with a cup of Sumac Tea* and a slice of Black Walnut Pie.*

¼   cup chopped wild leeks or wild onions, white parts only
4   cups strong chicken broth
2   cups boiled Jerusalem artichokes (page 146), peeled and sliced
1   cup light cream
     Salt and freshly ground pepper to taste

Garnish: *Chives, finely cut*

1. Simmer leeks until tender in the chicken broth, about 15 minutes.

2. Add Jerusalem artichokes and force soup through a sieve or food mill.

3. Add cream and salt and pepper to taste. Reheat just to simmering, if you're serving the soup hot; or chill and serve icy cold. Garnish with minced chives.

Serves 6.

CHILLED ROSE-HIP SOUP

This sweet soup is high in vitamin C, and it makes a delicious cool opening for a summer meal.

> 4 cups ripe rose hips, garden and wild kinds mixed, bruised with a rolling pin
> Water
> 1 cup sugar
> 2 tablespoons cornstarch

Garnish: ½ cup heavy cream, whipped at serving time

1. Cover rose hips with water in a saucepan, bring to a boil, and boil 10 minutes.
2. Strain through cheesecloth, discard hips, and return liquid to heat. Add enough water to make 4 cups.
3. Add sugar, bring to boil, and set pan off heat.
4. Mix cornstarch with ¼ cup water and stir into the soup. Return pan to medium heat and cook until soup is clear and lightly thickened.
5. Cool soup, then chill. Serve with a dab of whipped cream on each portion.
   Serves 4.

SWEET GOLDENROD SOUP

This is a hearty soup, especially appealing to the taste because of its slight anise flavor, and to the eye because of its golden color. Serve it with toast spread with Watercress Butter.*

> 4 cups chicken broth or, preferably, broth from cooking quail or duck
> 6 wild leeks, white parts only, or ½ cup chives, finely chopped

> ½ cup (packed) watercress leaves, finely chopped
> Peel of 1 lemon (yellow part only), shredded
> 1 or 2 cups of cooked chicken, quail, or duck, cubed
> ½ cup sweet goldenrod flowers, stripped from their stems
> ½ cup cubed Jerusalem Artichokes in Lemon Juice*

Garnish: *Sprigs of goldenrod and watercress*

1. Bring chicken broth to a boil in a large saucepan. Remove from the heat.
2. Add leeks or chives, watercress, lemon peel, and cubed chicken, quail, or duck. Stir and reheat to boiling.
3. Place goldenrod flowers and Jerusalem artichokes in a warmed soup tureen and pour hot soup over them.
5. Garnish with a sprig each of goldenrod and watercress and serve at once.
   Serves 6.

PURSLANE IN VEGETABLE SOUPS

In any soup recipe calling for okra, try substituting an equal amount of purslane, coarsely chopped. It will contribute a mucilaginous quality similar to that of okra, and the flavor is quite distinct but mild.

PURSLANE AND BACON SOUP

This stick-to-the-ribs soup can be made from either fresh or frozen purslane.

8   *slices bacon*
2   *cups purslane, rinsed, drained, and*
    coarsely chopped
3   *cups beef broth*
2   *cups water*
¼   *cup rice or quick-cooking barley*
1   *teaspoon salt*

1. Fry bacon until crisp, drain it on paper towels, and crumble. Reserve bacon fat in the skillet.
2. In the bacon fat cook the purslane over medium heat for 10 minutes, stirring occasionally. Set aside.
3. Bring beef broth and water to a boil in a saucepan, add rice or barley, and simmer until tender.
4. When rice or barley is done, add purslane and salt, bring soup to a boil, lower heat, and simmer for 10 minutes.
5. During last 3 minutes of cooking, add part of crumbled bacon.
6. Serve soup in a tureen, garnished with remaining bacon.

Serves 6.

PURSLANE AND TOMATO SOUP

Served with a toasted cheese sandwich, this hearty vegetable soup makes a most satisfying lunch or supper, especially if you finish with a chilled fruit dessert.

2   *tablespoons vegetable oil*
2   *cups purslane, rinsed, drained, and*
    coarsely chopped
2   *cups ripe tomatoes, peeled and coarsely*
    chopped
¼   *cup chopped chives*
1   *teaspoon finely chopped fresh basil, or ½*
    teaspoon crumbled dried basil
1   *tablespoon lemon juice*
3   *cups water*
1   *cup beef broth*

1. Pour oil into a large heavy pot and cook purslane, tomatoes, and chives over medium heat for 10 minutes, stirring occasionally.
2. Add basil, lemon juice, water, and beef broth. Bring to a boil, lower heat, cover, and simmer for 20 minutes. Serve hot.

Serves 6 to 8.

FRENCH ONION SOUP

½   *cup (1 stick) butter*
2   *cups thinly sliced wild onions, white*
    parts only
6   *cups strong beef bouillon*
1   *teaspoon salt, or to taste*
¼   *teaspoon freshly ground pepper, or to*
    taste
2   *cups bread cubes, toasted until quite dry*
    (plain croutons), or 8 slices of very
    crisp toasted French- or Italian-type
    bread
6 to 8 *tablespoons grated Parmesan cheese*

1. Melt butter in a large saucepan and cook onions in it, stirring them over medium heat till golden yellow.
2. Add bouillon and salt and pepper to taste and bring to a boil. Lower heat to medium and cook 15 minutes.
3. Distribute toasted bread cubes or slices of toast among 8 soup bowls and pour soup over them. Top each bowlful with grated cheese and serve immediately.

Serves 8.

CREAM OF SORREL SOUP

This slightly tart soup is a great beginning for a light fish supper, and its color is quite pleasingly green.

1½ cups Puréed Sorrel*
2 cups chicken broth
2 tablespoons flour
1½ cups milk
    Salt and freshly ground pepper to taste

Garnish: ½ cup commercial sour cream, grated nutmeg

1. Place sorrel purée and chicken broth in a saucepan and bring quickly to a boil. Remove from heat.
2. Stir flour into ½ cup of the milk until smooth.
3. Add the flour paste, then the remaining milk, to the sorrel broth. Season with salt and pepper and heat thoroughly, simmering long enough to cook the flour thickening.
4. Serve hot in individual mugs, each topped with a dab of sour cream sprinkled with nutmeg.

SORREL SOUP

2 strips bacon
½ cup chopped wild onions or leeks, white parts only
4 cups strong chicken broth
2 cups (packed) sorrel, washed, stems removed, and chopped
½ teaspoon salt, or to taste
    Freshly ground pepper to taste

Garnish: Sprigs of parsley

1. Fry the bacon until crisp. Then drain and crumble it, keeping the fat in the skillet.

2. In the bacon fat cook the onions or leeks gently until soft and golden yellow.
3. Bring chicken broth to a boil. Add sorrel, salt, pepper, and cooked onions or leeks. Lower heat, cover, and simmer for 20 minutes.
4. Pour soup into a tureen and garnish with crumbled bacon and a sprig of parsley. Serve hot.
Serves 6.

VIOLET GREENS SOUP

2 cups (packed) of heart-shaped violet leaves, stems removed
1 cup (packed) watercress, coarse stems removed
4 tablespoons butter or margarine
4 wild leeks (white parts), finely chopped
2½ cups water
4 tablespoons cornstarch
2 cups heavy cream
    Salt and freshly ground pepper to taste

Garnish: Handful of violet blossoms, stems removed

1. Rinse and drain the violet leaves and watercress. Chop the leaves.
2. Melt butter in a skillet over low heat and cook the greens and the leeks for about 15 minutes, stirring often. Set off heat and add 2 cups of the water.
3. Mix cornstarch with remaining ½ cup water and stir into the skillet of greens.
4. Return to medium heat and bring to a boil, stirring until thickened.
5. Gradually add cream and continue to heat till thoroughly warmed. Season with salt and pepper.
6. Pour into a warmed soup tureen. Adorn the top with violet flowers just before serving.
Serves 6.

WATERCRESS AND SOUR CREAM SOUP

3   cups buttermilk
2   cups (loosely packed) watercress, rinsed,
     drained, and coarsely chopped
2 or 3 drops Tabasco or other hot pepper
     sauce
1   cup commercial sour cream
     Salt, if needed

Garnish: Sprigs of watercress

1. In the jar of an electric blender, blend buttermilk and watercress at low speed for 3 minutes, or until smooth.
2. Add hot pepper sauce and sour cream and blend again at medium speed until mixed. Taste, and add salt, if needed.
3. Chill thoroughly and serve cold in individual bowls, garnished with watercress sprigs.
Serves 8.

CHILLED WOOD SORREL SOUP

4   cups strong beef bouillon
6   Jerusalem artichokes, peeled, boiled (page
     146), and coarsely chopped
1   cup wild leeks, white parts only, boiled
     until tender and chopped
2   cups (packed) wood sorrel leaves, washed
     and shredded
1   cup light cream
     Salt and freshly ground pepper to taste

Garnish: Wood sorrel leaves and flowers

1. Combine bouillon, Jerusalem artichokes, leeks, and wood sorrel in a sauce-

pan, bring to a boil, and cook over medium heat for 5 minutes.
2. Add cream, stir, and remove from heat. Season with salt and pepper.
3. Chill and serve icy cold, garnishing each individual serving with a sorrel leaf and flower.
Serves 6.

HOT WOOD SORREL SOUP

½   cup (packed) mustard or winter cress
     leaves, rinsed and drained
¼   cup wild leeks, white parts only
¼   cup wild onions, white parts only
½   small head of cabbage, about 1 ½ cups
     when shredded
3   tablespoons butter
½   teaspoon sugar
4   cups strong beef bouillon
1   cup (packed) wood sorrel (oxalis) leaves,
     rinsed and drained
     Salt and freshly ground pepper to taste

Garnish: Wood sorrel leaves

1. Chop mustard or winter cress, leeks, onions, and cabbage and mix together.
2. Melt butter in a 3-quart saucepan, add chopped vegetables, and cook over medium heat, stirring often, until well wilted.
3. Add sugar and bouillon, cover pan, and simmer soup for 1 hour.
4. Add wood sorrel leaves and more water if needed to cover vegetables, return to the boiling point, turn down heat, and simmer soup for 10 minutes.
5. Season with salt and pepper and serve hot, garnished with a few sorrel leaves.
Serves 6.

VEGETABLES

GREENS

Recipes using greens, our most abundant wild food, make up a good part of this section on vegetables. Often I will speak of "greens" generally and not specify which plant to use. Most greens, though they vary in flavor and texture, can be interchanged in recipes, and most greens, just because of their differences in taste and texture, blend well. There will be some recipes that call for combining only two greens, and others that use one kind only because of the subtle tastes of certain plants. In most cases I will say only "greens," and you can use in the recipe your own favorite, or whatever is most available.

Among the vegetable recipes that follow, you will find basic directions for cooking each of the "pot greens" discussed in this book. Some greens need longer cooking than others, but generally you can cook together, if you like, any combination of greens that require about the same cooking time. The vegetable recipes begin with some of my favorite ways of using either combined or interchangeable greens. Other greens recipes will be found farther along in the section under their own names—dandelion, pokeweed, and so on.

Some greens plants need special preparation for cooking, others don't. Information on such special preparation will be given in this section when it is needed.

As to nutrition: research has been done into the vitamin and mineral content and general nutritiousness of many wild greens, and it has been found that the wild growers are higher in nutritional value than most cultivated greens plants.

The Basic Cooking of Wild Greens

For a whole list of greens *(see below)*, the basic preparation and cooking method is the same; some will take a little longer than others to become tender, however. Follow these directions for greens to be served with a simple seasoning of butter, salt, and pepper, or for greens to be drained and used in any of my recipes that call for them in cooked form.

Pick the leaves from any tough stems of the plants and discard such stems and any leaves that are obviously tough or insect-infested. Wash the greens carefully through two or three waters, or more if necessary. (I find that warm water cleans them best.) Drain them well in a salad basket or on a thick towel.

Put the greens into a saucepan and add very little water—the leaves contain considerable water of their own, and additional water will cling to them after washing. Cook over medium-high heat, forking the leaves over in the pot occasionally so they'll cook evenly, until they're done to your taste. Salt them to taste, about half a teaspoon of salt to a quart of raw greens, and add any other seasonings you like if you're serving the greens as a vegetable. If you're using them in a recipe, check the recipe before draining them—some recipes call for the juice, too.

This method is fine for amaranth, chickweed, dock, lamb's quarters, mustard, pepper grass, purslane, violet leaves, wild lettuce, winter cress, and wood sorrel. To cook chicory, dandelion, henbit, milkweed, plantain, pokeweed, sorrel, sow thistle, or watercress, see individual recipes in the following pages.

SOUFFLÉ OF MIXED GREENS

This festive dish can well serve as a main course when accompanied by a salad and your favorite bread. Finish off the menu with a not-too-sweet dessert, such as fresh fruit or fruit cup. The soufflé can be made with any of the greens you like best; it is particularly good when an assortment of greens is used.

    2   tablespoons butter
    ¼   cup minced wild leeks or wild onions
        (white parts only) or chives
    2   cups cooked greens (page 132), drained
        and chopped
    2   tablespoons flour
        Salt and freshly ground pepper to taste
    ½   teaspoon dill seed
    ½   teaspoon crumbled dried basil or 1 ½
        teaspoons minced fresh basil
    2   cups fine dry bread crumbs
    ½   cup heavy cream
    8   egg whites
    ½   teaspoon cream of tartar
    6   egg yolks, beaten only until mixed
    ¼   cup grated Swiss-type or Parmesan
        cheese

1. Preheat oven to 350°.
2. In a large skillet, melt butter over medium heat and cook leeks, onions, or chives until limp. Remove from heat.

3. Add greens. Sprinkle with flour, salt and pepper, dill, and basil, add crumbs, and stir well with a fork.
4. Gradually add cream, return pan to medium heat, and simmer till thickened. Set off heat.
5. Beat egg whites with cream of tartar until they form stiff peaks on the lifted beater, starting with slow speed and gradually increasing the speed of beating.
6. Stir egg yolks into bread crumb and greens mixture.
7. Gently fold the greens mixture into the stiff egg whites, sprinkling in the cheese as you fold.
8. Pour into a buttered 2-quart soufflé dish or casserole and bake for 30 minutes, or until firm.
Serves 8.

GREENS ITALIANO

This is a very filling dish and is the only vegetable you'll need with a meat-pie dinner, for instance. Follow it with a light dessert.

    1   large clove of garlic, finely chopped
    ¼   cup chives, finely chopped
    3   tablespoons oil, preferably olive oil
    4   cups cooked mixed greens (page 132),
        drained and chopped
    1   small can (8 ounces) tomato sauce
    1   teaspoon salt, or to taste
        Freshly ground black pepper to taste

1. In a small skillet, cook garlic and chives gently in the oil until tender but not browned.
2. Pour tomato sauce over the greens in a saucepan, season with salt and pepper, and heat.
3. Add the oil and herbs and toss well. Serve hot.
Serves 8.

CREAMED GREENS

Simple, hearty, and easily prepared, this dish is good with any main course of meat, poultry, or fish. We serve it with pot roast and finish with a light dessert, usually fresh fruit.

    2   tablespoons flour
    4   cups cooked and drained greens, either
            dandelion, chicory, or mustard (see
            recipes), or a combination
    ½   cup heavy cream
    1   cup beef bouillon
    1   teaspoon salt
        Freshly ground black pepper to taste
    2   tablespoons butter

1. Sprinkle flour over the greens in a saucepan and mix well.

2. Pour in cream and bouillon. Stir well.

3. Cover, bring to a boil, then lower heat and simmer 10 to 15 minutes, stirring occasionally. Season with salt and pepper.

4. Pour into serving dish and top with bits of butter. Serve hot.

Serves 8.

GREENS CREAMED WITH WILD ONIONS OR LEEKS

    2   tablespoons butter
    1   cup small wild onion bulbs or chopped
            wild leeks, white parts only
    1   tablespoon flour
    ½   cup heavy cream
    2   cups cooked greens (particularly good is
            a combination of chickweed and mus-
            tard with pokeweed—see basic recipes
            for cooking)
    2   hard-cooked eggs, chopped

1. Melt butter in a skillet and cook on-

ions or leeks over low heat until tender, about 10 minutes; do not allow to brown.

2. Push onions to one side of the skillet and sprinkle flour into the butter. Stir until there is a smooth paste and remove from heat.

3. Gradually add cream and return pan to low heat. Cook, stirring, until sauce is thick.

4. Stir in the greens and heat the mixture thoroughly.

5. Pour into serving dish and garnish with chopped eggs. Serve hot.

Serves 6.

GREENS LOAF

This loaf is perfect for people who want to serve a green vegetable plus a starch in one dish. To recycle leftovers, simply refrigerate the remainder of the loaf and slice it half an inch thick. Fry the slices in butter and serve with either a tomato or a cheese sauce.

    2   tablespoons butter
    ¼   cup celery leaves, chopped
    1   tablespoon flour
    2   cups cooked greens (page 132),
             drained (reserve juice) and chopped
    ¼   cup juice in which the greens were
             cooked
    1   egg, well beaten
    1½   cups cooked and cooled rice
    1   teaspoon salt, or to taste
    ¼   teaspoon celery seed
    2   slices bacon

1. Preheat oven to 400°.

2. Fry celery leaves in butter over low heat until wilted but not browned.

3. Sprinkle with flour and blend well.

4. Add greens, cooking juices, and beaten egg; stir over low heat until warm.

5. Pour into mixing bowl with rice, salt, and celery seed; mix well.

6. Pack into greased 9×5-inch loaf pan and place bacon strips on top.

7. Bake 30 minutes, or until firm and lightly browned, and unmold to serve hot.
Serves 8.

SOUTHERN-STYLE WILTED GREENS

This is my own way of "wilting" such greens as mustard, lamb's quarters, dock, and watercress, preferably mixed. Some people hereabouts prefer the more traditional way of merely pouring the hot bacon fat, vinegar, and seasonings over the tender greens and serving them without further cooking.

4 *slices bacon, cut into narrow crosswise strips*
6 *wild leeks, both white parts and the tender part of greens, coarsely chopped*
About 2 quarts tender raw greens, washed and thoroughly drained
¼ *cup vinegar*
Water, as needed
Salt (about 1 teaspoon) and freshly ground pepper to taste

1. Fry bacon until crisp, using a large heavy saucepan; remove bacon bits and reserve.

2. Add leeks to fat in pan and fry over medium heat till soft but not browned.

3. Add greens gradually and cook, stirring them with a fork, until they appear clear green in color.

4. Add vinegar and as little water as needed to keep the greens from sticking and cook them until tender, stirring occasionally; a few minutes are usually sufficient.

5. Season with salt and pepper to taste and serve hot, topped with the bacon.
Serves 8 to 10.

GREENS IN A TART SAUCE

6 *tablespoons butter*
1 *tablespoon chopped wild leeks or wild onions, white parts only*
4 *cups lamb's quarters or pokeweed, cooked (see their basic recipes) and barely drained*
3 *tablespoons white vinegar*
1 *teaspoon salt, or to taste*
¼ *teaspoon freshly ground pepper, or to taste*
4 *hard-cooked eggs, chopped fine after reserving 3 or 4 sliced rounds for garnishing*

1. Melt the butter in a large skillet and brown the leeks or onions.

2. Add greens, vinegar, salt, and pepper to the skillet and simmer for 15 minutes, turning the greens occasionally.

3. Drain greens, stir in chopped eggs, and serve hot with a few egg rounds as a garnish.
Serves 8.

AMARANTH

To serve as a green vegetable, amaranth leaves are cooked for about 10 to 12 minutes, or until tender, by the basic method given on page 132. Some like to serve these greens, after seasoning them, with vinegar or with lemon wedges.

AMARANTH GREENS WITH BACON

Similar in flavor to beet greens, amaranth greens are given a somewhat Oriental character by this recipe.

> 2   *quarts green amaranth leaves, washed and drained*
>   *Hot water, as needed*
> 2   *slices bacon, cut into squares*
> 4   *tablespoons cider vinegar*
> 1   *tablespoon soy sauce, imported if available*
>   *Salt and freshly ground pepper to taste*

1. Boil greens in water barely to cover for 15 minutes.
2. Drain off half the water.
3. Return to heat and add bacon, vinegar, soy sauce, salt, and pepper.
4. Simmer until tender, about 10 minutes. Serve hot.
Serves 8.

AMARANTH GREENS WITH BRANDIED ORANGE SAUCE

With its sweet-and-tart brandied sauce, this greens dish goes well with a fish or fowl main course. We usually complete the menu by serving a tray of raw carrot sticks, celery, and cauliflower sections, followed by a freshly baked pie and a cup of tea or coffee.

> 3   *cups cooked amaranth greens (page 132), salted to taste*
> ½   *can (6-ounce size) frozen orange-juice concentrate, thawed*
> ¼   *cup water*
> ¼   *cup brown sugar, packed*
> ¼   *cup fruit brandy, preferably apricot or peach*
> 1   *teaspoon grated or chopped fresh ginger root (½ teaspoon if dried)*
>   *Freshly cooked hot rice or egg noodles to serve 8*

1. Combine greens, orange-juice concentrate, and water in a saucepan and bring to a boil. Lower heat to medium.
2. Add brown sugar, brandy, and ginger root.
3. Simmer 10 minutes. Serve hot over rice or egg noodles.
Serves 8.

ASPARAGUS

Pick only asparagus spears that are pale green and tender for most of their length. Break off the tough part as far down as the stalk snaps easily. Wash spears thoroughly in warm water.

There are several good ways to cook asparagus. One is to lay the stalks flat in a large skillet or other shallow pan and add boiling salted water to cover (some people use just half an inch or so of water). Cover the skillet and cook the asparagus, till just tender—the time may vary from 10 to 20 minutes.

Another way is to cook the spears standing up. I happen to have a sky-blue 9-inch-high enamel coffee pot which I love to use. I stand the asparagus upright in this and cover the lower part of the spears with an inch or two of boiling salted water. If overcooked, asparagus is difficult to remove from a narrow tall pan, but we like our asparagus cooked as little as possible, so this works well for us. If you will tie your asparagus into small bunches, about ten to a bunch, they can be removed from any pot much more easily. I use knitting wool to tie mine, but any coarse string will do; small twine is inclined to cut the outside stalks.

ASPARAGUS RING

This is a particularly delightful dish when the center of the ring is filled with a cheese sauce to be spooned over the portions cut from the ring. To make the sauce, add grated sharp cheddar-type cheese to taste and a little Cayenne pepper to White Sauce.*

3 *eggs, separated*
1 *cup milk or light cream*
3 *tablespoons butter*
3 *tablespoons flour*
4 *cups cut-up cooked asparagus, salted to taste and drained thoroughly*

1. Preheat oven to 375°.
2. Beat egg whites until stiff enough for a meringue (very stiff peaks).
3. Mix milk or cream and egg yolks well.
4. Melt butter in a skillet over low heat and stir in flour to make a paste. Remove from heat.
5. Gradually stir the milk and egg mixture into the butter and flour paste.
6. Return skillet to low heat, stirring continually until sauce thickens heavily—about 10 minutes.
7. Remove from heat and add asparagus.
8. Fold egg whites into the mixture

and pour into greased 9-inch ring mold.
9. Set the mold in a pan of boiling water (water should reach about halfway up the sides of mold) and bake for 30 minutes, or until a knife blade comes out clean.
10. Unmold ring onto a warmed platter and serve hot.
Serves 6.

ASPARAGUS CANTONESE

3 *tablespoons oil, preferably peanut*
2 *or 3 bulbs wild garlic, peeled and lightly crushed*
1 *tablespoon sliced wild ginger root, or 2 teaspoons dried ginger root, cut up and soaked in warm water to soften, then drained*
20 *to 30 spears asparagus, cut into thin diagonal slices*
1 *cup sliced or chopped fresh mushrooms (I use Judas's ears)*
Salt to taste
Water, as needed

1. Heat oil in a skillet (one having a lid) over medium-high heat.
2. Add garlic and ginger and cook for a few seconds, stirring—don't brown.
3. Add asparagus and mushrooms, raise heat to high, and cook, tossing constantly with a large spoon, for 2 to 3 minutes, or until asparagus is bright green and vegetables are coated with oil.
4. Add salt to taste and about ½ cup water. Cover, lower heat to medium, and steam until asparagus is just tender-crisp, perhaps 5 minutes or less (test often); don't overcook. If needed, add a little more water during cooking.
5. Serve immediately, accompanied by hot rice.
Serves 6.

ASPARAGUS IN EGG SAUCE ON TOAST

¼ cup butter
¼ cup flour
1 cup hot milk
1 cup strong chicken broth
6 sliced hard-cooked eggs
1 tablespoon chives, finely chopped
1 teaspoon salt, or to taste
   Freshly ground black pepper to taste
4 cups cooked asparagus, cut into 1½-inch
   lengths
6 slices crisp, hot toast
6 slices crisply fried bacon, drained and
   crumbled

1. Melt butter in saucepan over low heat and blend in flour.
2. Whisk in milk and chicken broth. Cook over medium heat, stirring constantly, until mixture is thick, 5 to 10 minutes.
3. Continuing to stir, add chopped eggs, chives, salt, and pepper.
4. Add asparagus and heat thoroughly.
5. Serve on hot toast, topped with the crumbled bacon.
   Serves 6.

ASPARAGUS AND CHEESE SHORTCAKE

3 tablespoons butter
¼ cup chopped wild onions, white parts
   only
4 tablespoons flour
1 teaspoon salt
   Freshly ground black pepper to taste
2 cups hot milk
½ cup shredded cheddar-type cheese

30 spears of asparagus
1 batch of B.J.'s Biscuits,* cut into 3-inch
   rounds and freshly baked according
   to directions
2 hard-cooked eggs, sliced into rounds

1. Melt the butter in a skillet and fry the onions over medium heat till tender but not browned, about 10 minutes.
2. Push the onions to the side of the pan and add flour, stirring it into the butter until a thick paste is formed.
3. Remove from the heat. Add salt and pepper and gradually add the milk, stirring or whisking constantly until smooth.
4. Return to the stove over low heat and cook until thickened, about 5 to 10 minutes. Add cheese.
5. Add the asparagus spears to the sauce. Cover and cook over low heat 15 minutes, or until asparagus is tender.
6. Arrange split hot biscuits on a warm platter and top them with the asparagus and sauce. Garnish with egg slices and serve hot.
   Serves 6.

ASPARAGUS PIE

Asparagus pie is a good accompaniment for any type of broiled meat, especially beef or venison steaks. For hearty eaters you might add boiled and buttered Jerusalem artichokes, and I'd serve a fruit cup for dessert.

3 tablespoons butter
3 tablespoons flour
1 cup hot milk
2 chicken bouillon cubes
1 tablespoon minced chives
¾ teaspoon salt, or to taste
⅛ teaspoon freshly ground pepper, or to
   taste

4 *cups cooked asparagus, cut into 1-inch*
  pieces
4 *hard-cooked eggs, chopped*
  Baked Pie Shell,* cooled
½ *cup shredded sharp cheddar-type cheese*

1. Preheat oven to 400°.
2. Melt butter in a saucepan over low heat and blend in flour.
3. Add hot milk, stirring constantly, and cook over medium heat until mixture is thickened, 5 to 10 minutes.
4. Add bouillon cubes to sauce and stir until dissolved. Add chives, salt, and pepper, mixing well.
5. Add asparagus and remove pan from heat. Add chopped eggs.
6. Pour filling into baked pie shell and sprinkle top with shredded cheese.
7. Bake until cheese topping begins to brown, about 10 minutes.
8. Cut into wedges and serve at once.
Serves 4 to 6.

BRACKEN AND OTHER FERN FRONDS

The young, tender, tightly curled fronds—croziers or fiddleheads—of brack-en (or brake ferns) and of ostrich and cinnamon ferns are all prepared in the same way. Rub off the fuzz (or, for some ferns, the scaly coating) of the young, crisp fronds, wash them, and place them, lying flat, in a saucepan or skillet with a small amount of boiling salted water. Bring water again to a boil. Turn to low heat, cover, and simmer for 10 to 20 minutes, or until fronds are just tender (time will depend on the size and kind of fronds). Season with butter, salt, and pepper to taste, or serve with lemon juice or any sauce that would be suitable for asparagus.

BRACKEN FRONDS À LA ORANGE

2 *cups (packed) freshly picked young fronds*
  (fiddleheads) of bracken or other edible
  ferns, defuzzed and washed
4 *cups chicken broth*
1 *seedless orange, peel and all, processed to*
  a pulp in an electric blender
2 *eggs, beaten till foamy*
2 *slices of bacon, fried until crisp, drained,*
  and crumbled

1. Cover bracken fronds with 2 cups of the chicken broth, bring to a boil, cover, and simmer 5 minutes.
2. Mix the orange pulp with eggs in a saucepan.
3. Gradually add the remaining 2 cups of broth to egg mixture and heat, stirring constantly over low heat, until thick.
4. Pour cooked fronds and their broth into the thickened egg mixture.
5. Simmer gently, stirring occasionally, for 10 minutes.
6. Pour into individual soup bowls and top with crumbled bacon. Serve hot.
Serves 4 to 6.

BURDOCK

The basic cooking method for all parts of the burdock is the same. To cook the peeled roots, the flower stems (stripped of their skin), or the washed and drained young leaves, place the plant parts in a saucepan and cover with water. Add a teaspoon of baking soda per quart of water, bring the water to a boil, and pour it off. (The water will turn very green.) Cover with fresh water and boil until the vegetable is tender. Leaves will be done in a few minutes; stems or roots will take longer, up to 15 or 20 minutes. The use of soda in cooking vegetables is looked upon with disfavor by nutritionists, but in the case of burdock it is helpful in breaking down the fibers of the plant and making it more tender.

PARSLIED BURDOCK ROOTS

A substantial vegetable dish to serve with duck, quail, goose, or other poultry or wild fowl.

　　Water, as needed
4　cups sliced burdock roots, precooked (above)
¼　teaspoon salt

6　tablespoons butter
　　Freshly ground black pepper to taste
½　cup minced parsley
　　Lemon juice to taste

1. Pour a little water into a small saucepan and heat precooked burdock roots well.
2. Drain and add the salt, butter, pepper, parsley, and lemon juice. Stir well, reheat if necessary, and serve hot.
　　Serves 8.

BURDOCK ROOT PATTIES

4　cups sliced burdock roots, precooked (see above)
½　cup sliced wild onions or leeks, simmered in a little water until soft, then drained
1　egg, well beaten
½　cup dry bread crumbs
　　Salt to taste
1　tablespoon fresh parsley, finely chopped
　　Butter for frying

1. After burdock roots have been precooked, press them through a food mill or strainer to remove the stringy portions.
2. Mix the burdock, onions or leeks, egg, and bread crumbs. Add salt to taste.
3. Shape into patties and sprinkle with parsley; press parsley into surface.
4. Heat the butter in a skillet over medium heat until foam begins to die down and fry the patties till golden brown, turning them once. Serve hot.
　　Serves 8.

BURDOCK ROOTS IN BRANDIED ORANGE SAUCE

This is an elegant dish meant to be served with other elegant foods such as roast pheasant or duck, and perhaps followed by a jellied salad, such as an aspic containing watercress, or Asparagus Vinaigrette* as a salad course. If you have frozen berries on hand, a delicious finish for the meal would be a blackberry, raspberry, or strawberry pie topped with ice cream (see *Index*).

4 cups burdock roots, precooked (page *140*)
  Salt to taste
½ can (6-ounce size) frozen orange-juice concentrate, thawed
2 tablespoons light-brown sugar
2 tablespoons cornstarch
¼ cup warm water
¼ cup Cognac or other fine brandy
  Thin slices of orange for garnishing

1. Cut precooked burdock roots into bite-sized pieces. Add salt to taste.
2. Combine orange-juice concentrate and brown sugar and simmer together for 5 minutes in a heavy skillet or saucepan.
3. Mix cornstarch with water and add to juice mixture.
4. Add burdock roots to orange sauce. Add Cognac or brandy and simmer 10 minutes.
5. Garnish with thin slices of fresh orange. Serve hot.
Serves 8.

BURDOCK ROOTS WITH PINEAPPLE CHUNKS

This somewhat sweet dish goes very well with venison steak or fried squirrel. A green salad is recommended as a companion dish.

2 tablespoons butter
¼ cup brown sugar, packed
1 teaspoon lemon juice
1 cup canned, drained pineapple chunks (reserve juice)
½ cup pineapple syrup drained from chunks
2 tablespoons cornstarch
2 cups burdock roots, cut into rounds and precooked until tender (page *140*)

1. Melt butter in skillet over low heat, add brown sugar and lemon juice, stir, and set aside.
2. Mix pineapple syrup with the cornstarch and stir well.
3. Add the pineapple and cornstarch mixture to the butter and sugar mixture.
4. Return to low heat and stir constantly until the mixture is a thick sauce—about 20 minutes.
5. Add the burdock roots and pineapple chunks to the sauce and heat through. Serve hot.
Serves 6.

GLAZED BURDOCK SLICES

4 cups burdock roots, cut into rounds and precooked (page *140*)
½ cup granulated sugar
½ cup light-brown sugar, packed
¼ cup butter
  Hot cooked rice to serve 8
  Minced parsley for garnishing

1. Drain hot burdock roots and pat them dry on paper towels.
2. Mix sugars and roll burdock rounds in mixture.
3. Melt butter in a heavy skillet.
4. Put sugared burdock slices into skillet and fry gently over low heat, turning often till completely glazed.
5. Serve on bed of hot rice. Garnish with minced parsley.
Serves 8.

CAT-TAILS

To prepare cooked cat-tail buds to use in a recipe or to eat hot as a vegetable, remove the sheaths from young cat-tail flowers and plunge the spikes into a large pot of boiling salted water and cook over high heat for 15 minutes. Drain and serve hot, to be eaten like corn on the cob; or cool until the spikes can be handled and, using the inverted bowl of a spoon, scrape the flesh (buds) off the spikes and spread them on paper towels to rid them of excess moisture. Four to five dozen spikes will yield about two cups of cooked buds.

The sprouts taken from the roots in the spring before they begin to grow upward should be scrubbed, peeled, and rinsed. They are then ready to slice raw into salads, or you can boil them until tender in salted water (about 15 minutes) and either season them and serve as a vegetable, or cool and season them with Vinaigrette Dressing* or other dressing as a cooked-vegetable salad.

Young cat-tail shoots, gathered before the plant is more than about two feet high, are the famous "Cossack asparagus." Peel off the tough outer sheath and you have uncovered a crisp whitish-green core, which may be as much as a foot or eighteen inches long. Serve the core in strips as a nibble, or cut it up for salads, or cook the shoots for 15 minutes or so in boiling salted water and serve them with butter as a vegetable.

SPANISH CAT-TAIL BUD PIE

My daughter Angel and I visited my brother in Spain one summer, and while there we did a good bit of foraging and comparing their wild foods to our own familiar plants. My sister-in-law, Rosina, and I came upon a huge marsh filled with cat-tails and proceeded to cook them in as many ways as we could think of. We all chose this recipe as a favorite; even six-year-old Joey found it delicious.

> *Flesh (buds) scraped from 4 or 5 dozen uncooked young cat-tail spikes, about 2 cups*
> ¼ *cup butter*
> 2 *small hot dried peppers (chili peppers)*
> 1 *large clove of wild garlic, finely minced*
>   *Salt to taste*
> 1 *cup sharp cheddar-type cheese, shredded*
>   *Pinch of chili powder, or to taste*

1. Preheat oven to 400°.

2. Put the cat-tail buds in a skillet with the butter and cook over medium heat for 10 minutes, stirring occasionally.

3. Add peppers, garlic, and salt and cook 5 minutes longer. Remove peppers.

4. Pour into baking dish and sprinkle with cheese and chili powder.

5. Bake 10 minutes and serve hot.

> *Serves 6.*

CHICKWEED

Chickweed is cooked (page 132) and used in the same way as most other wild greens. Remember, though, that the plant loses a great deal of its bulk in the cooking, so pick at least twice as much of the raw vegetable as you will need of the cooked greens. Be sure to wash chickweed well, as it tends to be sandy, and pack it well into the pan. It's rather mild in flavor, so it makes a good companion in a pot of stronger-tasting greens. Cooking time is about 10 minutes.

CHICORY

Chicory is a particularly bitter pot herb, so it is wise to depart a little from the basic cooking method for greens (page 132). Cover the leaves with water, return to a boil, and pour off this first water. Add a little fresh water and complete the cooking (10 to 15 minutes) for a better-tasting dish of greens.

DANDELION BUD OMELET

Particularly good for brunch or early supper, this omelet is light but filling. At Wildflower we often cut down the recipe in order to use a handful of flowers found after a two- or three-day warm spell in the middle of winter. It is delicious as is, or topped with fresh sweet butter and a wild-fruit jam or syrup.

6   *eggs*
½   *teaspoon salt*
¼   *cup (½ stick) butter*
2   *cups dandelion buds, stemmed, washed,*

and patted dry on paper towels
Freshly ground black pepper to taste
Opened dandelion flowers for garnishing

1. Beat eggs lightly with salt.
2. Melt butter in a 10-inch omelet pan or skillet over medium heat.
3. When foam dies down, add dandelion buds and cook until they begin to burst into open flowers. Raise heat to high.
4. Pour eggs over flowers and cook omelet, shaking pan constantly; as the omelet firms up around the edges, lift edges to allow the uncooked egg to run underneath.
5. Cook just until omelet is firm at the edges and still a bit soft in the center.
6. Sprinkle omelet with pepper, fold, and serve on a warmed platter, garnished with a little bunch of opened dandelion flowers.
    Serves 4.

FRIED DANDELION FLOWERS

Serve this surprisingly excellent yellow vegetable dish as part of a meal including a hearty meat pie, another vegetable, and a tossed green salad. For dessert, a simple cake.

3   *cups dandelion buds, stems removed*
    Butter for frying, ¼ to ½ cup
    Salt and freshly ground pepper to taste

1. Wash dandelion buds and drain well. Sprinkle with salt and pepper.
2. Heat butter in an iron skillet over medium heat until foam dies down.
3. Place buds a few at a time in the pan and cook just until flowers burst into bloom. Keep warm while rest of buds are being cooked. Serve hot.
    Serves 6.

DANDELION FLOWER FRITTERS

These fritters can be used in place of such a vegetable dish as corn fritters on any dinner menu. With fresh butter and honey, however, they are so delicious—as sunny-tasting as their ingredients—that we like to serve them for breakfast or brunch in place of pancakes. Once you've tasted these fritters you are likely to start encouraging the growth of dandelions on your lawn.

Cat-tail pollen (page 41) can be used to replace half of the flour in this recipe.

> Fat or oil for deep frying
> 1 cup flour
> 2 teaspoons baking powder
> Pinch of salt
> ½ cup milk
> 2 tablespoons powdered non-dairy creamer ("coffee lightener")
> 2 eggs
> 1½ cups dandelion flowers

1. Heat fat to frying temperature (350°) in a deep-fryer or a saucepan.
2. Sift together the flour, baking powder, and salt.
3. In another bowl, beat the milk, non-dairy creamer, and eggs together. Combine mixtures and whisk just until smooth.
4. Wash flowers and clip off any stems that may remain. Do this quickly so the flowers will not wilt. Pat flowers dry between paper towels.
5. Dip blossoms into batter and fry a few at a time until golden brown. Drain on paper towels and keep warm while frying remaining flowers.
6. Serve immediately when all are done.

Serves 8.

DANDELION GREENS

Like chicory, dandelion greens tend to be bitter, so it's a good idea to blanch or parboil them before proceeding with the basic cooking method for greens (page 132). Chop or tear up the washed leaves, place in a pot, and add boiling water to cover. Bring the greens to a boil and drain well, then add fresh boiling water and cook for about 15 minutes. Drain, then season and serve as you would other pot herbs.

DAY-LILY BUDS

Here's the basic cooking method for the buds: Rinse and drain unopened day-lily buds and clip off any stem remnants. Place buds in a saucepan and add water barely to cover. Bring quickly to a boil, cover, and simmer 20 minutes. The buds are now ready for use in recipes calling for the cooked flowers; or they may be drained and served as a simple vegetable dish after being salted, peppered, and buttered.

SAUTÉED DAY-LILY BUDS

A delicious vegetable, with a flavor akin to green beans but milder. A variation of this recipe is made by adding ¼ cup chopped wild onions or leeks when you begin to cook the buds.

> 4 tablespoons (½ stick) butter
> 2 cups day-lily buds, rinsed, drained, and patted dry
> ¼ cup water, or as needed
> ½ teaspoon salt
> Freshly ground black pepper to taste

1. Melt butter in a skillet over medium

heat. Add the buds and fry them gently until lightly browned.

2. Add a small amount of water and salt and pepper to taste.

3. Cover and simmer over very low heat until buds are tender, 10 to 15 minutes. Drain and serve hot.

Serves 4.

DAY-LILY BUDS ORIENTAL STYLE

3 cups day-lily buds, rinsed, drained, and patted dry with paper towels
1 cup water
1 tablespoon mild vinegar
¼ cup pecans or almonds, chopped
1 tablespoon soy sauce, preferably imported
  Salt to taste
  Hot boiled rice to serve 6

1. Combine day-lily buds and water in saucepan and bring to boil.

2. Simmer gently 15 minutes, or until buds are tender.

3. Drain off most of water, leaving only a tablespoonful or two.

4. Add vinegar, nuts, soy sauce, and salt to taste. Stir well and serve hot over rice.

Serves 6.

DAY-LILY FRITTERS

Follow the recipe for Dandelion Flower Fritters,* substituting 1½ cups cooked, well-drained day-lily buds for the dandelions. Remove as much moisture as possible from the day lilies before dipping them into the batter.

DOCK

The basic cooking method for dock is the same as that for most greens (page 132). Dock does not cook down as much as some greens, so you need not pick a great deal more than you will require when it has been cooked. Although I prefer dock mixed with other pot herbs, it will do for a one-plant dish. Chop the leaves coarsely before cooking them. They'll take about 20 minutes.

HENBIT

Henbit is one green that I definitely prefer to use in a mixed-greens pot. Used alone, the taste is a bit too minty to be palatable, I think; but you may feel differently, so try it alone by all means. Snip the small shoots close to the ground. Wash these well and chop them coarsely. Place them in a pot of already boiling water and boil 5 minutes. Pour off half the water and add more fresh boiling water. Bring to a boil again and immediately lower the heat, cover, and simmer for 10 minutes. Add salt and pepper to taste and serve the drained henbit with thin slices of lemon.

JERUSALEM ARTICHOKES

These knobby little tubers are a bit difficult to clean and to peel, but are well worth the endeavor. After digging the artichokes, shake as much earth from them as possible. Dunk them in a sink of water for scrubbing with a stiff vegetable brush. If there are too many protuberances on the roots, you may want to slice off some of them to facilitate the cleaning job. The peel is thin, and because of this and the knobbiness of the vegetable, the peeling job is a little more bothersome than peeling potatoes.

After the Jerusalem artichokes have been peeled, again wash them and either leave them whole or slice or chop them coarsely. Place them in a pot with water just to cover and bring them to a boil. Reduce the heat to medium, cover, and continue to cook vigorously until tender, at most about 25 minutes. Now you have the makings for many a fine dish. This vegetable may be substituted for potatoes in many recipes. Salt should be added to taste during or after cooking, depending on how you're using the vegetable.

JERUSALEM ARTICHOKES IN LEMON JUICE

Jerusalem artichokes may be kept this way, ready for use in salads and other dishes, for several weeks. It will take about 8 hours for them to take on the tartness of the lemon juice.

12 to 14 Jerusalem artichokes, peeled
½ cup lemon juice
Water

1. Place the whole peeled Jerusalem artichokes in a pint jar.

2. Pour lemon juice over them and add water to fill the jar to the neck.
3. Tightly cap the jar and store in refrigerator.

PAN-ROASTED JERUSALEM ARTICHOKES

This versatile vegetable goes just as well with a beef roast as it does with roasted game—one needn't wait for hunting season to enjoy the combination. Sometimes I make a regular ground-beef meat loaf and place a layer of parboiled Jerusalem artichokes in the center of the loaf between layers of meat. The artichokes offer a delightful surprise in a common dish.

4 cups whole Jerusalem artichokes,
     scrubbed and peeled
  Boiling water to cover
  Salt and freshly ground pepper to taste
1 teaspoon lemon juice

1. Cover Jerusalem artichokes with boiling water, parboil 5 minutes, and drain well.
2. Add salt, pepper, and lemon juice. Shake saucepan to distribute seasonings evenly.
3. Place around roast in oven during last 25 minutes of cooking. Turn frequently in pan juices. Artichokes should be tender by the time roast is done.
  Serves 6.

FRIED JERUSALEM ARTICHOKES

Some people prefer to peel Jerusalem artichokes before slicing and frying them, but I seldom do; the thin skin enhances the slightly earthy flavor of this vegetable.

Unlike potatoes, they don't become crisp when they are fried, but they are every bit as tasty.

4 *tablespoons vegetable oil for frying, or amount needed*
4 *cups raw Jerusalem artichokes, scrubbed and sliced or chopped*
1 *teaspoon salt, or to taste*
Paprika

1. Heat oil in a large skillet and add the sliced or chopped Jerusalem artichokes. Add salt and stir.
2. Cook, stirring occasionally, over medium heat until browned.
3. Reduce heat, cover, and cook 15 to 20 minutes, or until tender when pierced by a fork. Serve hot, garnished with paprika.
Serves 6.

JERUSALEM ARTICHOKES IN ORANGE SAUCE

3 *tablespoons butter*
¼ *cup brown sugar, packed*
½ *cup granulated sugar*
½ *teaspoon chopped wild ginger root, or ½ teaspoon powdered dried ginger*
¼ *teaspoon salt*
½ *can (6-ounce size) frozen orange-juice concentrate, thawed*
2 *tablespoons cornstarch*
¼ *cup water*
4 *cups cooked Jerusalem artichokes (page 146)*

1. Preheat oven to 350°.
2. Melt butter in a heavy skillet over medium heat.
3. Add sugars, ginger, and salt. Cook, stirring, for 5 minutes and set off heat. Stir in orange-juice concentrate.
4. Stir cornstarch into water till well mixed.

5. Return skillet to low heat and gradually add cornstarch mixture, stirring and cooking until sauce is clear and thick.
6. Put Jerusalem artichokes into a shallow baking dish and pour the orange sauce over them.
7. Cover dish and bake for 20 minutes. Remove cover and continue baking for 10 minutes, or until top is slightly glazed. Serve hot.
Serves 8.

SCALLOPED JERUSALEM ARTICHOKES

2 *cups peeled, sliced raw Jerusalem artichokes*
½ *cup chives or wild leeks, minced*
1 *cup grated sharp cheddar-type cheese*
2 *tablespoons butter*
2 *tablespoons flour*
1½ *cups hot milk*
1 *teaspoon salt, or to taste*
Freshly ground black pepper to taste
½ *cup bread crumbs*

1. Preheat oven to 375°.
2. In a 1-quart baking dish, arrange Jerusalem artichokes in alternate layers with the minced chives or leeks, sprinkling each layer with cheese.
3. Melt butter in a skillet over low heat and add flour, stirring to make a paste. Remove from the heat.
4. Gradually stir the hot milk into the butter-flour mixture, return to low heat, and cook until thickened, stirring constantly. Add salt and pepper to taste.
5. Pour sauce over the casserole of vegetables and sprinkle with crumbs.
6. Bake 25 to 30 minutes, or until the artichokes are tender when pricked with a fork. Serve hot.
Serves 4.

JERUSALEM ARTICHOKES WITH BACON

4   *cups raw Jerusalem artichokes, peeled*
    Water to cover
    Salt to taste
4   *slices of bacon*
½   *cup diced or sliced wild onions or wild*
    leeks, white parts only
4   *tablespoons bacon fat*

1. Boil Jerusalem artichokes in salted water for about 10 minutes, or until half done.
2. While artichokes are boiling, fry the bacon, drain the slices and crumble them, reserving the bacon fat.
3. Drain partly cooked artichokes, pour cold water over them, and set aside.
4. Fry the onions or leeks in the bacon fat over medium heat until golden, not browned. (If you have less than the required amount of fat, add some cooking oil or butter.)
5. While onions or leeks are frying, slice the artichokes into rounds or cut them into small cubes.
6. Stir your diced or sliced artichokes into the onions or leeks.
7. Fry, tossing occasionally with a spatula, until golden brown and tender.
8. Put into serving dish and sprinkle the crumbled bacon on top. Serve hot.
Serves 8.

SHERRIED JERUSALEM ARTICHOKES

The wild Jerusalem artichoke is well tamed in this dish, which is delicious with baked ham as well as such wild meats as roast goose or pheasant. The sherry gives a nice zing to the otherwise somewhat bland vegetable, and the crisp nuts give a pleasing contrast in texture.

4   *cups hot, cooked Jerusalem artichokes*
    (page 146), salted to taste
½   *cup light cream*
½   *cup brown sugar, packed*
¼   *teaspoon ground cinnamon*
2   *tablespoons butter*
1   *egg, well beaten*
3   *tablespoons cream sherry*
1   *cup pecans*

1. Preheat oven to 375°.
2. Mash Jerusalem artichokes with a potato masher or press them through a colander; they should be nearly smooth.
3. Heat cream in a saucepan at a low temperature and add brown sugar, cinnamon, butter, egg, and sherry. Continue heating and stirring just until butter is melted.
4. Stir artichokes and pecans into the cream mixture and pour into a 2-quart baking dish.
5. Bake 40 minutes, or until top is evenly browned. Serve hot.
Serves 8.

CREAMED JERUSALEM ARTICHOKES

5   *cups cooked Jerusalem artichokes (page 146), sliced*
½   *teaspoon salt*
    Freshly ground black pepper to taste
1   *cup light cream*
1   *cup milk*
2   *tablespoons chopped chives*
½   *teaspoon chopped parsley*
½   *cup Parmesan cheese, finely grated*

1. Combine the Jerusalem artichokes, salt, pepper, cream, milk, and chives in a large heavy skillet.
2. Cook over medium heat, stirring

frequently, until a slightly thickened sauce is formed.

3. Pour into serving dish and sprinkle with parsley and Parmesan cheese. Serve hot.

Serves 8.

MINTED JERUSALEM ARTICHOKES

¼ cup butter
4 cups cooked Jerusalem artichokes (page 146)
½ cup fresh spearmint leaves, coarsely chopped
Salt and freshly ground pepper to taste

1. Melt butter in a saucepan over medium heat and add artichokes.
2. Heat thoroughly, tossing occasionally.
3. Add mint leaves, tossing lightly. Season with salt and pepper to taste and serve at once.

Serves 8.

JERUSALEM ARTICHOKES LYONNAISE

4 tablespoons (½ stick) butter
½ cup chopped wild onions, white parts only
2 cups peeled and chopped raw Jerusalem artichokes
Salt to taste
¼ cup water
1 to 2 tablespoons minced fresh parsley, or
1½ teaspoons crumbled dried parsley

1. Melt butter in a heavy skillet, add onions, and cook, stirring, for 10 minutes, or until onions are golden. Remove onions from pan, set aside, and reserve fat in pan.

2. Add Jerusalem artichokes to pan and cook over medium heat, stirring occasionally, until browned, then cover, lower heat, and continue cooking until tender, about 15 minutes. Stir occasionally.

3. Stir in fried onions and salt, add water, and cook 10 minutes longer, keeping the vegetables in a cake in the manner of hashed-brown potatoes.

4. Sprinkle with part of parsley, turn out on platter, and sprinkle with remaining parsley. Serve hot.

Serves 4.

HASHED-BROWN JERUSALEM ARTICHOKES

This is good served in place of potatoes at any meal, or serve it as Westerners serve hashed-brown potatoes, as a side dish for eggs at breakfast.

4 cups cooked Jerusalem artichokes (page 146), salted to taste
¼ to ½ cup Butter for frying

1. Let the cooked Jerusalem artichokes cool for a bit, then mash them with a potato masher, or chop them coarsely in an electric blender.

2. Shape the artichokes into patties and fry them in butter over medium heat until golden brown. Serve hot.

Serves 6 to 8.

LAMB'S QUARTERS

To serve this delicious wild plant as a simple green vegetable, follow the basic cooking instructions for greens (page 132). This green cooks down a lot, so be sure to gather at least twice the measure you'll need after cooking. Cooking time for the young leaves is 10 minutes or so.

HERBED LAMB'S QUARTERS

    3   slices bacon, fried until crisp, drained,
        and broken into bite-sized pieces
        (reserve fat)
 1½   cups sliced wild onions, white parts
        only
    4   cups (packed) lamb's quarters, washed
        and drained
  ½   cup chopped fresh parsley
 1½   teaspoons fresh rosemary leaves,
        chopped, or ½ teaspoon crumbled
        dried rosemary
  ½   teaspoon salt
  ¼   teaspoon freshly ground pepper
    2   tablespoons lemon juice

1. Place fat rendered from bacon in a saucepan and add onions, lamb's quarters, parsley, rosemary, salt, and pepper.

2. Cook over medium heat for about 10 minutes, or until bright green and tender, stirring occasionally.

3. Stir in lemon juice.

4. Turn into serving dish and sprinkle with bacon bits. Serve hot.

Serves 8.

LAMB'S QUARTERS WITH WILD RICE

Instead of wild rice, you can use either brown or regular white rice, cooked and cooled, in this recipe.

    2   cups cooked lamb's quarters (page 149),
        drained and salted to taste
  ¼   cup melted butter
    4   eggs, beaten until frothy
    2   cups cooked and cooled wild rice (page
        171)

    1   cup milk
    6   wild leeks, including 3 or 4 inches of
        green tops, chopped
    1   cup sharp cheddar-type cheese, grated
    1   tablespoon Worcestershire sauce
  ½   teaspoon each crumbled dried thyme,
        marjoram, and rosemary, or 1½
        teaspoons each of the chopped fresh
        herbs

1. Preheat oven to 350°.

2. Combine all ingredients thoroughly and pour into a greased 2-quart casserole.

3. Bake uncovered for 35 minutes, or until firm. Serve hot.

Serves 8.

LAMB'S QUARTERS IN SOUR CREAM

    4   cups cooked lamb's quarters (page 149),
        drained and seasoned to taste with
        salt and pepper
  ½   cup commercial sour cream
        Lemon juice to taste

1. Chop lamb's quarters coarsely and heat thoroughly in a saucepan.

2. Stir in sour cream and warm for another moment without letting the mixture boil.

3. Sprinkle with a few drops of lemon juice and serve at once.

Serves 6 to 8.

SWEET AND SOUR LAMB'S QUARTERS

    2   strips bacon
    1   cup minced chives
    1   tablespoon flour

2   cups cooked lamb's quarters (page 149),
      drained (reserve juice)
¾   cup cooking liquid drained from lamb's
      quarters
¼   cup cider vinegar
2   teaspoons sugar
1   teaspoon salt
¼   teaspoon freshly ground black pepper

1. Fry bacon in a skillet until crisp; drain, crumble, and set aside, leaving fat in pan.

2. Cook minced chives in bacon fat over medium heat, stirring, for 5 minutes.

3. Stir in the flour to make a paste and set skillet aside.

4. In a saucepan over medium heat, combine the liquid from the greens with the vinegar, sugar, salt, and pepper. Stir in the chives mixture.

5. Add the lamb's quarters and cook, stirring, until sauce thickens lightly; cook for an additional minute or two.

6. Serve at once with the crumbled bacon on top.
Serves 6.

WILTED LAMB'S QUARTERS WITH GARLIC

4   tablespoons olive oil
3   wild garlic plants, both bulbs and tops,
      finely chopped
4   cups (packed) lamb's quarters, washed
      and patted dry on paper towels
    Pinch of salt, or to taste
    Lemon juice to taste

1. Heat oil in skillet over medium heat without allowing it to smoke.

2. Add garlic and cook just a moment, until heated well.

3. Remove from heat, add lamb's quarters, and toss in skillet until just wilted.

4. Add salt and lemon juice to taste and toss again, briefly. Serve at once.
Serves 6 to 8.

SAVORY LAMB'S QUARTERS SEED

A few years back a friend was in Peru for several months, and when he came home he told me about a great wild cereal he had enjoyed. It didn't take long for me to identify the plant from his description and serve him the same cereal—seed from my garden patch which I'd let grow up into *Chenopodium album.* Upon tasting the dish it didn't take him more than one bite to ascertain that it was indeed the same cereal he had eaten in the Andes.

Another way to enjoy this tiny seed, with its unique flavor, is to pour the hot cereal into a loaf pan and chill it. Slice and fry in butter or other fat.

4   cups lamb's quarters seed (page 59)
2   cups water
¼   cup wild chives or wild garlic, finely
      chopped
    Salt to taste

1. Roast seed for 1 hour in a preheated 300° oven, then pound well in a mortar, or run through a grain mill to break the seed thoroughly.

2. Boil the water and gradually add the roasted seed. When boiling starts again, lower the heat.

3. Add chives or garlic and continue to simmer until you have a thick gruel, about 20 minutes.

4. Serve this as you would hot grits, with a dab of butter, or serve as a cereal, with butter and cream if you choose.
Serves 6.

LEEKS

Leeks, served plain, make a fine vegetable. They should be washed thoroughly. Cut off the roots and all but about 3 to 4 inches of the green tops and wash again if necessary to remove any grit. Lay the leeks in a shallow pan or skillet and add boiling water to barely cover them and salt to taste. Reduce heat and simmer for 15 minutes, or until just tender. Drain and use in a recipe, or, if to be served at once, season with butter and freshly ground pepper and, if needed, more salt.

BAKED LEEK AND CHEESE PUFF

Golden-brown and crusty on top, this mildly oniony dish is just right for luncheon, preceded by a clear soup and followed by fresh fruit.

8   *slices bread*
8   *slices cheddar-type cheese*
4   *cups cut-up wild leeks, including 2 to 4 inches of green tops, simmered in salted water until tender (about 15 minutes) and drained*
2   *eggs*
1½ *cups milk*
1   *teaspoon salt*
1   *teaspoon mild prepared mustard*
     Paprika

1. Preheat oven to 350°.
2. Arrange 4 slices of bread in bottom of a buttered square 9-inch baking dish.
3. Place a slice of cheese on each slice of bread. Spoon half of the leeks over cheese.
4. Repeat layers of bread, cheese, and leeks.
5. Beat together eggs, milk, salt, and

prepared mustard and pour over contents of baking dish. Let rest for 15 minutes.
6. Bake 30 minutes, or until puffed and brown.
7. Sprinkle with paprika and cut into four separate "sandwich" sections. Serve hot from the oven.
   Serves 4.

SCALLOPED LEEKS

4   *cups coarsely chopped wild leeks, including about 4 inches of the green tops*
½   *teaspoon salt, or to taste*
     Freshly ground black pepper to taste
2   *tablespoons poppy seed*
½   *cup milk*
1   *4-ounce package cream cheese*

1. Preheat oven to 350°.
2. Place chopped leeks in greased 1-quart baking dish.
3. Sprinkle with salt, pepper, and poppy seed.
4. Place the milk and cream cheese in a small saucepan over medium heat and stir until a smooth sauce is formed.
5. Pour sauce over leeks, cover, and bake 1 hour. Serve hot.
   Serves 6.

LEEK CUSTARD

2   *slices bacon, fried until crisp, drained, and crumbled (reserve fat)*
2   *teaspoons bacon fat*
3   *cups wild leeks, including some of the green part, cut into bite-sized pieces*
1   *cup water*
2   *eggs*

1   *large can (13 ounces) evaporated milk*
⅓   *cup water*
1   *teaspoon salt*
⅛   *teaspoon freshly ground black pepper*
1   *teaspoon crushed dried dill weed, or 3
     teaspoons chopped fresh dill leaves*

1. Preheat oven to 375°.
2. In a saucepan cook together bacon fat, leeks, and 1 cup water for about 10 minutes, or until leeks begin to be tender. Drain and set aside.
3. In a mixing bowl combine eggs, evaporated milk, ⅓ cup water, salt, pepper, and dill. Stir in bacon and leeks.
4. Pour into greased 1½-quart casserole and set in a larger pan of hot water; water should rise about halfway up the sides of casserole.
5. Bake custard until a knife blade inserted into the center comes out clean, about 35 minutes. Serve hot.
     Serves 6.

WILD LEEKS ON TOAST

20 *to 30 cooked wild leeks (page 152)*
1   *cup White Sauce**
½   *cup grated sharp cheddar-type cheese*
4 *to 6 slices buttered toast*
     Paprika

1. Preheat broiler.
2. Drain cooked leeks, leaving them in saucepan or skillet.
3. Pour white sauce over leeks and heat 5 minutes, or until warmed through.
4. Place toast on a heatproof platter or a cookie sheet and arrange leeks on toast, spooning sauce over them. Sprinkle with cheese.
5. Broil until cheese melts and bubbles.
6. Sprinkle with paprika and serve at once.
     Serves 4 to 6.

BAKED SUGAR-AND-SPICE LEEKS

4   *cups cooked leeks (page 152), well
     drained*
3   *tablespoons brown sugar*
3   *tablespoons granulated sugar*
¼   *teaspoon ground cinnamon*
¼   *teaspoon ground nutmeg*
3   *tablespoons melted butter*
½   *cup chopped pecans or black walnuts
     Pinch of ground dried ginger*

1. Preheat oven to 350°.
2. Put drained leeks into a buttered 1½-quart baking dish.
3. Mix brown sugar, granulated sugar, cinnamon, nutmeg, and butter. Add nuts.
4. Sprinkle over and between leeks.
5. Bake 20 to 30 minutes, or until heated through, and sprinkle with ginger before serving.
     Serves 8.

MILKWEED

Preparing milkweed is arduous and I find it not worth the bother for any part except the flower buds and unripe seed pods, which no other vegetables can top for taste. You may, however, not feel this way and may want to go to the trouble of using the young shoots and leaves as well. Here is the method I've found best for all parts of the milkweed.

Bring a large pot of water to a boil and keep it boiling. Put the milkweed in a smaller pot and pour in boiling water to cover. Boil for 1 minute, then pour off the water. Again add boiling water to cover and again boil for 1 minute. Repeat this process until all bitterness is gone—taste to make sure. At most, three or four blanchings are sufficient, and one or two may be enough. Remember to keep the supply of water boiling, otherwise the bitterness tends to "set" in the plant.

To cook young shoots or leaves, flower buds, or unripe seed pods after all bitterness has been removed, give the milkweed a final cooking in boiling, salted water until tender, 10 to 20 minutes. Drain and either use in a recipe calling for the cooked vegetable, or season and serve with butter. Milkweed shoots or buds are also good served hot with Vinaigrette Dressing.*

MILKWEED BUDS MEXICALI

When in Baja California on a hike, our party came upon a country road simply lined with purple-blossomed milkweed. We began picking the unopened buds and soon had enough for a good dish, for which we found some of the other ingredients as we walked along. We prepared this dish in the field with no trouble.

¼   cup cooking oil
1   wild garlic bulb, quartered
1   pod dry hot pepper (chili pepper)
½   cup chopped wild onions or wild leeks, white parts only
4   cups milkweed flower buds, blanched (see above), and drained
½   teaspoon salt, or to taste
¼   cup water

1. Put oil in a heavy skillet. Add garlic, chili pepper, and onions or leeks and fry over medium heat, stirring often, till onion is tender but not browned—about 10 minutes.

2. Remove garlic quarters and hot pepper pod.

3. Add milkweed flower buds, salt, and water.

4. Cover and cook over medium-high heat for 5 minutes.

5. Serve at once, with corn chips as an accompaniment.

Serves 4.

MILKWEED PODS WITH BLACK WALNUTS

This is a delicious and most unusual dish; the flavor of the black walnuts blends well with the unique taste of milkweed pods. Serve it, if you can, with a plain venison roast and a green salad, plus a light dessert.

2   cups black walnut meats
1   cup fine dry bread crumbs
¼   cup (½ stick) butter
½   teaspoon salt, or to taste
¼   teaspoon crumbled dried thyme, or ¾ teaspoon chopped fresh thyme

½ teaspoon crumbled dried basil, or 1 ½
teaspoons chopped fresh basil
Freshly ground black pepper to taste
3 cups of milkweed pods, blanched to
remove bitterness (page 154),
drained, and salted to taste
Water, as needed

1. Preheat oven to 300°.
2. Toast nuts in a shallow pan in oven for 30 minutes, stirring occasionally. Remove nuts and raise oven setting to 350°.
3. Mix bread crumbs with salt, thyme, basil, and black pepper.
4. Put into a buttered 1½-quart casserole a layer of milkweed pods, a layer of nuts, and a sprinkling of the herbed crumbs. Continue layering the dish in this manner, ending with remaining crumbs.
5. Sprinkle with just enough water to moisten topping—less than ¼ cup.
6. Cover and bake for 30 minutes, removing the cover during the last 10 minutes to allow browning. Serve hot.
Serves 8.

MUSHROOMS

Mushrooms are delicate victuals and most of them require a short cooking time to save their flavor. Meadow mushrooms, chanterelles, sulphur shelf, Judas's ears, shaggy manes, puffballs, and oyster mushrooms require no special treatment before cooking. If they are quite clean, simply wipe them with a cloth. If washing is needed, do it quickly and pat them dry with paper towels.

Morels, however, should be washed well and placed in a pan of boiling water to which salt has been added, ¼ cup salt to a quart of water, and let stand for 5 minutes. Then pour off the water and pat the morels dry, or drain them well on paper towels, before proceeding with your recipe.

When sulphur shelf or oyster mushrooms are used, it is good to slice them thinly before frying, for these thick, fleshy mushrooms will otherwise take a longer cooking time than other kinds. Be sure to use only the tender portions of these two fungi—older parts of both can be quite tough or woody.

MUSHROOMS IN SOUR-CREAM SAUCE

This is an excellent mushroom dish to serve with fish. It is also delightful on its own, served over crisp toast.

4 tablespoons (½ stick) butter
½ cup chopped wild onions or wild leeks,
including a little of the green parts
2 tablespoons flour
2 cups mushrooms (chanterelles or sliced
oyster mushrooms or meadow mushrooms are particularly good),
if necessary rinsed and patted dry
1 cup commercial sour cream
¼ cup milk
Salt and freshly ground pepper to taste

1. In a large iron skillet melt the butter over medium heat and fry the onions or leeks till golden brown.
2. Sprinkle flour over the onions or leeks and blend well over low heat.
3. Add mushrooms, cover skillet, and simmer 15 minutes, stirring frequently.
4. Remove from the heat and stir in sour cream and milk slowly. Season to taste with salt and pepper.
5. Return skillet to low heat and just warm mushrooms and sauce well before serving; don't allow the sauce to boil. Serve hot.
Serves 4.

MUSHROOM AND RICE CASSEROLE

6   tablespoons butter
1   cup wild onions or leeks, white parts only, coarsely chopped
1   cup sweet peppers, finely chopped
2   cups mushrooms, rinsed if necessary, patted dry, and coarsely chopped (meadow mushrooms and oyster mushrooms are particularly flavorful in this casserole)
2   cups Boiled Wild Rice* or 1 cup each cooked wild rice and cooked long-grain white rice, salted to taste
¼   teaspoon crumbled dried thyme or ¾ teaspoon finely chopped fresh thyme
¼   teaspoon crumbled dried marjoram or ¾ teaspoon chopped fresh marjoram
¼   teaspoon ground cumin
1   teaspoon crumbled dried parsley or 3 teaspoons finely chopped fresh parsley
½   cup strong chicken broth
½   cup dry bread crumbs
1   cup grated cheese, either mozzarella or a very mild cheddar type

1. Preheat oven to 350°.
2. Melt butter in a skillet and cook onions over medium heat until translucent. Remove onions with a slotted spoon and set aside. Leave butter in pan.
3. Cook peppers in the same pan until softened. Remove with slotted spoon and set aside, again keeping the butter in pan.
4. Add mushrooms to pan and cook, stirring, for 5 minutes. Remove with slotted spoon and set aside. Reserve butter and pan juices.
5. In a small saucepan combine rice, thyme, marjoram, cumin, parsley, and chicken broth. Cook over low heat for 10 minutes, or until warmed through. Drain, reserving the broth.

6. In a greased 2-quart casserole place a layer of the herbed rice, then a layer each of onions, peppers, and mushrooms. Repeat, ending with mushrooms as the top layer.
7. Combine the butter and vegetable juice from the skillet and the broth from the rice and pour over the contents of the casserole.
8. Top with bread crumbs, then the cheese.
9. Bake 30 minutes, or until the cheese topping is brown and crusty. Serve hot.

Serves 8.

FRIED MUSHROOMS

This method of cooking is good for meadow mushrooms, sulphur shelf, morels (after they have been blanched—page 155), chanterelles, puffballs, shaggy manes, and oyster mushrooms. The oyster mushrooms and sulphur shelf may take a longer time to cook and should be covered while they cook so that the juices will be retained in the skillet to be absorbed into the mushrooms. You may want to cook only the caps of the meadow mushrooms, and the chanterelles will probably be too small to require chopping.

4   tablespoons (½ stick) butter
2   cups mushrooms, washed if necessary, drained, patted dry, and chopped coarsely
Salt and pepper to taste

1. Melt butter over medium heat in a heavy skillet.
2. Gently pour mushrooms into butter and cook until the mushrooms just begin to brown around the edges. (See note page 155 if you are cooking oyster mushrooms or sulphur shelf.) Turn them with a broad spatula or a slotted spoon, being careful

not to break the mushrooms.

3. Cook for about 5 minutes on second side. Season and serve hot, or use in a recipe calling for fried or precooked mushrooms.

Makes about 1½ cups.

DEVILED MUSHROOMS

A meal can be made around this substantial dish, which is particularly good when prepared with either oyster or meadow mushrooms. Serve the casserole with a fresh green tossed salad and follow it with a cup of tea and a hearty dessert. It's also a great vegetable accompaniment when game is served as a main dish.

2   *cups fresh mushrooms*
1   *cup water*
1   *tablespoon salt*
    Juice of 1 lemon
2   *tablespoons butter*
1   *cup fine dry bread crumbs*
4   *tablespoons finely chopped onions, white parts only*
1   *cup light cream*
2   *eggs*
¼   *teaspoon grated nutmeg*
¼   *teaspoon Cayenne pepper, or to taste*

1. Preheat oven to 350°.
2. Cover mushrooms with water, salt, and lemon juice and let them soak for 10 minutes. Drain and pat dry.
3. Melt butter in a skillet, add bread crumbs and onions, and fry over medium heat, stirring, for 10 minutes.
4. Add mushrooms and cook 10 minutes longer, stirring frequently.
5. Beat cream and eggs together thoroughly.
6. Put mushroom mixture into a buttered shallow baking dish and pour in the egg and cream mixture.

7. Sprinkle with nutmeg and Cayenne pepper.
8. Bake for 30 minutes, or until golden brown and somewhat firm.

Serves 6.

MUSHROOM CASSEROLE

This is very filling and can well be served as a main course. Accompanied by a green salad and followed by a rich dessert, it makes a fine meal.

¼   *cup (½ stick) butter*
¼   *cup flour*
3   *cups hot milk*
1½   *teaspoons salt*
     Freshly ground black pepper to taste
3   *tablespoons Worcestershire sauce*
2   *cups Fried Mushrooms**
½   *cup diced green pepper*
1   *4-ounce can pimientos, drained and chopped*
4   *hard-cooked eggs, sliced*
2   *cups shredded cheddar-type cheese*

1. Preheat oven to 325°.
2. Melt butter in a heavy iron skillet. Add flour and stir constantly over low heat until lightly browned.
3. Gradually stir in hot milk and cook, stirring, till thickened. Cook for a moment longer, remove from heat, and stir in salt, pepper, and Worcestershire sauce.
4. Gently stir in mushrooms, green pepper, and pimientos. Fold in sliced eggs carefully.
5. Pour into well-oiled 2-quart casserole.
6. Bake for 40 minutes, or until top is brown.
7. Top with shredded cheese, return to oven for 5 minutes to let cheese melt, and serve hot.

Serves 6 to 8.

MUSHROOMS BAKED IN CREAM

2   *cups fresh mushrooms (meadow mush-*
    rooms, chanterelles, or morels
    are recommended)
    Salt to taste
1   *cup heavy cream*
2   *tablespoons butter*

1. Prepare mushrooms for cooking as directed on page 155.
2. Preheat oven to 400°.
3. Place mushrooms in shallow baking dish and add salt to taste.
4. Pour cream over mushrooms and dot with butter.
5. Bake 15 minutes and serve hot.
   Serves 4.

MUSHROOM OMELET

6   *tablespoons butter*
1   *cup firm fresh meadow mushrooms,*
    rinsed if necessary, patted dry, and
    cut into thick slices
1   *teaspoon lemon juice*
    Salt, as needed
    Freshly ground pepper to taste
8   *eggs*

1. Melt half of the butter in a heavy skillet over medium heat and add mushrooms, lemon juice, and salt and pepper to taste. Cook for 2 or 3 minutes, stirring briskly. Set aside to cool somewhat.
2. Beat eggs lightly with additional salt (about ½ teaspoon) and a little pepper. Stir in cooked mushrooms and their juices.
3. Heat a 12-inch omelet pan or skillet over high heat and melt the remaining butter (3 tablespoons), turning pan to coat bottom and sides. Don't let butter brown.

4. When pan and butter are thoroughly hot, pour in omelet mixture and stir rapidly with the flat of a fork for a moment, shaking the pan briskly back and forth. Cook omelet until softly set on top.
5. Fold omelet and turn out onto a warmed platter. Serve at once.
   Serves 4.

MORELS BAKED WITH HERBS

1   *tablespoon butter*
1   *cup chopped wild leeks or wild onions,*
    in either case with part of the green
    tops
¼   *teaspoon crumbled dried marjoram or ¾*
    teaspoon chopped fresh marjoram
3   *teaspoons chopped fresh parsley*
¼   *teaspoon crumbled dried thyme or ¾*
    teaspoon chopped fresh thyme
¼   *teaspoon crumbled dried basil or ¾*
    teaspoon chopped fresh basil
½   *teaspoon salt*
    Freshly ground black pepper to taste
1   *teaspoon Worcestershire sauce*

1   *egg, slightly beaten*
¼   *cup cream sherry*
¼   *cup toasted slivered almonds or coarsely
      chopped pecans or chinquapins*
½   *cup crisply toasted bread cubes or
      packaged plain croutons*
30 *morels, blanched (page 155), drained,
      and slit down one side
      Vegetable oil*

1. Preheat oven to 350°.
2. Melt butter in a skillet and fry the onions or leeks over medium heat till white part is pale yellow.
3. Add the marjoram, parsley, thyme, basil, salt, pepper, Worcestershire sauce, egg, sherry, and almonds.
4. Heat mixture through, stirring.
5. Pour over croutons and let soak till they are well moistened, then mix well.
6. Brush the outside of the morels with a little vegetable oil.
7. Stuff the hollows of the mushrooms with the herbed mixture.
8. Arrange morels in a shallow baking dish in a single layer, slit sides up. If there is any stuffing left over, put it in the baking dish.
9. Bake for 15 minutes, or until morels are tender. Serve hot.
   Serves 4 to 6.

STUFFED MORELS BAKED IN CREAM

1   *4-ounce package cream cheese*
½   *cup crumbled blue cheese*
20 to 30 *morels, blanched (page 155),
      drained, and slit down one side*
2   *tablespoons butter*
1   *cup dry bread crumbs*
¼   *teaspoon finely chopped chives*
¼   *cup cream sherry*
½   *cup heavy cream*

1. Preheat oven to 350°.
2. Combine cream cheese and blue cheese and stuff the cavities of the morels with the mixture.
3. Melt butter in a skillet over low heat, add bread crumbs and chives, and cook, stirring, until well heated.
4. Place half of the crumb mixture in the bottom of a shallow 1-quart casserole.
5. Add stuffed morels, making sure the slit sides are up.
6. Sprinkle with remaining crumb mixture, then with the sherry.
7. Pour a little of the cream over each morel.
8. Bake for 30 minutes, or until the stuffing begins to puff from the slits of the browned mushrooms. Serve hot.
   Serves 4 to 6.

MORELS STUFFED WITH CHEESE

¼   *cup dry bread crumbs*
¼   *cup mozzarella or Muenster cheese,
      grated*
¼   *teaspoon crumbled dried basil or ¾
      teaspoon minced fresh basil*
¼   *teaspoon fennel seed (optional), well
      bruised*
12 *morels, blanched (page 155), drained,
      and slit down one side*
4   *tablespoons butter, melted*

1. Preheat broiler.
2. Mix the bread crumbs, cheese, and herbs and stuff the morels.
3. Place morels in a shallow broiling pan with their slit sides up and brush generously with the butter.
4. Broil about 6 inches from the heat for 5 or 6 minutes, or until the filling is hot through and the cheese has melted. Serve at once.
   Serves 4.

BAKED MORELS WITH FISH STUFFING

2 tablespoons butter
¼ cup wild leeks or chives, chopped
½ cup flaked cooked fish, preferably salmon
¼ cup dry bread crumbs
½ teaspoon crumbled dried thyme or 1½ teaspoons minced fresh thyme
Salt to taste
20 to 30 morels, blanched (page 155), drained, and slit down one side
Vegetable oil

1. Preheat oven to 350°.
2. Melt butter in small skillet and cook leeks or chives over medium heat until well wilted, about 5 minutes.
3. Combine fish, crumbs, the leeks or chives with their cooking butter, thyme, and salt and toss with a fork until well mixed.
4. Stuff morels and arrange, slits upward, in a greased shallow baking dish. Brush morels lightly with vegetable oil.
5. Bake 10 to 15 minutes, or until lightly browned. Serve hot.

Serves 4 to 6.

FRIED PUFFBALLS

Cooked this way, puffballs have a flavor that, to me, is like that of country-fried potatoes. They're wonderful with a steak—add a green salad and a frozen dessert, and your dinner will be fine enough for a king.

¾ cup milk
1 egg
1 cup flour
Salt and freshly ground pepper to taste
10 large (teacup-sized) puffballs, sliced

¼-inch thick and with the skin peeled from the slices
Butter for frying

1. Beat milk and egg together until blended.
2. Mix flour, salt, and pepper together and spread on a plate.
3. In a skillet, melt over medium-high heat enough butter to cover the bottom.
4. When butter is hot but not brown, dip enough puffball slices to fill the pan into the egg mixture one at a time, then into the flour, and again into the egg.
5. Fry slices over medium-high heat until brown, turning them once to brown both sides. Keep warm while dipping and frying the remaining puffballs, adding butter to the pan when it's needed. Serve hot.

Serves 8.

WILD MUSHROOMS TETRAZZINI

This mushroom and pasta dish makes a good and filling main course. When it's served with a tossed salad and a fruit pie, meat will never be missed from the menu.

1 16-ounce package fine spaghetti or spaghettini
6 tablespoons butter
3 cups oyster mushrooms, cut into thick (¼ inch) slices
½ cup wild leeks or chives, finely chopped
3 tablespoons flour
1½ teaspoon salt
½ teaspoon freshly ground black pepper
2 cups hot milk
¼ cup dry sherry
⅓ cup chopped parsley
1½ cups mozzarella cheese, cut into small pieces

1. Preheat broiler, or preheat oven to 450°.

2. Cook spaghetti until just tender in a large pot of boiling salted water. Drain and pour into a buttered large shallow ovenproof dish, cover with foil, and set aside to keep warm.

3. In a 3-quart saucepan, melt butter and cook mushrooms and chives over medium-low heat until mushrooms are tender, about 5 minutes.

4. Over low heat, add flour, salt, and pepper, blending them smoothly into the butter. Continuing to cook and stir, gradually add milk, then sherry. Cook until thickened, then cook a moment or two longer.

5. Add parsley and 1 cup of the cheese, reserving the rest.

6. Continue to cook this sauce, stirring constantly, until the cheese has melted. Remove from heat.

7. Pour the sauce over the spaghetti in the oven dish and spread with the remaining ½ cup of cubed cheese.

8. Broil 10 to 12 inches from the heat just until the spaghetti and sauce are hot and cheese is melted, watching carefully. (Alternatively, dish can be heated and browned on the top rack of a preheated 450° oven.) Serve at once.

Serves 8.

MUSTARD GREENS

The young leaves of mustard are well worth cooking by themselves as a green, and you'll notice that some of my recipes calling for mixed greens suggest mustard as part of the mixture. Cook mustard, after stripping off any stems that may not be tender, according to the basic recipe on page 132; the greens will be done in about 10 to 12 minutes.

ONIONS

If you're lucky enough to have a good supply of wild onions available for the foraging, you'll find you can use them in any recipe calling for tame onions. Also, as you'll notice in the following recipes, wild onions and leeks can often be interchanged in recipes with fine results.

ONION OR LEEK PIE

Plan a dinner using this with a poultry main course, a green vegetable or a salad, and a great dessert, and look for a great success.

    1   recipe Standard Pie Crust*
    1   cup grated sharp cheddar-type cheese
    2   cups cooked wild onion bulbs or chopped
        and cooked wild leeks (including 2 or
        3 inches of green tops), salted and
        peppered to taste
    1   egg yolk, beaten
    ½   cup milk
    ¼   teaspoon paprika
    2   teaspoons chopped parsley or 1 teaspoon
        crumbled dried parsley

1. Preheat oven to 375°.

2. Roll out pastry for lower crust and fit into a 9-inch pie pan.

3. Into the pie crust sprinkle alternate layers of cheese and onions or leeks, beginning and ending with cheese.

4. Beat egg yolk with milk, paprika, and parsley and pour over filling. Roll out top crust and place over filling. Seal edges and slash top crust in several places. Bake for 40 minutes, or until crust is firm and golden brown.

Serves 6.

GLAZED WILD ONIONS

This is a particularly good side dish to serve with barbecued trout or broiled fish of any kind. It works with the white part of wild leeks too.

¼ cup dry white wine
2 tablespoons sugar
2 tablespoons butter
2 cups small wild onion bulbs, boiled till tender in salted water and drained well

1. Heat the wine, sugar, and butter in a heavy skillet until sugar has dissolved. Add onions.

2. Cook over medium heat for about 15 minutes, stirring often, until onions are glazed to a golden-yellow color. Serve hot.

Serves 4.

WILD ONIONS WITH APPLES

During coon- and possum-hunting time this recipe comes to mind, for it's delicious with those meats. If you don't have wild meat, this would be a fine accompaniment for a fresh pork roast.

2 tablespoons vegetable oil
2 cups wild onion bulbs, thinly sliced
6 cooking apples, peeled, cored, and cut into quarters
2 teaspoons salt
2 tablespoons sugar
Water, if needed

1. Pour oil into a skillet and fry onions over medium heat till yellow and tender.

2. Add apples, salt, and sugar.

3. Cover and steam for 15 minutes, stirring occasionally. Add a little water if necessary to keep from sticking. Serve hot.

Serves 6.

WILD ONIONS PIQUANTE

Lovely served as a brunch dish, this is also a good substantial dish for everyday luncheons.

1 cup grated sharp cheddar-type cheese
2 cups wild onion bulbs, boiled until tender in salted water and drained (reserve broth)
½ cup broth drained from cooked onions
1 tablespoon Worcestershire sauce
3 tablespoons wine vinegar
3 tablespoons butter
Salt and freshly ground pepper to taste
6 slices crisp toast

1. Over low heat, melt cheese in onion broth.

2. Add Worcestershire sauce, vinegar, and butter.

3. Stir the onions into the sauce and reheat. Taste, and add salt and pepper if needed.

4. Serve hot over crisp toast.

Serves 6.

PEPPER GRASS

Pepper grass makes a good pot herb, either alone or in combination with other greens. To cook it, follow the general instructions for greens on page 132; cooking time will be about 8 to 10 minutes.

PLANTAIN

This pungent green is a fine addition to a mixture of wild greens served as a vegetable, or it can be cooked and served alone. Gather plenty, for you'll lose a good part of the bulk in preparing plantain for cooking.

To prepare the leaves, start at the base of each leaf and pull out the strings, or cut them out with a pair of small, sharp scissors. This is a big job, but just make yourself a cup of fragrant tea, get set in a comfortable place, maybe where you can see the bird feeder, and go to work. You'll be well rewarded.

Plantain is tougher than some other greens, so it will require a little more time in the boiling salted water; about 20 minutes should be enough. Sometimes I bring it to a boil, drain the water, then cook it for about 15 minutes in fresh water; it tastes even better when parboiled this way. Season the cooked greens with more salt, if needed, plus butter and pepper.

POKEWEED

This is one of the mild plants and far more delicious than most garden vegetables, but any discussion of pokeweed—"poke salad"—must be accompanied by a warning about the preparation of the plant for eating. Parts of the plant are not only edible but choice, but other parts—the roots, berries, and the fully mature leaves after the flower head has formed—should be avoided. They are "strong medicine," capable of making the eater ill. So never sample the roots, berries, or fully matured leaves. The stalk, after peeling, the young shoots when they're 6 to 8 inches high, and the leaves, gathered before the flower head has formed, are all delectable and completely safe.

The preliminary preparation of •the thick poke stalks is simple—just peel off the thick, purplish outer skin (it strips off easily). It's then ready to use in any of the recipes that call for poke stalks, although it may be parboiled if you wish. To prepare the young shoots and leaves, wash them and trim off any opened leaves from the stems of the shoots. If the young leaves have large center ribs, I usually remove them with the kitchen shears before parboiling the leaves—such ribs tend to be tough.

Put the shoots or young poke leaves in a pot, cover with water, bring to a boil, and drain thoroughly. Add fresh water, bring to a boil, add salt to taste, and lower the heat. Cover the pot and simmer the vegetable 5 minutes, or until tender. When done, drain and season and serve. Some like to cook poke with butter, pepper, and other seasonings for a longer time. And try serving the shoots warm, with Vinaigrette Dressing (Index). If parboiled poke is called for, it's ready to use after the first water has been drained off.

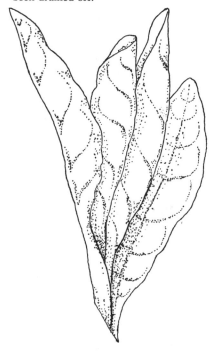

POKEWEED SPROUTS AU GRATIN

About 30 6-inch poke sprouts with their leaves tightly curled, parboiled (page 163) and drained
1 cup grated cheese (any kind will do, but a sharp cheddar type is preferable)
   Paprika
   Salt and freshly ground pepper to taste
2 cups White Sauce*
½ cup cracker crumbs
3 tablespoons butter

1. Preheat oven to 350°.
2. Put a layer of poke sprouts in a greased 9- or 10-inch baking dish.
3. Sprinkle layer with half of the grated cheese, paprika, salt, and pepper, and cover with half of the white sauce.
4. Repeat layering of sprouts, cheese, seasoning, and sauce to make two layers in all.
5. Top with cracker crumbs and dot with bits of butter.
6. Bake for 40 minutes, or until sauce is bubbling and the top well browned. Serve hot.
Serves 6.

POKEWEED WITH WINE SAUCE

2 tablespoons butter
3 cups pokeweed (leaves, sprouts, or peeled stalks), chopped and parboiled 10 minutes, then boiled in fresh water until tender and drained
1 teaspoon salt
¼ teaspoon grated nutmeg
¼ teaspoon ground cinnamon
½ cup chopped mushrooms, cooked in a little butter until tender
2 tablespoons cornstarch
⅓ cup Madeira or other wine of a similar type
⅓ cup heavy cream
6 strips bacon, fried until crisp, drained, and crumbled

1. Melt butter in a large skillet and add pokeweed, salt, nutmeg, cinnamon, and mushrooms. Heat thoroughly over medium heat.
2. Mix the cornstarch, wine, and cream and pour into the skillet.
3. Let sauce thicken over medium heat, stirring occasionally.
4. Pour into a serving dish and serve hot, topped with bacon.
Serves 6.

POKEWEED STALKS AMANDINE

4 cups pokeweed stalks, peeled and finely diced
1 tablespoon chopped chives
1 bulb of wild leek or wild garlic, finely chopped
   Water, as needed
½ cup (1 stick) butter
½ cup strong chicken broth (canned concentrated broth is good)
1 cup light cream
   Salt and freshly ground pepper to taste
2 tablespoons cornstarch
¼ cup water
1 cup sliced blanched almonds

1. In a saucepan place the pokeweed with the chives and the leek or garlic and enough water to cover. Bring to a boil, then simmer until vegetables are tender, about 15 minutes. Drain vegetables.

2. Return vegetables to pot and add butter, broth, cream, and salt and pepper. Bring to a simmer and cook for a minute or two.

3. Stir together the cornstarch and ¼ cup water and add to vegetables, stirring; cook until thickened, then cook an additional minute or two.

4. Pour into a serving dish and top with the almonds. Serve hot.

Serves 8.

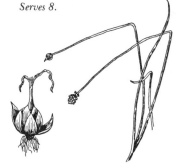

BRAISED POKEWEED STALKS

4 *cups pokeweed stalks, peeled, parboiled (page 163), and cut into ½-inch pieces*
½ *cup wild leeks or wild onions, white parts only, finely chopped*
2 *teaspoons minced parsley*
¾ *teaspoon crumbled dried marjoram or 2 teaspoons fresh marjoram, chopped*
¾ *teaspoon crumbled dried basil or 2 teaspoons fresh basil, chopped*
2 *teaspoons salt, or to taste*
  Sprinkling of freshly ground pepper
6 *slices bacon, fried until crisp, drained, and crumbled*
1 *cup chicken broth*
1 *cup dry bread crumbs*
2 *tablespoons butter*

1. Preheat oven to 350°.

2. Mix the pokeweed, leeks or onions, parsley, marjoram, basil, salt, pepper, bacon, chicken broth, and half of the bread crumbs.

3. Pour into greased 2-quart casserole and cover.

4. Bake for 20 minutes.

5. Uncover casserole and sprinkle the remaining crumbs on top. Top with bits of butter and bake uncovered 15 minutes longer, or until well browned. Serve hot.

Serves 8.

POKEWEED STALKS ORIENTAL STYLE

2 *tablespoons oil, preferably peanut*
3 *cups pokeweed stalks, peeled and sliced diagonally about ½ inch thick*
½ *cup sliced mushrooms (oyster mushrooms or chanterelles are particularly good)*
1 *teaspoon salt, or to taste*
  Freshly ground black pepper to taste
2 *tablespoons soy sauce, imported if available*
½ *cup sliced Jerusalem Artichokes in Lemon Juice,* or one 5-ounce can of water chestnuts, drained and sliced*
2 *cans crisp chow mein noodles, warmed on a platter placed in an oven set at very low heat*

1. Heat oil in a skillet over low heat.

2. Add pokeweed, mushrooms, salt, pepper, and soy sauce. Cook over low heat, tossing occasionally, for 15 minutes, or until vegetables are tender.

3. Add Jerusalem artichokes or water chestnuts and stir.

4. Shape noodles into a nest on the platter, spoon in the hot vegetables, and serve at once.

Serves 6.

PRICKLY PEAR PADS

The pads of prickly pears, as well as the fruits, can be eaten. The interior of the pads is mucilaginous, like okra, and may not be palatable to some. I have used prickly pear pads to thicken soups which I make on field trips, and indeed the unfamiliar taste is quite acceptable in fowl or fish stews. In the field I simply wrap several of the prickly pads in foil, being careful to avoid the stickers, and place them over low coals on the grill and let them stay all day. By evening the tough outer skin, with its thorns, pulls right off.

In the kitchen the skins are more simply removed by placing the pads in an oven set at 375° for 40 minutes. Then split the skin, pull it off, and you have the remaining soft flesh to use as a soup thickener or vegetable.

PRICKLY PEAR PADS WITH YUCCA SEEDS

3   tablespoons oil
½   cup wild onions, finely chopped
½   cup green peppers, finely chopped
1   cup stewed or canned tomatoes
16   prickly pear pads, fried as described in Prickly Pear Pads in a Zesty Sauce (above)
1   cup Boiled Yucca Seeds*
½   cup soft bread crumbs
1   tablespoon finely chopped parsley
4   slices bacon

1. Preheat oven to 375°.
2. Heat oil in a skillet and cook onions and green peppers gently till soft. Add tomatoes.
3. Place 8 fried pads in a shallow baking dish and top with ½ cup boiled yucca seeds, then repeat the layers.
4. Pour tomato sauce over the vegetables. Top with bread crumbs, then parsley, then bacon strips.
5. Bake for 20 minutes, or until bacon is cooked but not too crisp. Serve hot.

Serves 8.

PRICKLY PEAR PADS IN A ZESTY SAUCE

Serve this saucy dish with any dark-meat game or with beef.

Sauce:
3   tablespoons oil
½   cup finely chopped green peppers
½   cup wild onions, finely chopped
1   bulb wild garlic, finely chopped
2   cups stewed or canned tomatoes
1   teaspoon chili powder
1   teaspoon sugar
½   bay leaf
¼   teaspoon ground cloves
1   teaspoon salt
     Freshly ground pepper to taste

Prickly Pears:
16   prickly pear pads, each 4 or 5 inches long with skins removes (see above)
½   cup yellow cornmeal
¼   cup flour
½   teaspoon salt
     Freshly ground pepper to taste
1   egg, well beaten
½   cup milk
     Vegetable oil for frying

1. Make sauce: Heat oil in a heavy skillet and cook peppers, onions, and garlic gently for 5 minutes, or until soft but not browned.
2. Add tomatoes, chili powder, sugar, bay leaf, cloves, salt, and pepper and cook

over low heat for 45 minutes, or until thick. Stir occasionally.

3. Preheat oven to 350°.

4. Fry prickly pear pads: Combine cornmeal, flour, salt, and pepper.

5. Combine beaten egg and milk.

6. Heat oil (about ¼ inch deep) in a skillet over medium-high heat.

7. Cut pads in half. Dip pieces first into egg mixture, then into the dry ingredients.

8. Fry the pads over medium heat for 3 or 4 minutes on each side, cooking them until browned.

9. Place pads in a shallow baking dish and cover with sauce.

10. Bake for 20 minutes. Serve hot.

Serves 8.

PURSLANE

Both the leaves and succulent stems of purslane, picked over and washed, are fine for cooking as greens. Follow the master recipe on page 132; cooking time is usually about 10 minutes.

Use the cooked purslane as a vegetable course, seasoned with salt, pepper, and butter, or try it as an ingredient in a recipe calling for cooked greens.

PURSLANE AND BACON CASEROLE

3 *cups cooked purslane (page 132), drained and salted to taste*

10 *slices bacon, fried until crisp, drained, and crumbled*

½ *cup light cream*

1 *cup cracker crumbs*
Paprika

1. Preheat oven to 350°.

2. Place half of purslane in a 1½-quart casserole and sprinkle with half of the bacon. Add remaining purslane and pour cream over it.

3. Top first with cracker crumbs, then the rest of the bacon. Sprinkle with paprika.

4. Bake for 25 minutes, or until firm. Serve hot.

Serves 6 to 8.

PURSLANE WITH EGGS

4 *tablespoons (½ stick) butter*

2 *cups purslane, washed and drained*

½ *cup wild onions or leeks, chopped*
Salt and freshly ground pepper to taste

6 *eggs, well beaten*

1. Melt butter in a large skillet over medium heat.

2. Add purslane and leeks and cook for 10 minutes, stirring often.

3. Cover, turn heat low, and cook for 5 minutes more. Season with salt and pepper.

4. Uncover, add eggs, and cook, stirring, until eggs are as firm as you like them.

Serves 6.

PURSLANE AND MIXED GREENS CASSEROLE

2   cups cooked purslane (page 167)
½   cup cooked watercress or mustard greens
      (see basic recipes)
¼   cup cooked dandelion or chicory greens
      (see basic recipes)
    Salt and freshly ground pepper to taste
¾   cup White Sauce*
½   cup grated American cheese
½   cup dry bread crumbs

1. Preheat oven to 350°.
2. Combine purslane with other greens in a saucepan, heat carefully, and drain. Season with salt and pepper to taste.
3. Add white sauce and stir well.
4. Put a layer of creamed greens in a 1½-quart casserole and sprinkle with part of the grated cheese, then bread crumbs. Repeat, with cheese as the last layer.
5. Bake 15 minutes, or until cheese topping has melted. Serve hot.
    Serves 6.

SORREL

The basic way to cook sorrel is simple and quick. Pick over and wash the greens and remove the stems. For each fairly well packed quart of leaves, bring a cup of water to a boil and add 1 teaspoon of salt and the sorrel. Return to a boil and cook for 5 minutes, or until done.

PURÉED SORREL

This purée is highly thought of as a base for poached fish. It is also the basis of Cream of Sorrel Soup.*

3   cups (packed) sorrel, washed, drained,
      and stems removed
1   teaspoon salt
    Freshly ground pepper to taste
1   cup water
2   tablespoons lemon juice

1. Place sorrel in a saucepan and add salt and pepper.
2. Add water, cover, and bring quickly to a boil. Lower heat and simmer for 10 minutes, or until sorrel is tender.
3. Drain sorrel in a colander (reserve liquid) and place it in the jar of an electric blender.
4. Add lemon juice and run blender at medium speed until a smooth purée results. If necessary, add a bit of the drained cooking water to get the desired consistency.
    Makes 1½ to 2 cups.

SORREL AND JERUSALEM ARTICHOKE BAKE

4   tablespoons butter
¼   cup chopped wild onions, white parts
      only
3   cups cooked and drained sorrel (page
      132)
2   cups Jerusalem artichokes, peeled,
      cooked (page 146), chopped coarsely,
      and salted to taste
½   cup light cream
½   cup dry bread crumbs
½   cup mild cheddar-type cheese, grated

1. Preheat oven to 350°.
2. In 1 tablespoon of the butter, cook the onions over medium-low heat until soft and golden yellow.
3. Combine onions with the sorrel and Jerusalem artichokes and place in a 2-quart casserole.

4. Pour cream into dish.

5. Dot top with remaining 3 table-spoons butter and top with first the bread crumbs, then the cheese.

6. Bake for 30 minutes, or until hot through and topping is brown.

Serves 8.

SOW THISTLE

To be at their best as greens, the leaves of sow thistle should be picked as young as possible, always before the plant's flowers open. The flavor tends to be strong, so parboiling is a good idea. Cover the potful of washed leaves with water, bring to a full boil, and drain well; then proceed with the basic cooking method outlined on page 132. Cooking time is usually about 20 minutes.

SPRING BEAUTY TUBERS

Spring beauty tubers are a special delight any time they are served. Their nutty flavor is unlike that of any other vegeta-bles, and because they are so very small and difficult to dig one feels particularly rewarded when enough are obtained to make the main ingredient of a dish.

SPRING BEAUTY TUBERS AU GRATIN

The definitely nutlike flavor of this dish makes it a particularly savory companion for chicken or fish.

2 *tablespoons butter*
1 *cup chopped wild leeks, including about 4 inches of green tops*

2 *cups spring beauty tubers, boiled (page 169), peeled, and seasoned to taste with salt and pepper*
1 *cup shredded mild cheddar-type cheese*
½ *cup cracker crumbs*
¼ *cup milk*
2 *tablespoons butter*

1. Preheat oven to 350°.

2. Melt butter in a skillet and cook chopped leeks over medium heat until soft.

3. Place layer of tubers in a 2-quart casserole, add a layer of leeks, and sprinkle with ½ cup of the cheese, then ¼ cup cracker crumbs.

4. Add another layer of tubers, sprinkle with remaining cheese, pour milk over the layers, and top with remaining ¼ cup of crumbs. Dot with bits of butter.

5. Bake for 30 minutes, or until hot through and golden brown on top. Serve hot.

Serves 6 to 8.

BOILED SPRING BEAUTY TUBERS

1½ *cups water*
½ *teaspoon salt*
2 *cups spring beauty tubers, washed but not peeled*
   Cold water, as needed

1. Bring 1½ cups water to a boil, add salt, and add tubers.

2. Return to a boil, lower heat, cover, and cook until tubers are soft when pres-sed gently.

3. Drain tubers and cover with cold water. When they can be handled easily, slip off the skin. You'll then have small white pearls of goodness which may be used in several ways.

HASHED BROWN SPRING BEAUTY TUBERS

2 *cups boiled spring beauty tubers (page 169), peeled, if desired, and salted to taste*
Butter for frying

1. Mash tubers coarsely, either with or without skins.
2. Form into 8 small flat patties.
3. Fry in butter over medium heat until golden brown, turning once.
    Serves 4.

VIOLET GREENS

Among the most delicious and widely available greens are the leaves of the violets—the heart-shaped or roundish kinds, not the branched leaves of the bird-foot violet, whose flowers are the edible part. Gather plenty of leaves, pull off any coarse stems, and cook like other greens, page 132. Cooking time will be about 10 minutes.

WATERCRESS

Cook watercress exactly like spinach and you'll have a delicious green vegetable dish, ready to season with butter, salt, and pepper and enjoy for its tangy "bite."

Like spinach, watercress cooks down a lot, so allow at least 2 quarts of picked-over cress, moderately packed down, to serve four to six. Remove any thick stems, but keep the small ones. Cook in a large pot over medium-high heat, using only the water left on the leaves from washing, and turn the cress with a fork often until it is well wilted and done to your liking; it will take only a few minutes. Drain, if necessary, and either use in a recipe calling for cooked greens or season and serve at once.

CREAMED WATERCRESS LOAF

This green loaf is easily sliced for serving. The tangy bite of the cress goes well with such mild-flavored meats as quail or chicken.

3 *cups cooked watercress (see above), drained and salted to taste*
4 *hard-cooked eggs, finely chopped*
½ *cup dry bread crumbs*
1 *cup heavy cream*

1. Preheat oven to 350°.
2. In a large mixing bowl combine watercress, eggs, and bread crumbs, mixing thoroughly.
3. Pour into a greased 9 × 4-inch loaf pan. Pour in cream, cutting through mixture every inch or so with a knife so cream will penetrate well.
4. Bake for 30 minutes, or until firm. Serve hot.
    Serves 6.

WATERCRESS OMELET

Substituting 1 cup of sliced and parboiled wild leeks for the watercress will give you an entirely different tasting, but equally delicious, omelet. Either kind is an ideal luncheon dish.

1 cup watercress leaves, very finely
  chopped
½ teaspoon freshly ground pepper, or to
  taste
1 teaspoon lemon juice
1 teaspoon salt
8 eggs
4 tablespoons (½ stick) butter
½ cup sour cream, at room temperature
  Watercress sprigs for garnishing

1. Toss together chopped watercress, pepper, lemon juice, and salt.

2. Beat eggs just until well mixed and stir in the watercress mixture.

3. Heat a 12-inch omelet pan or skillet over high heat and add butter, shaking and turning to coat bottom and sides (don't let butter brown).

4. Pour in omelet mixture and stir the eggs rapidly with the flat of a fork for a moment, at the same time shaking pan briskly back and forth; cook just until softly set on top.

5. Fold omelet and turn out on a platter. Spoon sour cream over the top, garnish with sprigs of watercress, and serve at once.

Serves 4.

WATERCRESS QUICK-COOKED THE CHINESE WAY

This is a recipe from a city-dwelling friend who uses "tame" watercress and garlic, plus fresh ginger from the tropics, but we find that our wild materials, too, make a delicious dish.

3 tablespoons vegetable oil, preferably
  peanut
1 or 2 bulbs of wild garlic, peeled and
  flattened
2 or 3 slices of fresh ginger root (optional),
  flattened
2 quarts (fairly well packed) watercress,
  washed, well drained, and with the
  coarse stems removed
  Salt to taste

1. In a very large skillet (the Chinese use a wok) heat the oil until quite hot but not smoking.

2. Add the garlic and ginger and toss in the oil for a second or two, no more—don't let them brown.

3. Add the watercress and toss vigorously, mixing it with the oil and cooking it rapidly over high heat for 2 to 4 minutes, or until it's wilted and done to your taste (it's best when it still has a hint of crispness).

4. Sprinkle with salt, toss again, and fork into a serving bowl, leaving any excess juice behind. Serve at once.

Serves 4 to 6.

BOILED WILD RICE

1 cup wild rice
4 cups water
1 teaspoon salt

1. Wash the rice thoroughly in cold water twice—this is to remove the wild smoky taste.

2. Bring water to a boil and add salt. Add rice slowly as water boils.

3. Boil gently without stirring for 20 to 25 minutes, or until rice is tender.

4. Drain in a sieve or colander and rinse with very hot water. Rice is now ready to serve or to use in a recipe.

Serves 4.

WINTER CRESS

Cooked by the basic method for greens (page 132), winter cress leaves (they should be picked young) will be done in just a few minutes. Try serving them with lemon or vinegar in addition to a seasoning of butter, salt, and pepper; or pass Vinaigrette Dressing* to be poured over the drained hot greens.

WOOD SORREL

Acid-flavored and refreshing, wood sorrel is a good addition to a pot of mixed greens; you can use both the leaves and the stems. If you want to serve wood sorrel as a separate green, don't overdo the size of the servings; the plant contains oxalic acid, which is completely harmless in small quantities but is poisonous in large doses, so it isn't a good idea to consume more wood sorrel at one time than an ordinary moderate helping. Cook the greens by the method described on page 132; they'll be done very quickly.

WOOD SORREL AND RICE

The amounts given will fill a 1½-quart ring mold, if you want to serve it this way. Fill the center of the ring with creamed mushrooms for an exceptionally satisfying main-course dish.

  1   *cup uncooked rice*
  2   *cups chicken stock*
 ½   *cup wood sorrel, both leaves and stems*
      Salt and freshly ground pepper to taste
      Additional wood sorrel leaves and flowers for garnishing

1. Put rice in a heavy pot and add chicken stock; it should cover rice.
2. Bring to a boil, then lower heat and simmer 15 minutes with the pot closely covered.
3. Remove rice from heat, add sorrel, stir well, cover again, and let stand 10 minutes. Taste, and add salt and pepper if needed.
4. Serve in a mound, garnished with wood sorrel leaves and flowers.
    Serves 4.

WOOD SORREL AND CABBAGE

  2   *cups wood sorrel leaves (remove any flowers, because they turn dark when cooked)*
  2   *cups shredded cabbage*
  1   *cup chopped celery*
  2   *chopped wild leeks, white parts only, or ¼ cup chopped chives*
 ½   *sweet medium-sized green pepper, sliced into ¼-inch strips*
 ¼   *cup white vinegar*
      Water, as needed
  2   *eggs, beaten*
 ½   *teaspoon mustard seed*
 ¼   *teaspoon paprika*
 ½   *cup light cream*
      Salt and freshly ground pepper to taste
      Paprika for garnishing

1. Combine wood sorrel leaves, cabbage, celery, leeks or chives, green pepper, and vinegar in a saucepan, cover with water, bring to a boil, and cook over high heat for about 10 minutes. Set aside.
2. Stir eggs, mustard seed, paprika, and cream together in a saucepan and stir over low heat just until thickened; be careful not to let sauce curdle. Season with salt and pepper.

3. Drain vegetables and put into a serving dish.
4. Pour the sauce over the vegetables and sprinkle with more paprika. Serve hot.
Serves 8.

YUCCA

One look at the Spanish bayonet or yucca plant and you'd be justified in doubting its usefulness as food. But the flowers are delicious when candied (Index), and the seeds make a good vegetable dish, either alone or combined with prickly pear pads (Index).

BOILED YUCCA SEEDS

2   *cups unripe yucca seeds*
1   *cup water*
1   *tablespoon butter*
1   *teaspoon salt*
¼   *cup leeks, white parts only, chopped*

Combine all ingredients, bring to a boil, lower heat, cover pot, and simmer 10 minutes, or until seeds are tender. Serve hot.
Serves 4.

SALADS AND SALAD DRESSINGS

APPLE-SPEARMINT SALAD

Be prepared for exclamations of admiration and eager requests for your recipe when you serve this salad. There is seldom a time in the Arkansas Ozarks when it's too cold for spearmint to be found. If that found growing in the open ground has frozen or died back because of cold weather, I search the running creeks and spring headwaters where I recall having seen this mint growing in companionship with watercress. If I can't get 2 cups of spearmint, I use less and add more apples.

    6   crisp red or yellow apples, washed
            Juice of 2 lemons
    2   cups (packed) spearmint leaves, washed
            and drained
    ½   cup raisins
    ½   cup black walnuts or pecans, broken up
    ½   cup Mayonnaise*

1. Wash apples and cut into small pieces, removing the cores but leaving the skins on.

2. Sprinkle lemon juice on the apples. (This keeps them from turning dark and also brings out the flavor.)

3. Tear or snip the spearmint leaves into small bits. (This increases the mint flavor.)

4. Toss apples with the raisins, nuts, and mint leaves.

5. Now add the mayonnaise and toss the salad briskly.

6. Serve in a sparkling-clear glass salad bowl.

Serves 8.

ASPARAGUS ASPIC

When making almost any kind of a savory aspic, try using, as part of the liquid, the juice left over from boiling mushrooms or from cooking such greens as mustard, lamb's quarters, dock, or any combination. In this recipe you could use some of the asparagus cooking water to replace plain water.

    ½   cup hot water
    ½   teaspoon salt
    ½   cup cider vinegar
    ½   cup sugar
    2   tablespoons lemon juice
    1   envelope unflavored gelatin
    1   cup cool water
    2   cups asparagus, cooked (page 136),
            drained, cooled, and coarsely chopped
    ½   cup pecans, coarsely chopped

1. In a saucepan mix the hot water, salt, ¼ cup of the vinegar, the sugar, and the lemon juice and bring to a boil. Set aside to cool for 10 minutes.

2. Meanwhile, sprinkle gelatin into the cool water and let it soak for 5 minutes or so.

3. Add warm vinegar mixture gradually to the gelatin, stirring until gelatin has dissolved. Add remaining ¼ cup vinegar. Cool until mixture begins to thicken a little.

4. Stir in chopped asparagus and pecans.

5. Pour aspic into a 6-cup mold or a 9 × 4-inch loaf pan and chill for at least 3 hours, or until firm.

6. To remove aspic from mold, quickly dip the outside of the mold into a bowl or sink filled with hot water. Invert a serving dish over the mold and, holding them together, turn them right side up. The salad should slip right out. If it doesn't, dip the mold into hot water again for just a few seconds.

Serves 6.

CHILLED ASPARAGUS SALAD WITH CHIVES

> 3 *cups strong beef bouillon*
> 30 *to* 40 *spears of asparagus*
>   *Oil, preferably olive*
>   *White vinegar*
> ¼ *cup chopped chives*
>   *Salt and freshly ground pepper*

1. Bring the bouillon to a boil in a large skillet and add asparagus spears, laying them flat.

2. Cover skillet, lower heat, and cook asparagus until just tender, 10 to 15 minutes.

3. Lift asparagus out of pan, drain, arrange on a platter, and chill.

4. Just before serving, sprinkle asparagus with oil, vinegar, chives, salt, if needed, and pepper.

Serves 8.

ASPARAGUS VINAIGRETTE

Asparagus-sprouting time is the surest sign that winter is gone. This recipe gives us a change of pace from the many hot asparagus dishes we eat at the height of the season, when the shoots are picked two to three times a week. This salad can also be served as a first course.

> 30 *to* 40 *asparagus spears, cooked and chilled*
> *Vinaigrette Dressing**

1. Arrange asparagus on a chilled platter and sprinkle with vinaigrette dressing.

2. Refrigerate until serving time, preferably not more than 2 hours.

Serves 8.

BRACKEN-FROND SALAD

2   cups young bracken or other fern fronds,
      defuzzed, washed, drained, and
      cut up coarsely
1   cup watercress sprigs, loosely packed
1   cup mustard leaves, loosely packed
¼   cup fresh chanterelles or pickled chan-
      terelles (see Index for Pickled Mush-
      rooms*)
¼   cup chopped chives
¼   cup blue cheese, crumbled
2   strips bacon, cooked until crisp, drained,
      and crumbled
4   tablespoons white vinegar
      Salt and freshly ground pepper to taste

1. Break fern fronds into bite-sized
pieces.
2. Mince watercress with sharp knife.
3. Tear mustard leaves into bite-sized
pieces.
4. Wash chanterelles, if fresh, and snip
off any tough stems. Drain pickled mushrooms, if used.
5. Toss bracken fronds, watercress,
mustard leaves, mushrooms, chives, and
cheese together in a salad bowl.
6. Sprinkle crumbled bacon over the
salad, then sprinkle it with vinegar, salt,
and pepper. Toss again.
   Serves 8.

COOKED CAT-TAIL SPROUT SALAD

3   cups cat-tail sprouts, cleaned (page
      142), boiled in salted water until
      tender, drained, and chilled
2   hard-cooked eggs, cooled, peeled, and
      coarsely chopped
½   cup chopped wild onions, white parts
      only

¼   cup black olives, chopped
¼   cup hickory nuts or pecans, finely
      chopped
4   tablespoons Mayonnaise*

1. Combine sprouts, most of the
chopped eggs (reserve a spoonful for
garnish), onions, olives, and nuts in a salad
bowl. Toss well.
2. Add mayonnaise and toss again until
well combined.
3. Serve in a wooden bowl, garnished
with the reserved chopped eggs.
   Serves 6.

CAT-TAIL SPROUT SALAD

2   cups cat-tail sprouts, scrubbed and
      peeled (page 142)
½   cup chopped wild leeks, white parts only
1   wild garlic bulb, finely chopped
1   tablespoon dried dill seed
½   cup chopped pecans
      Salt and freshly ground pepper to taste
      Green Mayonnaise*

1. Combine cat-tail sprouts, leeks,
garlic, dill seed, and pecans and toss well.
2. Add salt and pepper, then add
enough green mayonnaise to dress the
salad to your taste and toss again.
   Serves 6.

CHICKWEED AND CRESS SALAD

2   cups (packed) chickweed, finely chopped
1   cup (packed) watercress, coarsely chopped
1   cup (packed) winter cress, coarsely
      chopped
4   hard-cooked eggs, cooled, peeled, and
      coarsely chopped
      Onion and Sour Cream Dressing*

1. Place chickweed, watercress, and winter cress in a large wooden bowl and toss well.
2. Gently mix chopped eggs into greens.
3. Pour dressing over salad, toss again, and serve at once.
Serves 8.

WILTED DANDELION SALAD

4 cups (well packed) young dandelion leaves, rinsed and drained
¼ cup chopped chives
4 slices bacon, fried until crisp, drained, and crumbled (reserve fat)
¼ cup hot bacon drippings
¼ cup cider vinegar

1. Pat dandelion greens dry with paper towels.
2. Combine greens with chives in a wooden bowl.
3. Heat bacon fat and vinegar in a skillet and pour over greens, tossing quickly.
4. Add crumbled bacon and serve immediately.
Serves 6.

DANDELION SALAD

4 cups (packed) very young dandelion leaves, washed, drained, patted dry with paper towels, and chilled Vinaigrette Dressing*, as required
2 hard-cooked eggs, sliced

1. Toss dandelion leaves with dressing until leaves are barely coated.
2. Serve in a crystal bowl, garnished with hard-cooked egg slices.
Serves 6.

JERUSALEM ARTICHOKE SALAD

Here is a salad using Jerusalem artichokes. This root vegetable begins to sprout (and sometimes rot) in the ground as early as April, so dig and use them as often as feasible in fall and winter, for a long hot artichokeless summer lies ahead. Try them uncooked in salads, too—see the recipe for Violet and Wood Sorrel Salad.*

4 cups cooked Jerusalem artichokes (page 146), cooled, peeled, and sliced
¼ cup chopped wild onions (white parts) or chives
3 hard-cooked eggs, cooled, peeled, and coarsely chopped
4 tablespoons green olives, chopped
¼ cup chopped sweet pickles or sweet pickle relish
¼ cup Mayonnaise*
2 tablespoons Prepared Mustard,* or commercial prepared mustard
¼ teaspoon cumin seed, crushed slightly
½ teaspoon dill seed
¼ teaspoon crumbled dried rosemary, or 1 teaspoon chopped fresh rosemary
½ teaspoon grated lemon peel
Salt and freshly ground pepper to taste
Paprika

1. Place Jerusalem artichokes, onions or chives, eggs, olives, and chopped pickles in a large salad bowl and toss together gently.
2. Beat together the mayonnaise, mustard, cumin seed, dill seed, rosemary, lemon peel, salt, and pepper.
3. Pour dressing over salad and toss gently but thoroughly.
4. Serve in a crystal salad bowl, garnished with paprika.
Serves 6 to 8.

PURSLANE AND WOOD SORREL SALAD

Purslane is a "people plant"—it is more often found in yards and gardens than in the fields. At Tameweed next door I have on occasion picked enough purslane from the crevices of the rock steps and patio to make this salad, but the plant has not yet graced our grounds.

2 cups (packed) purslane leaves, tender shoots, and stems, rinsed and drained
1 cup (packed) rinsed, drained, and chopped wood sorrel
1 tomato, peeled and coarsely chopped
2 wild leeks, white parts only, chopped
  Vinaigrette Dressing*
  Salt and freshly ground pepper (optional)
2 hard-cooked eggs, sliced

1. Combine purslane, wood sorrel, tomato, and leeks and toss well with dressing to taste. If desired, add more salt and pepper.
2. Serve in a wooden bowl, topped with slices of egg.
Serves 6.

SLAW WITH CHIVES

1 cup finely chopped chives
3 cups crisp cabbage, finely chopped
1 cup cottage cheese
¼ cup green olives, chopped, or Elderberry Capers*
1 tablespoon poppy seed
¼ cup Mayonnaise,* or amount desired
2 tablespoons white vinegar
  Additional chopped chives for garnishing

Combine all the ingredients, except the garnish, in a wooden bowl and toss well.

Garnish with additional chopped chives and serve at once.
Serves 8.

HOT SPRING BEAUTY SALAD

2 strips bacon
  Fat drained from cooked bacon
½ cup chopped wild leeks, including about 4 inches of green tops
2 tablespoons sugar
3 tablespoons white vinegar
3 tablespoons water
2 cups spring beauty tubers, boiled (page 169), peeled, and salted and peppered to taste
¼ cup chopped raw chinquapins
  Paprika

1. Fry bacon until crisp and remove from skillet to a paper towel. Reserve bacon fat.
2. In reserved fat, fry chopped leeks over medium heat until tender but not browned. Drain off fat.
3. Add sugar, vinegar, and water to leeks and reheat.
4. Add the spring beauty tubers and chinquapins to the skillet and continue to heat until warmed through.
5. Place in a warmed bowl, crumble the bacon over the top, and sprinkle with paprika. Serve at once.
Serves 4.

VIOLET AND WOOD SORREL SALAD

1 cup (packed) violet leaves (the heart-shaped kind) and flowers, rinsed and well drained

2 cups (packed) wood sorrel (leaves, stems, and flowers), rinsed and well drained
1 cup Jerusalem artichokes, peeled and finely chopped
2 tablespoons lemon juice
2 tablespoons Mayonnaise*

1. Toss violet and wood sorrel leaves and flowers together.
2. Add Jerusalem artichokes and toss again.
3. Blend mayonnaise and lemon juice and pour over salad. Toss until well blended and serve immediately.
Serves 6 to 8.

WATERCRESS AND CHANTERELLE SALAD

This colorful salad is a good accompaniment for a main course of fish.

1 cup fresh chanterelles
4 cups (packed) watercress sprigs, tough stems removed, rinsed and drained well
¼ cup chives, finely chopped
3 tablespoons wine vinegar
3 tablespoons oil, preferably olive
1 teaspoon coarse salt

1. Wash chanterelles if necessary, drain, and pat dry on paper towels.
2. Combine chanterelles, watercress, and chives in a salad bowl; chill.
3. Just before serving, toss salad with the wine vinegar, oil, and coarse salt.
Serves 6.

ESPECIALLY SPICY COMBINATION SALAD

Definite specifications for making combination salads are not really useful. They are endlessly variable—if one wild green isn't available, another kind will work fine. If you have only one or two wild greens, you may want to add garden lettuce or a head of romaine. Let your taste be your guide: experiment with combinations till you find out which you like most. In this and the following recipes for combination salads I will indicate quantities and kinds of green ingredients, but these suggestions are just a general guide—keep in mind that changes can be made to suit your taste or fancy.

1 cup watercress sprigs, packed
1 cup mustard leaves, packed
1 cup wood sorrel, flowers and all, packed
1 cup henbit leaves, flowers and all, packed
¼ cup pepper grass tops, flowers, and unripe seed, packed
2 hard-cooked eggs, cooled, peeled, and chopped
1 wild garlic bulb, finely chopped
2 slices bacon, fried until crisp, drained, and crumbled
¼ cup chopped chives
½ teaspoon chili powder
3 tablespoons white vinegar
3 tablespoons salad oil
Salt and freshly ground pepper to taste

1. Wash the watercress, mustard leaves, wood sorrel, henbit leaves, and pepper grass, drain them well, pat dry on paper towels, and tear them into bite-sized pieces (or snip them with kitchen shears). Chill, if desired.
2. Place all the ingredients except vinegar and oil in a salad bowl; toss well but gently.
3. Sprinkle with oil and toss; then sprinkle with vinegar, salt, and pepper, toss again, and serve at once.
Serves 6.

EARLY SPRING GREEN SALAD

Lemon juice alone is sufficient dressing for this salad—the flavor of these greens is such that no additional seasoning is needed.

½   cup (packed) plantain leaves, strings
      removed (page 163)
1½ cups (packed) wood sorrel
      leaves, coarsely chopped
1   cup young dandelion leaves
¼   cup spearmint leaves, chopped coarsely
2   cups watercress, coarsely chopped
      Juice of 1 lemon, strained

1. Wash all the greens and drain well. Chop the wood sorrel coarsely.
2. Place all the greens in a mixing bowl and toss together.
3. Transfer to a crystal bowl and sprinkle with lemon juice. Serve at once.
   Serves 8.

RED AND GREEN TOSSED SALAD

1   cup mustard leaves, packed
1   cup red amaranth leaves, packed
1   cup watercress sprigs, packed
2   cups raw Jerusalem artichokes, peeled
      and sliced thinly into rounds
½   cup (packed) plantain leaves, strings
      removed (page 163)
      Juice of 1 lemon
¼   cup Mayonnaise*
½   teaspoon paprika

1. Wash, drain, and pat dry the mustard and amaranth leaves, and watercress and tear or snip the greens into bite-sized pieces.
2. Add the Jerusalem artichokes and

prepared plantain leaves and toss with the greens in a salad bowl.
3. In a small bowl, mix the lemon juice, mayonnaise, and paprika.
4. Pour dressing over salad, toss, and serve at once in individual bowls.
   Serves 8.

ONION AND SOUR CREAM DRESSING

Although this is called a dressing here, it is a dual-purpose mixture. Delicious for potato or Jerusalem artichoke salads, here at Wildflower we also often serve it as a dip for potato or corn chips.

2   tablespoons butter
4   tablespoons minced wild onions or leeks
      (white parts) or chives
½   teaspoon salt, or to taste
1   tablespoon lemon juice
½   cup commercial sour cream
½   teaspoon paprika
      Freshly ground pepper to taste

1. Melt the butter in a skillet over low heat and cook the onions, leeks, or chives until soft but not browned at all, about 5 minutes. Add salt.
2. Mix lemon juice into the sour cream and put into a small saucepan.
3. Add cooked onions to the cream mixture and heat carefully over low heat, stirring, until just warmed through.
4. Stir in the paprika and pepper.
   Makes about ¾ cup.

VINAIGRETTE DRESSING

This is a flexible recipe—the proportions of ingredients may be adjusted to taste, and of course it can be doubled or tripled and herbs or other additional seasonings can be added, too.

6   *tablespoons olive oil*
2   *tablespoons wine vinegar*
½   *teaspoon salt, or to taste*
    Freshly ground black pepper, to taste

Whisk or shake ingredients together until well blended. May be kept, refrigerated, for several days.
Makes about ½ cup.

MAYONNAISE

Basic Mayonnaise

2   *egg yolks*
1   *teaspoon Dry Mustard* or commercial dry mustard*
½   *teaspoon salt*
1   *teaspoon sugar*
4   *tablespoons vinegar*
1   *cup olive oil*

1. With a wire whip, beat the egg yolks in a fairly small bowl until thick and lemon yellow.
2. Add mustard, salt, sugar, and 2 tablespoons of the vinegar. Mix well and pour into the jar of an electric blender.
3. Blend at medium speed while adding oil a few drops at a time at first; gradually increase the rate of pouring oil as the mixture thickens.
4. With the blender off, add remaining 2 tablespoons of vinegar. Turn blender on at high speed for 1 minute, or until vinegar is blended in.
5. Chill well before serving.
Makes 1½ cups.

Chive Mayonnaise

Blend 4 tablespoons of chopped chives into 1 cup of Mayonnaise (*above*).

Mayonnaise for Fruit Salad

1   *cup Mayonnaise (above)*
2   *tablespoons orange juice*
2   *tablespoons pineapple juice*
2   *tablespoons honey*
Mix well and serve with fruit salad.

Cress Mayonnaise

¼   *cup finely chopped watercress*
1   *cup Mayonnaise (above)*

1. In electric blender, purée cress 1 minute at high speed.
2. Add mayonnaise and blend briefly, until just mixed.
3. Serve over a combination salad or with Jerusalem Artichoke Salad (Index) instead of the dressing in that recipe.

GREEN MAYONNAISE

This is a quick and easy dressing for a combination salad or a salad of lettuce alone.

1   *wild garlic bulb*
1   *tablespoon minced fresh dill head (unripe seed head) or 1½ teaspoons dried dill seed*
2   *tablespoons chopped chives*
1   *egg yolk*
1   *teaspoon Dry Mustard* or commercial dry mustard*
2   *tablespoons white vinegar*
¼   *cup olive oil*
¾   *cup olive oil*

1. In jar of an electric blender place garlic, minced dill or dill seed, chives, egg yolk, dry mustard, vinegar, and ¼ cup olive oil.
2. Blend at low speed until smooth.
3. Very gradually, blending at low speed, add the ¾ cup of oil and blend 1 minute, or until smooth and thick.
Makes about 1 cup.

SAVORY AND SWEET SAUCES

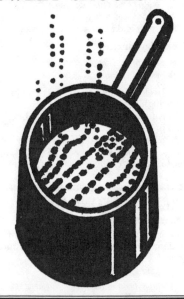

WILD GARLIC BUTTER

There are many uses for this savory butter—it's great when spread on fresh hot bread (or a heated loaf of French- or Italian-type bread), and it's an enhancement for broiled or roasted venison or other meat, or for fish. It will keep for months in the freezer, or for four days or so in the refrigerator.

1 *pound butter, softened at room temperature*
1 *wild garlic plant, both bulb and top, finely chopped*
½ *teaspoon salt*
Freshly ground black pepper to taste

1. Cream butter with minced garlic, salt, and pepper.
2. Pack into a bowl or a wooden butter mold, cover closely, and refrigerate or freeze.
3. Remove from refrigerator or freezer just before serving and turn out of mold onto serving dish. (A towel wrung out of hot water and placed around the mold for a moment will loosen the butter.)
   Makes about 2 cups.

WATERCRESS BUTTER

If you don't want to mold your watercress butter, shape it into small balls, each enough for a serving, and freeze them until serving time. Whatever shape it's in, this makes a zesty butter sauce for any kind of broiled or fried fish.

½ *pound (2 sticks) butter, softened at room temperature*
½ *cup (packed) finely chopped watercress leaves*

1. Cream butter thoroughly with watercress, using the back of a spoon to mash and blend the mixture.
2. Pack butter into a mold or a bowl and place in the refrigerator or freezer until firm again.
3. To remove from mold, wring a towel out of hot water and wrap it around the mold until the butter slips out easily when inverted onto a dish.
4. Refrigerate until serving time.
   Makes about 2 cups.

MUSHROOM BUTTER

Mushroom butter is a surprising taste addition when spread on a plain broiled steak, and it's particularly good on plainly cooked poultry. For canapés, spread this butter on melba toast or plain crackers. (If chanterelles are used, save a few tiny ones to use raw as a garnish.)

¼ cup (½ stick) butter
1 cup cubed or sliced wild mushrooms (meadow mushrooms, puffballs, or chanterelles)
½ cup (1 stick) additional butter
2 tablespoons commercial sour cream
Freshly ground black pepper to taste
¼ teaspoon salt
4 tablespoons sherry

1. Melt ¼ cup butter in a small skillet over medium heat. Add mushrooms and cook, stirring until tender. Cool.
2. Combine mushrooms and any juice with the ½ cup of butter and the sour cream, salt, and sherry in the jar of an electric blender and blend until smooth, about 1 minute.
3. Chill slightly before serving.
Makes about 1 ½ cups.

MUSHROOM–SOUR CREAM SAUCE FOR MEAT

Particularly good with venison or squirrel, this sour-cream mushroom sauce would also be delicious with any other meat. It makes a fine main course when served on toast for a "ladies' lunch," accompanied by a good salad.

2 tablespoons butter
1 cup mushrooms (shaggy manes, oyster mushrooms, sulphur shelf, or meadow mushrooms), cleaned and chopped
2 tablespoons flour
½ cup beef bouillon
½ cup commercial sour cream
Salt and freshly ground pepper to taste

1. Melt butter in a skillet or saucepan

and cook the mushrooms over medium heat until soft, about 5 minutes or more, depending on the kind.
2. Sprinkle flour over mushrooms and blend well.
3. Stir in beef bouillon and simmer sauce, covered, for 10 minutes, stirring occasionally.
4. Add sour cream and reheat without boiling. Season with salt and pepper and serve hot.
Makes 2 to 2 ½ cups.

JUDAS'S-EAR MUSHROOM SAUCE

Serve this delicious sauce over potatoes, rice, or toast, or with meat or poultry, or anything else that pleases you. If you can't find Judas's ears or other "tree ears," this sauce is fine when made with shaggy manes or meadow mushrooms.

2 cups beef bouillon
2 cups fresh Judas's-ear mushrooms, cleaned and cut into small pieces
2 tablespoons butter
2 tablespoons flour
Salt and freshly ground black pepper to taste

1. Bring bouillon to a boil, add mushrooms, and simmer, covered, for 30 minutes.
2. Melt butter in a skillet over low heat and stir in flour to make a smooth thick paste. Remove from heat.
3. Gradually add the mushrooms and their liquid to the contents of the skillet, stirring briskly.
4. Return skillet to medium heat and cook sauce, stirring constantly, until thickened; cook another minute or two.
5. Add salt and pepper to taste and serve hot.
Makes about 3 cups.

MUSHROOM SAUCE

Another delicious mushroom sauce—one we like with steak or with roast meat or game, and also on toast for a special breakfast dish.

3   tablespoons butter
½   cup wild onions or wild leeks (white parts) or chives, finely chopped
1   cup fresh mushrooms, finely chopped (meadow mushrooms, shaggy manes, chanterelles, sulphur shelf, or oyster mushrooms)
2   tablespoons flour
1   cup hot water, or amount needed
    Salt and freshly ground pepper to taste

1. Melt butter in a skillet, add onions, leeks, or chives, and cook, stirring, over low heat until tender.

2. Add mushrooms and cook until lightly browned. Turn heat low, cover skillet, and simmer 15 minutes or until mushrooms are tender, stirring occasionally.

3. Remove from the heat and push the vegetables to one side.

4. Sprinkle flour into the butter and juices in the skillet; stir until you have a thick smooth paste.

5. Return the skillet to low heat and, stirring constantly, gradually add hot water until the consistency of the sauce suits you. Cook for another minute or two after the sauce thickens.

6. Season to taste with salt and pepper. Serve hot.
   Makes about 2 cups.

WOOD SORREL SAUCE

Mildly tart, this is a particularly tasty sauce for fish or for boiled or steamed potatoes.

2   cups (packed) wood sorrel, rinsed, drained, and chopped
½   cup water, or as needed
1   cup hot White Sauce*
    Salt to taste

1. Cook the wood sorrel over low heat for 20 minutes with just enough of the water to keep it from sticking.

2. Purée the sorrel through a sieve or food mill or in a blender.

3. Combine the purée with the hot white sauce and reheat if necessary.

4. Add salt to taste and serve hot.
   Makes about 3 cups.

COTTAGE CHEESE SAUCE WITH CHIVES

This is a versatile sauce, good for hot boiled Jerusalem artichokes, fish balls, baked potatoes, or almost any kind of green vegetable.

½   pound cottage cheese, any kind
¼   cup commercial sour cream
½   teaspoon salt, or to taste
    Freshly ground black pepper to taste
3   tablespoons chopped chives, or to taste

1. Combine all ingredients in the jar of an electric blender and blend at high speed until very smooth.

2. Remove from blender to serving bowl. Chill if not to be served at once.
   Makes about 1½ cups.

JELLY SAUCE FOR GAME

If you should cook a possum, try this sauce with it. Jelly sauce is also particularly good with white meats, such as fresh pork, chicken, and rabbit.

½   lemon, peeled, seeds removed, and diced

1   *tablespoon chopped candied grapefruit
    peel*
1   *teaspoon butter*
¼   *cup sherry*
½   *cup Ground Cherry Jelly**
    Salt and freshly ground pepper to taste

Combine all ingredients, bring just to a boil, and serve hot with game.
Makes about 1 cup.

SPEARMINT SAUCE FOR MEAT

This traditional sauce for lamb is also especially good with possum, coon, rabbit, or waterfowl. It will keep indefinitely in the cupboard if sealed or for at least a month, unsealed, in the refrigerator.

1   *cup cider vinegar*
1   *cup water*
½   *cup honey*
½   *cup crumbled dried spearmint leaves, or
    1½ cups (packed) fresh spearmint
    leaves, finely chopped*

1. Combine vinegar, water, and honey in a saucepan and bring to a boil.
2. Add spearmint, remove from heat, and cover. Let stand about 10 minutes.
3. Pour into sterile bottles and cork or seal tightly.
Makes 2½ cups.

WILD PLUM SAUCE FOR MEAT

Drippings, with most of fat removed, collected from roasting venison, elk, other game, pork, or beef
Canned or stewed wild plums, seeded, about

½ *cup to each cup of meat juices*
Small amount of brown sugar, to taste
Dry Mustard* or commercial dry mustard, to taste
Salt, if needed

1. Measure drippings and combine with the wild plums in a skillet or saucepan and bring to a boil, stirring and mashing the fruit.
2. Season with brown sugar, dry mustard, and, if needed, a little salt. Serve hot.

SWEET AND SOUR SAUCE FOR FRIED FISH

3   *tablespoons corn oil or other vegetable oil*
4   *wild garlic bulbs, coarsely chopped*
1   *cup chopped wild leeks, white parts only*
½   *medium-sized red sweet pepper, chopped*
½   *medium-sized green sweet pepper, finely
    chopped*
½   *cup pineapple juice*
¼   *cup sugar*
3   *1-inch pieces of wild ginger root,
    scrubbed and finely chopped*
¼   *cup cider vinegar*
1   *tablespoon cornstarch*
¼   *cup water*
½   *teaspoon salt, or to taste*

1. Pour oil into a skillet, add garlic, leeks, and chopped peppers, and cook over medium heat, stirring, until vegetables are tender, about 10 minutes; do not brown.
2. Add pineapple juice, sugar, ginger root, and vinegar and simmer for 5 minutes.
3. Mix cornstarch and water and add gradually to the skillet, stirring over medium heat until sauce clears and thickens. Add salt to taste and serve hot.
Makes about 2½ cups.

PEPPER GRASS SAUCE

This rather thin, bright-green pepper sauce is a favorite of ours, either served plain or creamed into a few tablespoonfuls of soft butter as a dressing for fish.

    2   *cups unripe seed pods of pepper grass*
    1   *tablespoon vinegar*
        Salt and freshly ground pepper to taste
    ¼ *cup water*

1. Place all ingredients in the jar of an electric blender and blend on high speed, scraping down sides of jar occasionally, until a fairly smooth, thin paste is formed.
2. Strain through a fine sieve to remove any husks of the pods.
3. Store in refrigerator if not used at once. Serve at room temperature.
Makes about 1 ½ cups.

WHITE SAUCE

There are no "wild" ingredients in this sauce, but I'm including it here because it's called for in several recipes in this book. The sauce may be made thinner or thicker by using more or less milk; if quantity of liquid is changed, increase or decrease the seasonings accordingly.

    4   *tablespoons butter*
    3   *tablespoons flour*
    2   *cups hot milk*
    1   *teaspoon salt, or to taste*
    ¼ *teaspoon freshly ground pepper, or to taste*

1. Melt butter in a saucepan over low heat.
2. With a whisk or a wooden spoon, blend in flour, stirring constantly.
3. Gradually stir in hot milk, mixing smoothly.
4. Continue to cook, stirring constantly, until sauce is thick and smooth. Cook for an additional minute or two after thickening is complete (this is to prevent a taste of raw flour).
5. Add salt and pepper to taste.
Makes about 2 cups.

BERRY SAUCE

Equally good made with strawberries, blackberries, raspberries, mulberries, or ground cherries, this is a delectable sauce for filled pancakes—especially Cat-Tail Pollen Pancakes*—or for plain cake or pudding, or for ice cream.

    2   *tablespoons cornstarch*
    ¼ *cup water*
    2   *cups fresh berries (strawberries, blackberries, raspberries, or mulberries) or ground cherries*
        Water, as needed
        Sugar to taste

1. Combine cornstarch and ¼ cup water in saucepan.
2. Add berries and enough water to cover; stir.
3. Bring to a boil and cook, stirring, until sauce clears and thickens.
4. Add sugar to taste. Serve warm or cold.
Makes 2 ½ cups.

CHINQUAPINS IN RUM

If you can gather chinquapins, you'll find this sauce is delicious as a topping for vanilla ice cream. We also pour off the syrup to use on pancakes and use the nuts as a sweet snack.

    6   *cups water*
    6   *cups shelled chinquapins*

2 pounds brown sugar (4½ cups, packed)
1½ cups water
1½ cups light rum
½ seedless orange, thinly sliced
1 tablespoon finely chopped fresh wild ginger root

1. Bring water to a boil and add chinquapins.
2. Simmer until tender, about 40 minutes.
3. Drain, remove brown skins, rinse nuts, and pack in sterilized jars.
4. Combine brown sugar, water, and rum and bring to a boil.
5. Add orange slices and ginger root and let syrup return to the boil.
6. Pour over chinquapins in jars, making sure there is an orange slice in each jar.
7. Seal jars if to be stored indefinitely; or cover tightly and store for up to 2 or 3 weeks in the refrigerator.
Makes about 3 pints.

MINT DESSERT SAUCE

A good topping for ice cream, pound cake, or other plain cake.

¼ cup cider vinegar
1 cup water
½ cup crumbled dried spearmint leaves or 1½ cups (packed) chopped fresh mint leaves, finely chopped

2 tablespoons cornstarch
1 tablespoon lemon juice
1 to 2 tablespoons sugar, or to taste
¼ teaspoon salt

1. In a saucepan combine vinegar, ½ cup of the water, and ¼ cup of the dried mint or ¾ cup of the fresh, bring to a boil, lower heat, and simmer 5 minutes.
2. Strain and return the mint infusion to the saucepan.
3. Add remaining mint, the remaining ½ cup of water mixed with the cornstarch, and the lemon juice, sugar, and salt.
4. Bring just to a boil, stirring, and remove from heat. Chill before serving.
Makes about 1¾ cups.

MIXED FRUIT SAUCE

For this sauce you can use any mixture of wild fruits or berries except black cherries. If such fruits as wild plums or persimmons are used, of course you will want to remove any seeds or pits and chop them coarsely. If you use papaws, peel them before chopping.

4 cups mixed wild fruits or berries, rinsed and drained
Water
1 cup sugar, more or less

1. Place fruits in a saucepan and add water to cover.
2. Bring to a boil, lower heat, and simmer until soft.
3. Purée in blender, or press through a sieve or food mill.
4. Add sugar to taste and cook sauce over low heat until sugar is dissolved. Continue to simmer until sauce is the consistency you like.
5. Serve either hot or cold. Store in refrigerator.
Makes 2 to 3 cups.

BREADS, BISCUITS, MUFFINS, AND PANCAKES

GLADYS'S PERSIMMON BREAD

This sweet bread is really delicious when spread with cream cheese, or when served as a dessert with a topping of Caramel-Nut Frosting.*

½ cup shortening
¾ cup sugar
1 egg
2 cups flour
1 teaspoon baking powder
1 teaspoon baking soda
1 teaspoon ground cinnamon
½ teaspoon freshly ground dried ginger root or finely grated fresh ginger
½ teaspoon salt
1 cup persimmon pulp, either fresh, or frozen and thawed

1 teaspoon vanilla
½ cup chopped black walnuts or pecans

1. Cream together shortening, sugar, and egg and set aside.
2. Sift together the flour, baking powder, soda, cinnamon, ginger, and salt.
3. Gradually blend dry ingredients into the shortening mixture.
4. Add the persimmon pulp, vanilla, and nuts and mix to a stiff dough.
5. Pour into a greased 9 × 5-inch loaf pan and set aside for 20 minutes.
6. Meanwhile, preheat oven to 375°.
7. Bake for 50 minutes to 1 hour, or until a straw or toothpick comes out dry when inserted into the center. Cool for a few minutes, then turn out of pan to cool on rack.
   Makes 1 9-inch loaf.

JERUSALEM ARTICHOKE BISCUITS

6 Jerusalem artichokes, or enough to make ½ cup when cooked and mashed
1½ cups flour
½ teaspoon salt
4 teaspoons baking powder
¼ cup shortening
1 egg, beaten
1 cup milk

1. Boil artichokes in salted water until tender, drain, peel, and sieve or mash until smooth; you should have ½ cup.
2. Preheat oven to 400°.
3. Sift together flour, salt, and baking powder.
4. Rub shortening into dry ingredients until mixture is mealy, then add artichokes.
5. Combine egg and milk and mix with other ingredients to make a light dough.

6. Roll out on a floured board about ¼ inch thick (these should be thinner than regular biscuits) and cut into rounds.

7. Bake on an ungreased cookie sheet until golden brown, about 10 minutes. Serve hot.

Makes 16 to 18 2½-inch biscuits.

B.J.'S BISCUITS

This isn't a "wild" recipe, obviously, but I use these biscuits in preparing a number of dishes, so here's how to make them.

      2   cups flour
      3   teaspoons baking powder
    1½   tablespoons sugar
      1   teaspoon salt
      6   tablespoons shortening
      1   egg, slightly beaten
     ⅓   cup water
     ⅓   cup milk

1. Preheat oven to 400°.

2. Sift flour, baking powder, sugar, and salt together. Cut in shortening until mixture is mealy.

3. Mix the egg, water, and milk and add to the dry mixture. Stir only until just mixed—do not beat the dough.

4. On a floured board, knead dough 6 times, just until a unified mass is formed.

5. Divide dough in half. Pat out one half until it is about ¼ inch thick.

6. Cut rounds with biscuit cutter, pushing straight down—don't twist the cutter.

7. Repeat patting out and cutting other half of dough. Gather scraps, pat together, and cut out.

8. Place biscuits 1 inch apart on an ungreased cookie sheet and bake 12 minutes, or until golden brown. Serve hot.

Makes 14 to 16 2-inch biscuits.

ACORN MUFFINS

This was once a "hard-times" bread because acorns are so plentiful and cost nothing. Sweet or nut muffins can be made from this recipe by adding 4 tablespoons sugar to the dry ingredients, omitting the garlic or onion salt (substitute 1 teaspoon plain salt), and substituting melted shortening for the bacon fat. Add ½ cup of walnuts or pecans to the batter, if you like.

      1   cup acorn flour (page 25)
      1   cup cornmeal
      1   cup flour
      3   teaspoons baking powder
      1   teaspoon onion or garlic salt
      1   egg, slightly beaten
    1½   cups milk
      2   tablespoons bacon drippings, melted

1. Preheat oven to 425°.

2. Sift together the acorn flour, cornmeal, flour, baking powder, and the onion or garlic salt.

3. Beat egg and milk together; stir in bacon drippings.

4. Add liquid to dry ingredients and stir just until moistened; don't overmix.

5. Pour into well-greased muffin tins and bake 15 minutes, or until brown and crusty.

Makes about 18 muffins.

PLAIN OR JAM MUFFINS

2   cups flour
4   teaspoons baking powder
½   teaspoon salt
2   tablespoons sugar
1   cup milk
1   egg, lightly beaten
3   tablespoons vegetable oil or melted butter

1. Preheat oven to 400°.
2. Sift together flour, baking powder, salt, and sugar.
3. Combine milk and egg, add butter or oil, and stir into dry ingredients very briefly. Don't overmix—batter shouldn't be smooth.
4. Bake in greased muffin tins for 20 to 25 minutes, or until browned. Serve hot.
Makes 12 muffins.

Jam Muffins

Fill greased muffin tins to one-third of their depth with batter, drop a teaspoonful of jam, jelly, or marmalade into each, then add batter until cups are about three-quarters full. Sprinkle tops with a mixture of 1 part of cinnamon to 3 parts of sugar and bake as directed for plain muffins.

CORNMEAL NUT MUFFINS WITH PERSIMMONS

For an afternoon (or any time) snack, try these muffins with hot Spearmint Tea.*

⅔   cup flour
1⅓ cups yellow cornmeal
3   teaspoons baking powder
1   teaspoon salt
¼   cup sugar
½   cup black walnuts, hickory nuts, or pecans, finely chopped
2   eggs
1   cup milk
2   tablespoons bacon fat or other drippings, melted
¼   cup fresh persimmon pulp, either fresh, or frozen and thawed

1. Preheat oven to 400°.
2. Sift together the flour, cornmeal, baking powder, salt, and sugar. Stir in nuts.
3. Beat the eggs and milk together. Blend in drippings, then persimmons.
4. Stir liquid into dry ingredients just until blended; don't beat.
5. Spoon into greased muffin cups and bake 20 minutes, or until firm and browned.
Makes 12.

ACORN GRIDDLE BREAD

1   tablespoon butter
3   tablespoons wild leeks (white part) or chives, chopped
1   cup cornmeal
1   cup acorn flour (page 25)
½   teaspoon baking soda
1   teaspoon salt
1   teaspoon baking powder
1   tablespoon flour
1   cup buttermilk
1   egg, well beaten
1   teaspoon Tabasco or other hot pepper sauce

1. Melt butter in small skillet over low heat and cook leeks or chives until well wilted but not browned. Cool.
2. Sift together cornmeal, acorn flour, soda, salt, baking powder, and flour.
3. Add buttermilk and leeks or chives to dry ingredients and stir well.
4. Stir eggs and Tabasco sauce into batter.
5. Drop by tablespoonfuls onto hot

greased griddle and bake until bubbles at edges begin to break; turn and bake until the second side is golden brown.

Serves 4 or more.

CAT-TAIL POLLEN PANCAKES

Rolled and filled with Berry Sauce* or with any other fruit sauce, these pancakes are delicious for breakfast, brunch, or even for dessert. A spoonful of whipped cream on each roll is especially nice for dessert.

1   *cup cat-tail pollen (page 41)*
1   *cup flour*
1   *teaspoon baking soda*
¾   *teaspoon salt*
2¼   *cups buttermilk*
2   *tablespoons vegetable oil*
    Shortening or butter for frying

1. Sift together cat-tail pollen, flour, soda, and salt.
2. Stir together buttermilk and oil.
3. Add liquid ingredients to the dry mixture and set batter aside until it thickens, about 10 minutes.
4. Bake pancakes on hot greased griddle, turning them once and baking the other side as soon as the undersides are browned. Serve hot.

Makes about 1 dozen 6-inch pancakes.

CAT-TAIL FLIPS

These griddle cakes make a particularly delightful brunch dish; serve them with sweet butter and wild honey. If the sugar and spices are omitted, the cakes make a fine base for creamed fish or poultry.

Pancake Batter:
1¼   *cups flour*
2½   *teaspoons baking powder*

2   *tablespoons sugar*
1   *teaspoon salt*
1   *egg, slightly beaten*
¾   *cup milk*
3   *tablespoons vegetable oil*

Added Ingredients:
2   *cups cooked cat-tail buds (page 142)*
½   *teaspoon ground cinnamon*
¼   *teaspoon ground ginger*
    Shortening or butter for frying

1. Sift together the flour, baking powder, sugar and salt.
2. Beat together the egg, milk, and oil.
3. Stir liquids into dry ingredients.
4. Stir cat-tail buds, cinnamon, and ginger into batter.
5. Fry pancakes on heated griddle greased with shortening or butter, turning cakes once, when bubbles around edges stop breaking. Serve hot.

Makes about 20 4-inch griddle cakes.

ELDERBERRY FLOWER PANCAKES

1   *cup elderberry flowers, removed from stems*
2   *cups water*
3   *teaspoons salt*
1   *batch pancake batter from Cat-Tail Flips (above)*
    Shortening or butter for frying

1. Wash the flowers and let them soak for about 30 minutes in the water, to which the salt has been added.
2. Drain flowers and pat them dry with paper towels. Fold flowers gently into pancake batter.
3. Bake on a hot greased griddle, turning and baking the other side when bubbles ring the edges of the cakes.

Makes about 20 4-inch pancakes.

DESSERTS

APPLE AND JERUSALEM ARTICHOKE BAKE

  20   *Jerusalem artichokes, peeled and quartered (about 2 cups)*
    6   *hard crisp apples (Winesaps or Jonathans), peeled, cored and quartered*
       Cinnamon
    6   *tablespoons melted butter*
  ½   *cup maple syrup, or to taste*

1. Preheat oven to 375°.
2. Arrange the Jerusalem artichokes and apples in layers in a buttered 2-quart baking dish, sprinkling each layer lightly with cinnamon.
3. Pour the melted butter, then the maple syrup, over the layers.
4. Cover with a lid or aluminum foil and bake for 25 minutes.
5. Uncover dish and bake till light brown, about 15 minutes more. Serve either warm or cool.
    Serves 8.

WILD BERRY BREAD PUDDING

  ½   *cup butter, softened at room temperature*
  8   *slices bread, crusts removed*
      Berry filling for Fresh Wild Berry or Ground Cherry Pie*
  ¾   *cup heavy cream (optional)*
  2 *to* 3 *tablespoons sugar for cream (optional)*

1. Preheat oven to 350°.
2. Lightly butter 4 slices of bread on both sides and fit them into a 9-inch pie pan.
3. Mix the pie filling according to the recipe and pour into the lined pan.
4. Top with the other four slices of bread, lightly buttered on both sides.
5. Bake until golden brown, or about 15 minutes. Serve warm.
6. If desired, whip cream until stiff, beating in sugar if sweetening is wanted.
    Serves 4 to 6.

WILD BERRY ROLL

This marvelously tempting dessert can also be made with canned or frozen berries. The frozen berries should be thawed almost completely and any surplus juice drained off (save it for punch or another fruit drink); use the berries in the same way as the fresh ones. Drain canned berries of their juice and set them aside. Mix 1 cup of canned berry juice with the ½ cup sugar in the recipe and add 4 tablespoons of quick-cooking tapioca. Bring this mixture to a boil, cover it, and set it aside for 10 minutes. Then fold in the measured berries and cool mixture completely before spooning it over the dough.

2½ cups ripe blackberries or other wild
     berries (see note above if you
     use frozen or canned berries)
½ cup granulated sugar
½ cup light-brown sugar, packed down
     Dough for B.J.'s Biscuits*

Glaze (optional):

¼ cup confectioners' sugar
2 tablespoons lemon juice

1. Preheat oven to 350°.
2. Mix berries and sugar.
3. Roll biscuit dough into a rectangle about ⅓ inch thick, 9 inches wide, and 13 inches long.
4. Spread berries on dough and roll up, starting with one of the long sides.
5. Place on greased baking sheet, with the seam down. Bake until golden brown, or about 45 minutes.
6. If you decide to glaze the roll, mix the confectioners' sugar and lemon juice until smooth and spoon over the hot pastry.
7. Slice and serve hot, or transfer to a rack and cool before slicing and serving.

Serves 8 to 10.

BLACKBERRY FLUFF

1 quart blackberries (reserve 8 or 16 plump
     ones for garnish), rinsed and drained
1 cup water
1 cup sugar
1 teaspoon ground cinnamon
2 packages black-cherry gelatin dessert,
     prepared as directed on box, but with
     only 2 cups of water, chilled until
     partially congealed
1 pint Vanilla Ice Cream*
1 pint heavy cream
     Sugar to sweeten cream to taste

1. Combine blackberries, water, sugar, and cinnamon in a saucepan and simmer for 10 minutes, stirring occasionally.
2. Pour into a wire sieve and press through the juice and pulp. Discard seeds. Cool juices.
3. With an electric mixer, beat the chilled gelatin until foamy. Add ice cream and beat until blended. Add 3 cups of the blackberry juice.
4. Whip the cream, adding sugar to taste, and fold into the gelatin–ice cream mixture.
5. Pour into individual dessert dishes or glasses and refrigerate until jelled.
6. Garnish each serving with one or two fresh berries at serving time.

Serves 8.

FINE FLUMMERY

Flummery is a fancy name for several kinds of pudding as well as for cooked and thickened berries.

3 cups blueberries or other berries, rinsed
     and drained
2 cups water
4 tablespoons cornstarch
¼ cup cold water
¾ cup sugar
1 cup heavy cream (optional)
     Extra sugar (optional)

1. Simmer the blueberries in 2 cups of water for 10 minutes, or until berries are tender. Do not stir.
2. Mix cornstarch with ¼ cup water.
3. Stir cornstarch mixture into berries, mixing carefully, and simmer mixture 5 minutes longer.
4. Add sugar and set aside for 20 to 30 minutes.
5. Pour into a glass serving dish and chill. Serve cold, passing cream and extra sugar if you like.

Serves 6.

ELDERBERRY FLOWER FRITTERS

To make another kind of delicious dessert fritter, substitute 1 to 1½ cups of yucca flower petals for the elderberry flowers.

Fritter Batter:

- 1⅓ cups flour
- 2 teaspoons baking powder
- ¼ teaspoon salt
- ⅔ cup milk
- 1 egg, well beaten

Fat:

Deep fat or oil for frying

The Flowers:

- 24 elderberry flower clusters, all main stems removed, washed, drained, and patted dry on paper towels
  Confectioners' sugar

1. Sift together dry ingredients for fritter batter, then mix egg and milk. Gradually add dry ingredients to liquid and beat until smooth. Set aside.
2. Heat deep fat or oil for frying to 360° to 375°.
3. Dip flower clusters one at a time into fritter batter, letting surplus drain back into the bowl.
4. Fry a few at a time in hot fat just until golden brown. Drain on paper towels and keep warm.
5. Sprinkle the fritters with confectioners' sugar and serve while still warm.
Serves 6.

HUCKLEBERRY OR BLUEBERRY GRUNT

It is only in cookbooks of this generation that we begin again to find recipes for slumps and grunts. My ancestors, who moved to the South from New England, brought this version with them. Susan Blue, my niece, and her friend Wendy Keefer tried this recipe and they say that the mixture actually grunted as it boiled.

- 2 cups huckleberries or blueberries, washed and drained
- 1 cup sugar
- 1 cup water
- 1 cup flour
- 2 teaspoons baking powder
- ¼ teaspoon salt
- ½ cup milk, or amount needed
  Whipped cream (optional)

1. Combine huckleberries or blueberries, sugar, and water in a large saucepan that has a cover, bring to a boil, lower heat, and simmer for 10 minutes. Set aside.
2. Sift together flour, baking powder, and salt. Stir in enough milk to make a dough just soft enough to drop from the tip of a spoon.
3. Return berry sauce to the heat and bring it to a boil.
4. Drop dumpling dough from the tip of a teaspoon into the boiling sauce.
5. Reduce heat to medium and cook uncovered for 10 minutes.
6. Cover pan and cook 10 minutes more.
7. Serve hot, either plain or with whipped cream.
Serves 4.

MAYPOP ICE

Maypop Punch,* with whipped cream omitted
1 pint pineapple sherbet

1. Freeze punch in shallow pans or ice-cube trays until very firm.
2. Combine the frozen punch and

sherbet in the bowl of an electric mixer and beat at low speed until well blended.

3. Pour into tall dessert glasses and freeze just until mushy.

4. Garnish each serving with a slice of lemon, split and placed on the edge of the glass, and provide long iced-tea spoons.

Serves 8.

PAPAW CUSTARD

4 *cups milk*
4 *egg yolks, beaten until pale yellow*
1 *teaspoon vanilla*
1 *tablespoon cornstarch, mixed with 2 tablespoons of the milk*
2 *cups freshly sieved papaw pulp*
½ *cup confectioners' sugar*
Pinch of salt
Maraschino cherries for garnishing

1. In a heavy saucepan, place milk over low heat (first measure out 2 tablespoonfuls and mix with the cornstarch).

2. Beat together egg yolks, vanilla, and the cornstarch mixture.

3. Add egg-cornstarch mixture gradually to the warming milk and cook, stirring, until smoothly thickened (don't let custard boil); cook for 2 or 3 minutes more, then set off heat and cool.

4. Combine papaw pulp, sugar, and salt and stir gently into the cool custard.

5. Pour into individual serving dishes and refrigerate until firm. Serve garnished with maraschino cherries.

Serves 6.

PERSIMMON CUSTARD WITH MERINGUE TOPPING

2 *cups persimmon pulp, either fresh, or frozen and thawed*

1 *cup sugar*
2 *egg yolks, lightly beaten*
¼ *teaspoon ground cinnamon*
¼ *teaspoon grated nutmeg*
Pinch of salt

Meringue:

2 *egg whites*
Pinch of salt
¼ *cup sugar*

1. Preheat oven to 400°.

2. Beat together persimmon pulp, sugar, egg yolks, cinnamon, nutmeg, and a pinch of salt; blend well.

3. Pour into a buttered 9-inch square baking dish and place in a larger dish or pan. Pour in hot water to reach two-thirds up the sides of the custard dish.

4. Bake for 20 minutes, or until custard is almost done—it should be a bit soft in the center and the top crusty and shiny brown.

5. Meanwhile, make meringue: Beat egg whites with salt at high speed until foamy; continue to beat hard, adding sugar gradually, until stiff peaks are formed.

6. Spread meringue on custard, return to oven, and bake until meringue is lightly browned. Serve warm.

Serves 6 to 8.

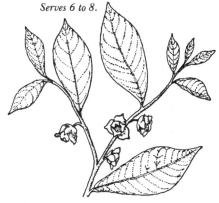

PERSIMMON SOUFFLÉ

1 *cup persimmon pulp, either fresh, or frozen and thawed*
½ *cup sugar*
3 *tablespoons lemon juice*
¼ *teaspoon salt*
5 *egg whites*

1. Preheat oven to 350°.
2. In a saucepan over low heat, stir the persimmon pulp with the sugar until sugar dissolves. Cool, then add lemon juice.
3. Add salt to egg whites and beat until stiff peaks form.
4. Fold the persimmon-sugar mixture into the egg whites just until blended.
5. Pour the mixture into a buttered 9-inch baking dish and place this dish in a larger pan. Add hot water to outer pan until it reaches two-thirds of the way up the inner dish.
6. Bake for about an hour, or until firm. Serve hot.
Serves 6.

PERSIMMON SHERBET

2 *cups water*
2 *cups sugar*
4 *cups persimmon pulp, either fresh, or frozen and thawed*
 Juice of 1 lemon, strained
½ *teaspoon salt*
2 *egg whites*

1. Boil water and sugar hard over high heat for 1 minute. Pour into bowl and set in refrigerator to chill.
2. When syrup is cold, add persimmon pulp, lemon juice, salt, and egg whites.
3. Pour contents into the can of an ice-cream freezer and surround can with a mixture of 1 part ice-cream salt to 6 parts of crushed ice.
4. Turn crank, or plug in freezer if electric, and churn until mixture is firm.
5. Remove the dasher, cover can, and pack more ice and salt around freezer can.
6. Alternatively, you can remove can from freezer, wipe the outside well, and set the covered can in the freezer until shortly before serving time.
Serves 8 or more.

BAKED PERSIMMON PUDDING À LA WILDFLOWER

3 *eggs*
1¾ *cups milk*
2 *cups persimmon pulp, either fresh, or frozen and thawed*
2 *cups flour*
1 *teaspoon baking soda*
1 *teaspoon salt*
½ *teaspoon ground cinnamon*
½ *teaspoon grated nutmeg*
½ *cup sugar*
2 *tablespoons melted butter*

Topping:

1 *cup heavy cream*
2 *to 4 tablespoons sugar, or to taste*

1. Preheat oven to 300°.
2. Beat eggs with a wire whip until well blended, then beat in milk, then persimmon pulp.
3. Sift together flour, baking soda, salt, cinnamon, nutmeg, and sugar.
4. Gradually beat dry ingredients into liquid mixture; beat until smooth.
5. Stir in melted butter.
6. Pour batter into greased shallow 9 × 13-inch baking pan.
7. Bake for 1 hour, or until nicely browned and slightly crusty. Cool in pan.
8. To serve, cut into squares and top each helping with cream, whipped until stiff with sugar to taste.

Serves 8 to 10.

INDIANA-STYLE PERSIMMON PUDDING

2 cups persimmon pulp, either fresh, or frozen and thawed
2 eggs
2¼ cups flour
1 cup sugar
1 cup brown sugar, packed down
1 teaspoon baking soda
1 teaspoon baking powder
1 teaspoon ground cinnamon
1 teaspoon ground allspice
½ teaspoon salt

Topping:

1 cup heavy cream for topping (optional)
2 to 3 tablespoons sugar for cream (optional)

1. Preheat oven to 350°.
2. Beat persimmon pulp and eggs together in a large bowl (of an electric mixer, if you have one).
3. Sift all dry ingredients together and add to persimmon mixture. Beat at low speed until smooth.

4. Pour into two greased round 9-inch baking pans.
5. Bake 50 minutes, or until browned and slightly crusty on top.
6. Serve warm, cut into wedges. Top each serving, if you like, with the cream, beaten until stiff and sweetened to taste.

Serves 12.

STEAMED PERSIMMON PUDDING

½ cup (1 stick) butter
½ cup sugar
2 eggs
1½ cups persimmon pulp, either fresh, or frozen and thawed
½ cup flour
½ teaspoon baking soda
2 teaspoons baking powder
¼ teaspoon salt

1. Cream together butter, sugar, and eggs. When very light, beat in persimmon pulp.
2. Sift together flour, soda, baking powder, and salt.
3. Gradually stir dry ingredients into creamed mixture; beat until smooth.
4. Pour into a greased 1-quart pudding mold with a cover, or into a gelatin mold of the same size. If gelatin mold is used, cover with waxed paper tied on with string.
5. Place on a rack in kettle containing 2 inches of hot water, put a tight cover on kettle, and steam for 1½ hours. Check occasionally and add more boiling water if necessary.
6. Let rest for 5 minutes, then invert mold onto a platter and unmold pudding. Serve hot.

Serves 8.

JELLIED PERSIMMON DESSERT

Because it's a fairly soft jelly, this is also an excellent topping for pudding or ice cream.

 2 *envelopes unflavored gelatin*
 ½ *cup water*
 ½ *cup sugar*
    Pinch of salt
2½ *cups persimmon pulp, either fresh, or frozen and thawed*
 1 *cup canned crushed pineapple, drained*

Topping:

 1 *cup heavy cream (optional)*
 ½ *cup chopped pecans (optional)*

1. Soften gelatin in the water for a few minutes in a heatproof bowl, then set bowl in a saucepan of hot water and heat, stirring, until gelatin dissolves.
2. Add the sugar and salt to the gelatin and stir until they dissolve.
3. Combine with the persimmon pulp and pineapple. Blend thoroughly, turn into sherbet glasses, and chill.
4. If you wish, serve topped with the cream beaten until stiff and mixed with the nuts.
Serves 8.

SPEARMINT, ORANGE, AND APPLE DESSERT

 3 *seedless oranges, cut up*
 3 *cups applesauce*
 1 *cup spearmint leaves, fairly finely chopped*
    Mint sprigs for garnishing

1. Pulverize the oranges, peel and all, in an electric blender.
2. Combine with applesauce and add mint.
3. Pour into a serving bowl or individual bowls and chill. Before serving, garnish with sprigs of mint.
Serves 8.

WILD STRAWBERRY DESSERT OMELET

Though sweet filled omelets have traditionally been served as a dessert, there's no reason why this couldn't be the main attraction at Sunday brunch.

Filling:

 2 *cups wild strawberries, rinsed, hulled, and drained*
 1 *tablespoon lemon juice*
 6 *tablespoons confectioners' sugar*
 ½ *cup heavy cream*
 ½ *teaspoon vanilla*

Omelet:

 8 *eggs*
 ¼ *teaspoon salt*
 4 *tablespoons granulated sugar*
 3 *tablespoons butter*

1. Prepare filling: Sprinkle strawberries with lemon juice and a little of the confectioners' sugar.
2. Beat the heavy cream until it begins to thicken.
3. Add vanilla and the rest of the confectioners' sugar and continue beating until stiff.
4. Fold in strawberries lightly.
5. Make omelet: Beat eggs with the salt and granulated sugar.
6. Heat a 12-inch omelet pan or skillet over high heat and add the butter, turning

pan to coat bottom and sides; don't let butter brown.

7. Pour in omelet mixture and stir rapidly for a moment with the flat of a fork, shaking the pan rapidly back and forth, then cook omelet until softly set on top.

8. Add the strawberry filling and fold omelet, sliding it immediately onto a warmed platter. Serve at once.

Serves 6.

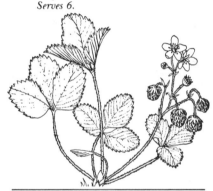

FROZEN WILD STRAWBERRY CREAM

1   *envelope unflavored gelatin*
1   *cup water*
¾   *cup Strawberry Syrup**
½   *cup heavy cream*
1   *6-ounce can frozen orange-juice concentrate*
1   *pint Vanilla Ice Cream**

1. Sprinkle gelatin over water in a small pan, then set over medium heat and stir constantly until gelatin dissolves.

2. Stir in strawberry syrup and chill until quite thick, almost firm.

3. Whip cream until stiff and set aside.

4. Whip gelatin mixture until frothy, using an electric or hand mixer.

5. Whip frozen orange-juice concentrate into gelatin, then stir or fold in the ice cream. Fold in whipped cream.

6. Pour into dessert glasses and place in freezer until firm.

Serves 6.

LORI'S STRAWBERRY CLOUD

My daughter Lori keeps this dessert well hidden in the freezer so that it is available for an after-date snack. She often freezes a double batch for dessert a week or two in advance of a wild-foods dinner party. This way her work is finished well in advance of party week, when the rest of us are all busy foraging and cooking.

1½   *cups wild strawberries, rinsed, hulled, and drained*
½   *cup sugar*
1   *egg white*
1   *teaspoon lemon juice*
1   *cup heavy cream*
1½   *cups vanilla-wafer or graham-cracker crumbs*

1. Place strawberries in the large bowl of an electric mixer and add sugar, egg white, and lemon juice.

2. Beat at low speed until well blended; then turn to high speed and beat for 20 minutes.

3. Whip cream until stiff and fold into strawberry mixture.

4. Place two-thirds of the crumbs in a 9 × 13-inch baking pan.

5. Spoon filling over crumbs and top with remainder of crumbs.

6. Cover closely with aluminum foil and freeze for a least 12 hours before serving.

Serves 8 to 10.

VIOLET CLOUD

This lovely frozen dessert with its tint of lavender is an elegant finish for a feast and it's also a delightful afternoon refreshment, served alone or with Ginger Sugar Cookies.*

    1 package of lemon-flavored gelatin
         dessert
    1 cup freshly picked violets, stems
         removed, packed lightly
    1 quart Vanilla Ice Cream*
    1 cup heavy cream
   16 Candied Violets*

1. Make up gelatin dessert according to the directions on the package. Chill until only partly set, not firm.

2. Put violets in the jar of a blender and run blender at high speed until they are almost liquid.

3. Take out about half of the violets and reserve them.

4. Add half of the ice cream to the violet purée in the jar and blend till it is a thick liquid. Empty the jar into a freezer container or metal bowl and repeat the blending with the rest of the ice cream and violets. Add to the first batch.

5. Put bowl of ice-cream mixture in freezer.

6. Whip cream until it forms stiff peaks.

7. Whip the partially set gelatin till it is frothy.

8. Quickly fold the whipped cream and the ice-cream mixture into the fluffed gelatin.

9. Pour into long-stemmed dessert glasses and refrigerate until firm.

10. At serving time, top each glass with a couple of candied violets.

Serves 8.

VANILLA ICE CREAM AND VARIATIONS

You can make as many flavors of ice cream as you have suitable fruits. I simply take this basic recipe for ice cream and add 1 cup of fresh crushed berries or other fruit. This works with strawberries, blackberries, mulberries, ground cherries, huckleberries, blueberries, and wild plums.

    1 quart light cream
   ¾ cup sugar
   ¼ teaspoon salt
    2 teaspoons vanilla

1. Combine all ingredients and stir until sugar is dissolved.

2. Place contents in the can of an ice-cream freezer and tighten lid.

3. Put a mixture of 1 part ice-cream salt to 6 parts crushed ice around freezer can.

4. Turn crank or plug in freezer, if electric, and churn until mixture is firm.

5. Remove the dasher, cover can, and pack more ice and salt around freezer can.

6. Alternatively, you can remove can from freezer, wipe the outside well, and set the covered can in the deep freeze until shortly before serving time.

Makes 1½ quarts.

CAKES AND COOKIES

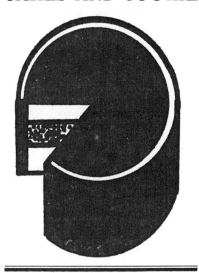

BLACK WALNUT JIFFY CAKE

A firm cake that keeps very well, Black Walnut Jiffy Cake is better when it's 24 hours or more old—it cuts better and the flavor of the nuts has permeated it by then. As it can be kept for a week to ten days when well wrapped and refrigerated, it's a particularly good bake-ahead dessert for a large party.

    2   cups sugar
    1   cup (2 sticks) butter, softened at room
            temperature
    2   cups flour, sifted
    1   cup black walnuts, ground
    ¼   teaspoon salt
    1   teaspoon vanilla
    1   teaspoon lemon extract
    5   eggs, at room temperature

1. Preheat oven to 350°.
2. Drop into the large bowl of an electric mixer all of the ingredients in the order of listing above.
3. Beat at high speed for 5 minutes, scraping down sides of bowl frequently.
4. Pour into greased and floured 9- or 10-inch tube pan.
5. Bake until a toothpick inserted deeply into cake comes out clean, about 1 hour and 15 minutes.
6. Let cool about 10 minutes in pan, then run a knife or narrow spatula around the sides and stem of pan. Turn out cake onto a wire rack, place another rack over it, and turn upright to cool.
7. When cold, wrap well to store. Serve in thin (about ¼ inch) slices.

Makes a 9- or 10-inch cake.

HUCKLEBERRY BUCKLE

    ¾   cup sugar
    ½   teaspoon ground cinnamon
    ¼   cup (½ stick) butter, softened at room
            temperature
        Basic dough for Coffee Cake*
    2   cups huckleberries or blueberries, washed
            and drained well and patted dry with
            paper towels

1. Preheat oven to 375°.
2. With a fork, work together the sugar, cinnamon, and butter to make a crumbly mixture. Set aside.
3. Fold huckleberries or blueberries into the coffee-cake dough and pour into a greased 8- or 9-inch square baking pan.
4. Sprinkle with the crumbly mixture.
5. Bake 45 to 50 minutes, or until firm and lightly browned.
6. Cut into 2- or 3-inch squares and serve warm.

Makes 9 to 16 servings.

HUCKLEBERRY OR BLUEBERRY CAKE

1   *cup sugar*
2   *eggs, well beaten*
3   *cups flour*
1   *tablespoon baking powder*
½   *teaspoon salt*
1½   *cups huckleberries or blueberries,
      washed and thoroughly drained, then
      patted dry with paper towels*
1   *tablespoon melted butter*
1½   *cups milk*

1. Preheat oven to 400°.
2. Beat sugar and beaten eggs together very well.
3. Sift together flour, baking powder, and salt, then combine with sugar-egg mixture.
4. Stir in huckleberries, then melted butter, then milk. Beat just enough to mix all ingredients thoroughly.
5. Bake in a greased 9 × 13-inch shallow cake pan until a toothpick inserted into center comes out clean, about 30 minutes.
6. Turn out onto a wire rack and cool. Cut into 20 pieces to serve.
Makes 20 servings.

UPSIDE-DOWN WOOD SORREL CAKE

This might be called a sweet-and-sour dessert. The wood sorrel provides a zesty tang in the otherwise sweet brown-sugar topping. We like the cake warm, with whipped cream.

2   *tablespoons butter*
1   *cup brown sugar, packed*
4   *cups wood sorrel, chopped*

1½   *cups flour*
¼   *teaspoon salt*
1½   *teaspoons baking powder*
¼   *cup shortening*
2   *eggs, well beaten*
½   *cup warm water*
1   *teaspoon vanilla*
    Pinch or two of cinnamon

Topping (optional):
1   *cup heavy cream, whipped
    and sweetened to taste*

1. Preheat oven to 350°.
2. In an 8-inch iron skillet melt butter over low heat and remove from stove. Add brown sugar, stirring well. Place sorrel in skillet and set aside.
3. Sift together flour, salt, and baking powder.
4. Cream shortening, beat well with eggs, then beat in warm water and vanilla.
5. Combine the dry mixture with the liquid mixture. Beat until a smooth batter is formed.
6. Pour over wood sorrel in skillet. Sprinkle with cinnamon.
7. Bake 50 minutes, or until a toothpick inserted into center comes out clean.
8. Let cool in pan for 5 minutes, then cover with a cake rack and invert pan and rack and let cake drop out. Serve while warm, or allow to cool. Top servings with whipped cream, if desired.
Serves 8.

STRAWBERRY AND WOOD SORREL SHORTCAKE

1   *recipe B. J.'s Biscuits**
1   *cup warm water*
3   *tablespoons cornstarch*
¾   *cup sugar*
1   *seedless orange, peel and all, pureed in
    an electric blender*

1¼ cups wild strawberries plus ¼ cup sugar, or a 10-ounce package frozen sweetened strawberries, thawed
3 cups wood sorrel leaves, coarsely chopped and packed lightly
1 cup heavy cream, whipped at serving time and sweetened to taste

1. Preheat oven to 400°.
2. Roll biscuit dough out ¼ inch thick and cut into eight 3- or 4-inch rounds.
3. Place biscuits on ungreased baking sheet and bake until golden brown, about 12 minutes. Cool on rack.
4. In a saucepan combine water and cornstarch and add sugar, puréed orange, strawberries and their juice, and the wood sorrel.
5. Bring to a boil, then cook 15 minutes over medium heat, stirring. Pour into bowl and cool in refrigerator for 30 minutes.
6. Pour fruit sauce over biscuit rounds on individual serving plates and top with whipped cream.
Serves 8.

WILD BERRY SHORTCAKE

This rich and delicious old-style shortcake may be made with strawberries, blackberries, blueberries, raspberries, or huckleberries.

Basic Shortcake Dough:

2 cups flour
3 teaspoons baking powder
1 teaspoon salt
2 tablespoons sugar
½ cup shortening
1 egg, slightly beaten
⅓ cup light cream
⅓ cup water

Berries and Topping:

4 tablespoons butter, softened at room temperature
4 cups lightly mashed wild strawberries, blackberries, blueberries, raspberries, or huckleberries, sweetened to taste
1 cup heavy cream, whipped and sweetened to taste

1. Preheat oven to 450°.
2. Sift flour, baking powder, salt, and sugar together.
3. Cut shortening into dry ingredients until mixture is mealy.
4. Beat together the egg, cream, and water and stir into the dry ingredients just until mixed—don't beat the dough.
5. On a floured board knead the dough 6 times, just until unified.
6. Divide dough in half. Roll out each half and fit into a greased round 9-inch cake pan.
7. Bake until light golden brown, about 15 minutes.
8. Cool in the pans about 5 minutes before removing.
9. On serving dish, place a layer of warm shortcake and butter generously.
10. Spoon from one-third to one-half of the berries over the layer and top with one-third of the whipped cream.
11. Top with second layer, then remaining berries. Garnish with the rest of the cream. Serve at once
Serves 6 to 8.

COFFEE CAKE—THREE VERSIONS

Basic Dough:

¼ cup butter, softened at room temperature
¾ cup sugar
1 egg
½ cup milk
2 cups flour
2 teaspoons baking powder
½ teaspoon salt

1. Preheat oven to 375°.
2. Cream together butter, sugar, and egg, then stir in milk.
3. Sift together flour, baking powder, and salt. Fold dry ingredients into creamed mixture.
4. Add your choice of topping or filling (see below) and bake as directed.

Jam-Nut Coffee Cake

Spread basic dough in a greased 8-inch square baking pan and dot with ¾ cup wild blackberry, raspberry, or strawberry jam. Sprinkle liberally with mixed cinnamon and sugar (1 part cinnamon to 3 parts sugar), then with ½ cup chopped pecans. With the back of a tablespoon, smooth the topping, pressing it into the dough. Bake 35 to 40 minutes, or until a toothpick inserted into the cake comes out clean. Remove from pan and cool partially on a rack. Serve warm.
Serves 6 to 8.

Honey-Nut Coffee Cake

Make basic dough and follow recipe for Jam-Nut Coffee Cake, substituting ½ cup honey for the jam and cutting the topping into the dough with a table knife, making cuts about ½ inch deep. Bake, cool, and serve as for jam-nut cake.
Serves 6 to 8.

Hidden Treasure Coffee Cake

Make basic dough and spread half of it in a greased 8-inch square baking pan. Spread it with ¾ to 1 cup of mulberry or May apple jam, then add remaining dough. Sprinkle top liberally with a mixture of 1 part ground dried ginger and 3 parts sugar. Bake, cool, and serve as described for jam-nut cake.
Serves 6 to 8.

B. J.'S BISCUIT CAKE

This upside-down cake may also be made with such other wild fruits as blackberries or strawberries. If berries are used, substitute ground cinnamon for the ginger.

4 cups ground cherries, rinsed and drained well
½ cup brown sugar, packed
1 teaspoon grated wild ginger root
½ recipe for B. J.'S Biscuits,* rolled ½ inch thick
1 cup heavy cream
2 to 3 tablespoons sugar, or to taste, for sweetening cream
Grated ginger root for garnishing

1. Preheat oven to 450°.
2. Fill a 9-inch pie pan with ground cherries. Sprinkle with brown sugar and 1 teaspoon grated wild ginger root.
3. Cover fruit with rolled-out biscuit dough and trim edges.
4. Bake until crust is firm and golden brown, about 15 minutes.
5. Loosen crust around edge of pan, invert a plate over cake, and turn cake out upside down on plate.
6. Serve warm, garnished with cream, whipped and sweetened, and additional ginger.
Serves 6.

HICKORY NUT CAKE

½ cup (1 stick) butter, softened at room
   temperature
1 cup sugar
1½ cups flour, sifted
½ cup milk
1 cup hickory nuts, coarsely chopped
1 teaspoon cream of tartar
1 teaspoon baking soda dissolved in 1
   teaspoon milk
3 egg whites
   Caramel-Nut Frosting* (optional)

1. Preheat oven to 350°.
2. Cream butter and sugar together thoroughly.
3. Fold in flour carefully, keeping mixture as light as possible.
4. Beat in milk, then add hickory nuts, cream of tartar, and dissolved soda; beat batter well.
5. Beat egg whites until they form stiff peaks, then fold them into the batter just until mingled; don't overmix.
6. Pour into greased and floured 9 × 5-inch loaf pan and bake until top is golden brown and a toothpick emerges dry when inserted into the center of cake, about 30 to 35 minutes.
7. Let cool in pan about 5 minutes, then remove and cool completely on a rack. Serve plain, or topped with caramel-nut frosting.
Makes a 9-inch loaf.

PERSIMMON FRUIT CAKE

Closely wrapped, this cake keeps as well as other fruit cakes. I like to wrap my cakes in cheesecloth soaked in apple cider and keep them in tightly sealed tins. This cake also freezes well, wrapped airtight in foil; I've kept it as long as two years this way.

½ cup (1 stick) butter, softened at room
   temperature
1 cup sugar
3 eggs
1 cup raisins
1 cup black walnuts, chopped
¼ cup drained and chopped maraschino
   cherries
¼ cup dates, chopped
1 teaspoon baking soda, dissolved in 1
   tablespoon hot water
1 cup persimmon pulp, either fresh, or
   frozen and thawed
1 teaspoon lemon extract
2¼ cups flour
   Pinch of salt
½ teaspoon ground cloves
1 teaspoon ground cinnamon

1. Preheat oven to 325°.
2. Cream butter, sugar, and eggs very thoroughly, beating until light.
3. Add raisins, black walnuts, cherries, and dates and mix well.
4. Mix dissolved baking soda, persimmon pulp, and lemon extract and add to creamed mixture.
5. Sift together flour, salt, cloves, and cinnamon.
6. Gradually blend dry ingredients into creamed mixture and stir until smooth.
7. Pour into 3 well-greased 9-inch loaf pans and bake for 1½ hours.
8. Cool in pans for 5 minutes, then turn out on racks to cool completely.
9. Wrap well to store or to freeze.
Makes 3 9-inch loaves.

PERSIMMON BUTTER FROSTING

This is an especially good frosting for any kind of spice cake.

½ cup (1 stick) butter
2 cups confectioners' sugar
   Pinch of salt
⅓ cup persimmon pulp, either fresh, or
       frozen and thawed
2 teaspoons lemon juice

1. Cream butter, then cream in the sugar and salt.
2. Stir in persimmon pulp and lemon juice.
3. Beat just until of a good consistency to spread.
   Enough for tops and sides of two 9-inch layers.

CARAMEL-NUT FROSTING

A versatile frosting: use it as a sauce over Gladys's Persimmon Bread* when served as a dessert, or as icing for a cake.

1½ cups sugar
1 cup hot water
1 tablespoon butter
½ teaspoon salt
½ teaspoon vanilla
3 tablespoons honey
1 cup chopped nuts (black walnuts,
       pecans, butternuts, or hickory nuts)

1. Place sugar in an iron skillet over low heat and cook it, stirring constantly, until it has changed to a light-brown syrup.
2. Stir in hot water and boil until syrup thickens (230° on candy thermometer).
3. Remove from heat and stir in re-maining ingredients. Beat until lukewarm and well thickened.
   Makes about 1½ cups.

BLACK WALNUT SQUARES

2 cups dark-brown sugar, packed
2 eggs
1 teaspoon vanilla
1 cup flour
½ teaspoon salt
¼ teaspoon baking soda
1 cup black walnuts, coarsely chopped

1. Preheat oven to 350°.
2. Beat together the brown sugar, eggs, and vanilla very thoroughly.
3. Into another bowl sift together the flour, salt, and soda.
4. Gradually beat flour mixture into sugar mixture, then add black walnuts.
5. Pour into a greased 9 × 13-inch cake pan.
6. Bake for 25 minutes, or until lightly browned and springy when pressed gently.
7. Cut into squares or rectangles while hot and leave in pan.
8. Remove from pan when cool. Serve while warm.
   Makes 12 to 16 servings.

BLACK WALNUT ROUNDS

1¼ cups butter, softened at room tem-
       perature
½ cup confectioners' sugar
2 cups flour
1 teaspoon rum flavoring
1 cup black walnuts, coarsely chopped

1. Preheat oven to 350°.

2. Cream butter and beat in sugar thoroughly. Then add flour, rum flavoring, and black walnuts in that order.

3. Roll into small balls (about ½ inch across) and place on ungreased cookie sheet, spacing them about 1 inch apart.

4. Flatten each ball with the bottom of a glass.

5. Bake 15 minutes, or until browned.

6. Cool on rack, sprinkling with confectioners' sugar while still warm.

7. When cool, store in an airtight container. If you'd like the cookies to be soft, store half a raw apple with them.

Makes 3 to 4 dozen.

NUT-BUTTER DROPS

I generally use black walnuts in these cookies because we have more black walnut trees than other nut trees. However, hickory nuts or butternuts work beautifully and each gives an entirely different taste. Chinquapins are fine, too, but should be roasted for 4 to 5 minutes in a 200° oven and finely chopped before use. Pecans make a delicately flavored cookie also.

½ cup (1 stick) butter, softened at room
    temperature
1 cup brown sugar, packed
½ teaspoon vanilla
½ teaspoon salt
2 cups flour
1 cup black walnuts or other nuts, chopped
    or broken into bits
    Confectioners' sugar

1. Preheat oven to 350°.

2. Cream butter, then cream in sugar, vanilla, and salt.

3. Add flour, mixing well. Add nuts.

4. Shape into small balls (about ½ teaspoon of dough) and place 1 inch apart on an ungreased baking sheet.

5. Bake about 15 minutes, or until golden brown.

6. Remove from pans and roll in confectioners' sugar while warm.

7. Cool well before storing in an airtight tin or cookie jar.

Makes 36 to 40 cookies.

LITTLE NUT FOLDS

1 cup butter
½ cup sugar
1 teaspoon rose water, if available
2 teaspoons vanilla
2½ cups flour
40 to 50 pecan halves or large pieces of
    black walnut meats
    Additional vanilla, as needed
    Sugar for sprinkling

1. Preheat oven to 350°.

2. Cream together butter, ½ cup sugar, rose water, and 2 teaspoons vanilla.

3. Add flour and mix well. Wrap dough and chill in refrigerator until firm.

4. Flour your hands and pinch off walnut-sized pieces of the dough. Then pat each piece of dough out until round and flat, about ¼ inch thick.

5. Place a nut half or chunk in the center of the round, folding dough over it from two sides in envelope fashion.

6. Space cookies 1 inch apart on an ungreased cookie sheet. Brush each lightly with additional vanilla extract just before placing pan in the oven.

7. Bake until golden brown, about 15 minutes.

8. Remove from oven, place cookies on a wire rack, and sprinkle them with sugar while warm.

9. When completely cool, store in an airtight tin or cookie jar.

Makes about 4 dozen cookies.

BRANDY-NUT BALLS

This is a particularly good recipe for using such strongly flavored nuts as black walnuts and hickory nuts. However, any other kind of nut is good, too; pecans or butternuts make a more delicately flavored cookie.

   1   *pound (4 sticks) butter, softened at room*
         temperature
   1   *egg*
   ¼   *cup sugar*
   2   *tablespoons brandy*
   1   *teaspoon vanilla*
         Pinch of ground cloves
   1   *cup black walnuts, finely chopped*
   6   *cups flour*
         Confectioners' sugar

1. Preheat oven to 325°.
2. Cream butter thoroughly, then add in turn, beating after each addition, the egg, sugar, brandy, vanilla, and cloves.
3. Beat in the black walnuts and flour.
4. Shape dough into balls the size of a walnut and place 1 inch apart on an ungreased cookie sheet.
5. Bake 15 to 20 minutes, or until golden brown.
6. Sprinkle with confectioners' sugar and allow to cool on cookie sheets.
7. Store with half an apple (to keep cookies soft) in an airtight container.
Makes about 7 dozen.

JAM-NUT COOKIES

You can spread the little cut-out doughnut centers with jam and bake them as miniature cookies. These cookies may be made with any berry jam or with persimmon or maypop marmalade.

Cookies:

   3½   *cups flour*
    ½   *teaspoon salt*
    1   *teaspoon baking powder*
    1   *cup shortening*
   1½   *cups sugar*
    2   *eggs, well beaten*
   1½   *teaspoons vanilla*

Filling:

    ½   *cup jam or marmalade*
    ½   *cup black walnut, hickory nut, or*
          pecan pieces

1. Sift together flour, salt, and baking powder and set aside.
2. Cream shortening and sugar together thoroughly.
3. Add beaten eggs and vanilla to creamed mixture and beat well.
4. Combine dry ingredients with the creamed mixture. Mix thoroughly, wrap dough, and chill for 30 minutes.
5. Preheat oven to 375°.
6. Divide dough in half.
7. Roll first half of dough ⅛ inch thick on a floured board and cut in 2½-inch circles.
8. Spread circles with jam or marmalade and sprinkle with nuts.
9. Roll second half of dough ⅛ inch thick and cut with a 2½-inch doughnut cutter. Place doughnut shape over the filling on each round.
10. Place on an ungreased baking sheet about 1 inch apart and bake 8 to 10 minutes, or until golden brown. Cool on racks.
Makes 2½ to 3 dozen cookies.

JAM-NUT SQUARES

   2   *cups flour*
   ½   *teaspoon salt*
   1   *teaspoon baking powder*

½ cup (1 stick) butter, softened at room
    temperature
1 cup sugar
2 eggs
½ teaspoon vanilla
½ cup jam (wild berry, ground cherry, or
    May apple)
½ cup pecans, finely chopped
1 cup light-brown sugar, packed
    Mixture of 3 teaspoons sugar and 1
    teaspoon cinnamon

1. Preheat oven to 350°.
2. Sift together the flour, salt, and baking powder.
3. Cream butter, then cream in sugar, eggs, and vanilla, beating thoroughly.
4. Spread half of dough in a greased 9 × 13-inch baking pan.
5. Mix jam, pecans, and brown sugar and spread over dough.
6. Cover with remaining dough.
7. Sprinkle top with cinnamon-sugar mixture.
8. Bake until golden brown, about 20 minutes.
9. Cool in pan and cut into small squares. Store in an airtight container.

Variation: Mint Squares

Follow recipe for Jam-Nut Squares but substitute ½ teaspoon of peppermint flavoring for vanilla. Omit brown sugar and jam and spread the first layer of dough with Spearmint Jelly (Index). Add nuts, or omit if you wish. You'll need about ¾ cup to 1 cup of the jelly.

PERSIMMON PINWHEELS

Persimmon Filling:

2 cups persimmon pulp, either fresh, or
    frozen and thawed
1 cup chopped pecans
½ cup sugar

Dough:

½ cup (1 stick) butter
½ cup brown sugar, packed
½ cup granulated sugar
1 egg, beaten
½ teaspoon lemon juice
2 cups flour
½ teaspoon baking soda
½ teaspoon salt

1. Make filling: Place persimmon pulp, pecans, and sugar in a saucepan, bring to the boiling point, and simmer for 5 minutes, stirring constantly. Cool.
2. Preheat oven to 350°.
3. To make dough, cream the butter, then cream again with the brown and granulated sugars.
4. Stir in beaten egg and beat until fluffy. Add lemon juice.
5. Sift together flour, baking soda, and salt.
6. Mix dry ingredients into the creamed mixture to make a smooth dough.
7. Roll dough into a rectangle measuring about 12 × 14 inches and spread with cooled filling.
8. Roll up to make 18-inch roll. Wrap in plastic or foil and chill for 1½ hours.
9. Cut into ¼-inch slices and place them 1 inch apart on greased cookie sheets.
10. Bake 15 minutes, or until golden brown.
11. Cool on racks and store in an airtight container.

Makes 4 to 5 dozen.

SPICED PERSIMMON COOKIES

1   cup shortening
1   cup sugar
1   egg
1   cup persimmon pulp, either fresh, or
       frozen and thawed
2   cups flour
1   teaspoon baking soda
1   teaspoon baking powder
½   teaspoon salt
½   teaspoon ground cinnamon
½   teaspoon grated nutmeg
½   teaspoon ground allspice
1   cup chopped pecans
1   cup raisins or chopped dates

1. Preheat oven to 325°.
2. Cream shortening, then cream in sugar, egg, and persimmon pulp.
3. Sift flour, soda, baking powder, salt, cinnamon, nutmeg, and allspice together.
4. Stir dry mixture into the creamed ingredients to make a stiff dough, then add pecans and raisins or dates.
5. Drop by teaspoonfuls onto greased cookie sheets, spacing the cookies 1 inch apart.
6. Bake 12 to 15 minutes, or until golden brown.
7. Cool on racks and store in an airtight container.
Makes about 40 cookies.

PERSIMMON COOKIES WITH CHOCOLATE CHIPS

½   cup butter or shortening
1   cup sugar
1½ cups persimmon pulp, either fresh, or
       frozen and thawed

½   teaspoon salt
1   teaspoon vanilla
1   egg
2   cups flour
1   teaspoon baking powder
1   teaspoon baking soda
1   teaspoon ground cinnamon
1   cup chopped black walnuts or hickory
       nuts
1   cup semi-sweet chocolate chips

1. Preheat oven to 350°.
2. Cream butter, then cream in sugar, then persimmon pulp.
3. Beat in salt, vanilla, and egg.
4. Sift together the flour, baking powder, soda, and cinnamon and gradually blend into the creamed mixture.
5. Add nuts and chocolate chips.
6. Drop by teaspoonfuls onto greased cookie sheets, spacing cookies 1 inch apart.
7. Bake from 12 to 14 minutes, or until golden brown.
8. Cool on racks and store in an airtight container.
Makes about 3 dozen.

JANET AND ANNE'S PERSIMMON COOKIES

Janet Edwards and Anne Hart were in the Biology Club group from the University of Central Arkansas that came to Wildflower not long ago to forage and cook. They concocted this recipe, and somehow most of the cookies managed to get eaten while the cooks were trying to save them for the group's wild-foods dinner.

I agree with Janet and Anne that the cookies should be eaten while warm and accompanied by a cup of hot Sumac Tea.* (Left-over cookies can be warmed and freshened in a low oven, if you happen to *have* any left over—I seldom do.)

1½ cups shortening
2   cups sugar
2   eggs
1   teaspoon vanilla
1   teaspoon ground cinnamon
1   teaspoon salt
1   cup persimmon pulp, either fresh, or
    frozen and thawed
1   teaspoon baking soda
4½ to 5 cups flour, as needed
1   cup chopped pecans
1   handful chopped black walnuts (optional)

1. Preheat oven to 400°.
2. Cream shortening and sugar together well, then, beating well after each addition, add eggs, vanilla, cinnamon, salt, persimmon pulp, and soda.
3. Stir in flour, pecans, and black walnuts, if you use them. (Dough will be stiff; it's easiest to mix it with your hands.)
4. Form balls of dough (about 1½ teaspoon each) and place them 1 inch apart on greased cookie sheets. Flatten balls with tines of a fork.
5. Bake until light brown, about 8 to 10 minutes.
6. Cool on racks and, if possible, serve while still warm.
Makes about 6 dozen.

GINGER SUGAR COOKIES

2½ cups flour
1   teaspoon baking soda
1   teaspoon ground cinnamon
2   teaspoons ground tropical ginger
    (commercial), or 3 teaspoons ground
    dried wild ginger root
½   cup butter
½   cup sugar
1   egg
1   cup molasses
½   cup commercial sour cream
    Sugar for sprinkling

1. Preheat oven to 350°.
2. Sift flour, soda, cinnamon, and ginger together and set aside.
3. Cream butter, add sugar, and cream together well. Beat in the egg, then the molasses, then the sour cream.
4. Gradually mix in the dry ingredients, stirring well. Knead into a smooth dough.
5. On a floured board roll dough very thin, about ⅛ inch, and cut out with a 2-inch cookie cutter.
6. Place cookies on an ungreased baking sheet and sprinkle with sugar. Bake for about 8 minutes, or until browned.
Makes about 6 dozen.

PIES, TARTS, AND TARTLETS

STANDARD PIE CRUST

2   *cups flour*
½   *teaspoon salt*
⅔   *cup shortening, preferably chilled*
6   *tablespoons cold water, or as needed*

1. Combine flour and salt in a large bowl.
2. Cut in shortening until mixture has the texture of coarse meal.
3. Sprinkle cold water over mixture a little at a time, stirring with a fork until dough is just moist enough to hold together when squeezed lightly.
4. Shape into a ball and divide in half. If desired, wrap dough in plastic and chill until needed.
5. Roll thin on a floured pastry cloth.
6. Use as your pie recipe or other recipe directs.

Makes enough pastry for two single-crust 9-inch pies or one double-crust 9-inch pie.

BAKED PIE SHELL

Using half of the dough for Standard Pie Crust (above), line a 9-inch pie pan and crimp the edges in whatever fashion you like best. Prick entire surface fairly closely with a fork and bake in a preheated 425° oven until golden brown and firm, usually 10 to 12 minutes. Cool before filling.

BLACK WALNUT PIE

Black walnut trees are prolific in the South, and a Southern lady's recipe file has never been complete without at least one pie made with this nut. Long before the day of "bought" nuts, cooks leaned heavily on the crop of black walnuts as well as that of pecans.

My older brothers and sisters recall that when they were young our father, "Dad Taylor" to us all, always took them nutting on Thanksgiving Day. They would pack a picnic lunch and Dad Taylor always carried along a 6-inch-wide plank with several holes bored in it, each about 1 to 1½ inches across. Some of the children would gather the nuts and pile them up, while others would hull the nuts by placing each one over a hole in the plank and giving it a couple of whacks with a large flat rock. The green or black hull would remain on top and the hard-shelled nut would drop through the hole.

After the nuts were hulled they were laid out to dry while everyone enjoyed the picnic lunch. Then they put the nuts in a tow sack and set off for home.

1   *recipe Standard Pie Crust**
4   *tablespoons butter, softened at room temperature*
1   *cup sugar*

4   tablespoons flour
3   eggs, well beaten
1   cup dark corn syrup (Karo)
½   teaspoon salt
½   teaspoon vanilla
1   cup black walnuts, coarsely chopped

1. Line a 9-inch pie pan with the pie-crust dough. Chill shell.
2. Preheat oven to 425°.
3. Cream butter, add sugar gradually, and beat until light and fluffy.
4. Beat in flour, then eggs, then corn syrup, salt, and vanilla. Stir in black walnuts.
5. Pour into the pie shell and top with shapes — rounds, leaves, or strips — cut from left-over pastry.
6. Bake for 10 minutes, then lower heat to 300° and bake 30 minutes longer, or until filling is firm.
7. Serve while still slightly warm, or allow to cool if you prefer.

Serves 8.

BLUEBERRY BILLY

If you like tartlets, try baking this filling in pastry-lined individual pans. Top each little tartlet with a single pastry cutout before baking.

1   recipe Standard Pie Crust*
4   cups fresh blueberries, rinsed and
       drained
1⅓ cups sugar
¼   teaspoon salt
2   tablespoons quick-cooking tapioca
4   tablespoons lemon juice
¼   teaspoon ground cinnamon
       Sprinkle of ground cardamom

1. Line a 9-inch pan with pastry and set aside. Reserve remaining pie dough.
2. Preheat oven to 425°.
3. Combine blueberries, sugar, salt,

tapioca, and lemon juice, mixing gently but well.
4. Pour into unbaked pie shell and sprinkle with cinnamon and cardamom.
5. Roll out remaining dough and cut out fancy shapes with cookie cutters and place them on top of filling.
6. Bake for 10 minutes at 425°, then for 20 to 25 minutes at 300°.

Serves 6.

FRESH WILD BERRY OR GROUND CHERRY PIE

This is a master recipe, so to speak, that can be used for any of the following fruits: ground cherries (these should be crushed), blueberries, huckleberries, mulberries, blackberries, or raspberries.

1   recipe Standard Pie Crust*
3   cups berries or ground cherries, washed
       and drained; ground cherries
       should be crushed
1⅓ cups sugar
⅓   cup flour
2   tablespoons butter

1. Preheat oven to 400°.
2. Roll out half of pie dough and line a 9-inch pie pan.
3. Combine whole berries or crushed ground cherries with the sugar and flour, stirring gently so as not to crush berries.
4. Pour into unbaked pastry shell and dot with butter.
5. Roll out top crust, cover pie, trim and crimp edge, and slash vents in top to allow steam to escape.
6. Bake for 30 to 40 minutes, or until crust is golden brown and the fruit juice bubbles out of the vents.

Serves 6.

GROUND CHERRY PIE

This unusual fruit pie is the perfect way to end a late fall meal. The sunshiny color of the ground cherries is a reminder of the summer past.

  1 *recipe Standard Pie Crust**
  3 *cups ground cherries, washed, drained, and chopped coarsely*
1⅓ *cups sugar*
  2 *tablespoons lemon juice*
  3 *tablespoons quick-cooking tapioca*
  ½ *teaspoon ground cinnamon*

1. Preheat oven to 400°.
2. Roll out half of pie dough and line a 9-inch pie pan.
3. Combine chopped ground cherries, sugar, lemon juice, and tapioca and stir well.
4. Pour filling into unbaked pie shell and sprinkle with cinnamon.
5. Roll out top crust, cover pie, trim and crimp edges, and cut vents to allow steam to escape.
6. Bake for 30 to 40 minutes, or until crust is golden brown and the juices bubble out of the vents.
   Serves 6.

IDAVONNE'S MULBERRY PIE

When my sister Idavonne lived in Afghanistan she renewed her taste for mulberries. From a tree in a nearby courtyard she picked an abundance of the large juicy white berries daily, in spite of a running contest between her, the birds, and the neighbor children as to who would get the most and best mulberries. This pie recipe is one she came up with.

  1 *recipe Standard Pie Crust**
  4 *cups ripe mulberries, stemmed, washed, and well drained*
     Juice of half a lemon
  1 *cup sugar*
  3 *tablespoons quick-cooking tapioca*
     Grated nutmeg

1. Preheat oven to 400°.
2. Line a 9-inch pie pan with pastry.
3. Fill pastry-lined pie pan with mulberries and sprinkle berries with lemon juice, then with sugar, tapioca and a sprinkling of nutmeg.
4. Top with second crust, sealing edges well and slitting the center to make steam vents.
5. Bake for 10 minutes, then reduce heat to 325° and bake 25 minutes longer, or until crust is golden brown. Cool on rack before serving.
   Serves 6.

PECAN PIE À LA WILDFLOWER

This pie is so very rich that it should be cut into smaller portions than most pies. It will serve eight amply and end a meal with a flourish.

  ½ *recipe Standard Pie Crust**
  ½ *cup (1 stick) butter*
  1 *cup sugar*
  3 *eggs, slightly beaten*
  ¾ *cup dark corn syrup (Karo)*
  ¼ *teaspoon salt*
  1 *teaspoon vanilla*
  1 *cup pecans, coarsely chopped*
  1 *cup commercial sour cream (optional)*

1. Roll out pie dough and line a 9-inch pan. Chill pastry shell thoroughly.
2. Preheat oven to 375°.
3. Cream butter; add sugar gradually and cream together until light and fluffy.

4. Beat in eggs, then corn syrup, salt, and vanilla; stir in pecans.

5. Pour into the pastry shell and bake 40 to 45 minutes, or until filling has become firm and crust is golden brown.

6. Serve while still slightly warm, with each portion topped with a spoonful of sour cream, if you like.

Serves 8.

PERSIMMON MERINGUE PIE

1 *cup sugar*
1 *tablespoon cornstarch*
½ *teaspoon salt*
2 *cups milk*
2 *egg yolks, beaten until thick*
1 *cup persimmon pulp, either fresh, or frozen and thawed*
1 *9-inch Baked Pie Shell**

Meringue:

2 *egg whites*
   Pinch of salt
2 *tablespoons sugar*

1. Mix 1 cup of sugar with the cornstarch and salt.

2. Heat milk in the top of a double boiler over boiling water until it reaches the simmering point.

3. Whisk the dry ingredients into the milk and cook until thickened, stirring constantly.

4. Beat a little of the hot mixture into the egg yolks, then pour eggs into the hot filling, stirring constantly.

5. Add persimmon pulp and cook over the hot water, still stirring, for 5 minutes. Let cool slightly.

6. Meanwhile, preheat oven to 425°.

7. Pour filling into baked pie shell.

8. Make meringue: Beat egg whites with salt at high speed until they form stiff peaks on the beater, beating in 2 ta-

blespoons sugar after whites begin to stiffen.

9. Pile meringue onto filling and bake pie until meringue is browned, about 10 to 15 minutes.

10. Cool on rack until lukewarm before serving.

Serves 6.

PARAMOUNT PERSIMMON PIE

½ *recipe Standard Pie Crust**
2 *cups persimmon pulp, either fresh, or frozen and thawed*
1 *egg*
1 *cup milk*
½ *cup sugar*
   Pinch of salt
1 *tablespoon cornstarch*

Topping:

1 *cup heavy cream for topping, whipped at serving time*
2 *or 3 tablespoons sugar for whipped cream (optional)*

1. Line a 9-inch pie pan with the pastry dough.

2. Preheat oven to 450°.

3. Beat persimmon pulp, egg, and milk together until well blended.

4. Mix sugar, salt, and cornstarch and beat into persimmon mixture.

5. Pour the mixture into unbaked pie shell and bake 10 minutes, or until edges of pie crust are firm.

6. Reduce oven temperature to 350° and bake 50 minutes longer, or until firm and crusted on top and crust is browned.

7. Serve while still slightly warm. At serving time, whip cream, sweeten it to taste, and either decorate pie with it, or spoon cream over each portion.

Serves 6.

WILD STRAWBERRY CREAM COOLER

At Wildflower, this strawberry pie and the one just above have somehow come to be called "pan pies" — the children's way of distinguishing these two favorites from fruit cobblers.

 1   *cup sugar*
 4   *cups wild strawberries, hulled, washed,*
      and drained
 1   *tablespoon cornstarch*
 2   *tablespoons water*
 2   *cups heavy cream*
 1   *9-inch Baked Pie Shell**
 2 *or 3 tablespoons sugar for sweetening*
      topping (optional)
      Additional strawberries and leaves
      for garnishing

 1. Sprinkle sugar over berries, stir gently, and set aside for 1 hour.
 2. Mix cornstarch and water and add to berry mixture.
 3. Pour into saucepan and cook over medium heat for 15 minutes, or until juices thicken and become clear. Cool.
 4. Whip 1 cup of the cream until stiff and fold into the cooled filling.
 5. Pour filling into shell and chill pie.
 6. At serving time, whip the remaining cup of cream, sweetening it if you like, and top the pie with it. Decorate the pie with a few berries and strawberry leaves.
 Serves 6.

"TASTE OF SUMMER" STRAWBERRY PIE

 ½   *recipe Standard Pie Crust**
 2   *egg yolks*
 1   *cup sugar*

 4   *cups wild strawberries, hulled, washed,*
      and well drained, or unsweetened
      frozen berries, partly thawed
 ¼   *cup fine dry bread crumbs*

Meringue:
 2   *egg whites*
      Pinch of salt
 2 *or 3 tablespoons sugar*

 1. Line a 9-inch pie pan with the pastry dough.
 2. Preheat oven to 325°.
 3. Whip egg yolks with 1 cup of sugar until the mixture is thick.
 4. Pour over strawberries and mix gently.
 5. Sprinkle bread crumbs into pie shell, then add berry mixture.
 6. Make meringue: In bowl of an electric mixer, whip egg whites with salt until stiff peaks are formed, adding 2 to 3 tablespoons sugar gradually during last half of beating.
 7. Top pie with meringue, spreading it out to touch the crust all around.
 8. Bake for 40 minutes, or until crust is firm and golden and peaks of meringue are browned.
 9. Cool on rack and serve within 2 hours; if held longer, crust may become soggy.
 Serves 6.

JELLIED WILD STRAWBERRY PIE

For dainty strawberry tartlets, bake individual shells as directed in the Jam Tartlets recipe. When they have cooled, fill them and chill them; at serving time, top each tartlet with whipped cream.

 1   *cup water*
 3   *envelopes unflavored gelatin*
 1   *cup sugar*
 4   *tablespoons cornstarch*

Red food coloring
4 *cups whole wild strawberries, hulled, washed, and drained*
1 *9-inch baked Pie Shell**

Topping:

1 *cup heavy cream, chilled*
Sugar for sweetening cream (optional)

1. In a saucepan put ½ cup of the water and sprinkle the gelatin over the top. Stir constantly over low heat until gelatin is dissolved. Add sugar and set aside.

2. Mix cornstarch with remaining ½ cup of water and stir into gelatin mixture. Tint mixture with 2 or 3 drops of red food coloring. Return pan to medium-low heat and stir until mixture thickens and clears. Cool to lukewarm.

3. Pour berries into the baked crust and cover them with the cooled filling.

4. Chill pie thoroughly. Near serving time, whip the cream, adding sugar if you like, and pile topping over the filling.

Serves 6.

WOOD SORREL PIE

Wood sorrel pie resembles rhubarb pie, both because of the reddish tint of the plant and because of its tartness. This pie is especially good served following a main course of fish, or after a light lunch of creamed mushrooms on toast.

1 *recipe Standard Pie Crust**
1 *egg, well beaten*
1 *cup sugar*
2 *tablespoons quick-cooking tapioca*
2 *cups chopped wood sorrel*
1 *cup canned pineapple chunks, plus pineapple juice to fill cup*

1. Preheat oven to 375°.

2. Line a 9-inch pie pan with pastry and set aside. Roll out pastry for top crust.

3. Beat together egg, sugar, and tapioca.

4. Add wood sorrel, pineapple, and pineapple juice to the egg and sugar mixture.

5. Pour filling into pie crust and cover with top crust; seal edges and make several slashes in top.

6. Bake 30 to 40 minutes, or until crust is firm and golden brown.

7. Cool on rack.

Serves 6.

JAM TARTLETS

By late winter—February in Arkansas—the pantry and freezer are low on fruits. Jam tartlets are the very thing then. This is a good use for the small amounts of jellies and jams in the bottoms of various jars in Wildflower's refrigerators, and tartlets are also a way to show off the less common fruit jams, those that are not made in abundance—May apple and ground cherry, for instance.

Nothing is more beautiful than a silver tray laden with these tartlets with fillings in every hue from pale pink to deep purple or clear golden yellow, and even green if mint jelly is included.

1 *recipe Standard Pie Crust,* chilled*
A variety of wild jams, jellies, and marmalades

1. Preheat oven to 425°.

2. Roll out pastry ⅛ inch thick and line 2-inch tartlet pans or small muffin tins.

3. Bake shells until golden brown, about 25 minutes. Cool on racks, still in their pans.

4. Just before serving fill tartlet shells with your choice of jams, jellies, or marmalades.

Makes about 24 2-inch tartlets holding 2 tablespoons of filling each.

B. J.'S BLACKBERRY TART

This recipe may be used for mulberries, huckleberries, or blueberries as well as blackberries. Adjust the spices and quantity of sugar to taste. Mulberries have a delicate flavor which should not be overshadowed with cloves and allspice. I use only ginger and cinnamon with this berry.

My family does not like ginger, cloves, or allspice with huckleberries or blueberries, so I use only cinnamon with these berries.

1	recipe Standard Pie Crust*
2	quarts ripe blackberries, washed and drained
1½	cups water
1	cup sugar, or to taste
2	teaspoons ground cinnamon
¼	teaspoons ground cloves
½	teaspoon ground allspice
¼	teaspoon ground ginger
4	tablespoons quick-cooking tapioca
4	tablespoons butter

1. Preheat oven to 350°.
2. Roll two-thirds of the pie pastry quite thin—⅛ inch or so—and cut into 24 3 × 3-inch squares.
3. Place pastry squares on an unbuttered baking sheet and bake until light brown. Set aside to cool.
4. Place berries in a large pot with the water and sugar, bring to a boil, and cook over medium heat for 10 minutes.
5. Mix cinnamon, cloves, allspice, and ginger with tapioca.
6. Place half of the cooled pastry squares in a 9 × 13-inch cake pan and pour half of the berry mixture over them.
7. Sprinkle with spice and tapioca mixture and dab with half of the butter, cut into small bits.

8. Repeat layers, ending with butter bits.
9. Roll remaining one-third of the dough thin and cut into decorative shapes—circles, leaves, or strips — and use as topping.
10. Bake 30 to 45 minutes, or until filling has thickened and the top is golden brown. Serve warm.
Serves 8 to 10.

JAM TART IN A NUT CRUST

1	recipe Standard Pie Crust*
¼	teaspoon ground cinnamon
1	cup finely ground pecans
	Grated rind of half an orange
2	cups strawberry, blackberry, mulberry, May apple, or ground cherry jam
	Confectioners' sugar

1. Make pastry, adding cinnamon to flour and adding pecans and orange rind to the fat and flour mixture before adding water. Chill dough until firm.
2. Preheat oven to 350°.
3. Remove about three-quarters of the dough, leaving the remainder in refrigerator.
4. Butter the bottom and sides of a 9-inch tart pan, pie pan, or round cake pan.
5. With your hands, press and spread the dough over the bottom and sides of pan to a thickness of about ¼ inch.
6. Spread jam in the pastry shell.
7. On a floured pastry board, roll remainder of dough into a rectangle about ¼ inch thick and cut into ½-inch strips. Lay strips over jam in a lattice pattern. Trim overhanging ends and crimp edges of tart.
8. Bake until crust is lightly browned, about 45 minutes. Cool.

9. Sprinkle with confectioners' sugar before serving.

Serves 6 to 8.

GLAZED BERRY TARTLETS

Many fruit and jelly combinations are good for these little tartlets. I suggest Wild Plum Jelly* or Wild Grape Jelly* with blackberries; Ground Cherry Jelly* with strawberries; Spearmint Jelly* over mulberries or blueberries; Venison Jelly* with mulberries; or Elderberry and Sumac Jelly* with elderberries.

> 2 cups fresh berries, rinsed and drained
> ½ cup sugar
> ½ to ¾ cup jelly (see note above)
> 12 tartlet shells, baked and cooled as described in Jam Tartlets*

1. Combine berries and sugar and set aside for 15 minutes.
2. Meanwhile, heat jelly in a small saucepan until melted. Preheat the broiler.
3. Spoon about 2 tablespoons of berries into each shell.
4. Top with enough heated jelly to cover the fruit.
5. Pop into broiler for 2 to 3 minutes, just until jelly bubbles.
6. Serve immediately.

Serves 12.

FRUIT-TOPPED CREAM TARTLETS

You can make these tartlets when you have small amounts of several different fruits or berries. They're especially good made with strawberries, blackberries, mulberries, or elderberries. If you'd like to make a fruit-topped cream pie, make a 9-inch Baked Pie Shell* instead of the tartlet shells, and fill, top, and garnish it in the same way. Don't try to make this dessert, large or small, too many hours ahead. Once the cream is in the shells it can be chilled for an hour or two, but the crust might get soggy if refrigerated longer.

Cream Filling:

> ¼ cup cornstarch
> ¾ cup sugar
> ½ teaspoon salt
> 2½ cups milk
> 3 egg yolks, slightly beaten
> 1 tablespoon butter
> 2 teaspoons vanilla

Shells:

> 24 tartlet shells, made as described in Jam Tartlets,* baked and cooled

Topping:

> 1½ to 2 cups fresh berries or cut-up fruit, sugared to taste
> 1 cup heavy cream
> 2 to 3 tablespoons sugar

1. Make filling: Combine cornstarch, sugar, and salt in a saucepan and stir in milk gradually.
2. Cook over medium heat, stirring constantly, until mixture thickens. Cook for another minute or two.
3. Blend half the hot mixture quickly into the egg yolks. Stir egg mixture back into the custard in the saucepan and cook again for 1 minute, stirring constantly, over medium heat.
4. Remove from heat and stir in butter and vanilla. Cool, stirring occasionally, until barely lukewarm.
5. Pour filling into tartlet shells, filling each halfway. Let cool completely.
6. Near serving time, top the cream filling with fruit or berries. Whip cream, adding sugar to taste, and garnish the tarts.

Makes 24 2-inch tartlets.

BEVERAGES

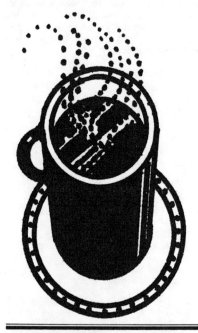

BLACK CHERRY PUNCH

2   *cups black cherries, stemmed and washed*
         Water to cover cherries
4   *cups water*
1   *teaspoon chopped wild ginger root*
1   *2-inch cinnamon stick, broken up*
¼   *cup lemon juice*
1   *cup sugar, or to taste*
         Spearmint for garnishing, if available

1. Place black cherries in a saucepan, cover with water, and bring to a boil. Reduce heat and simmer, covered, for 5 minutes. Set aside.

2. In another saucepan combine 4 cups water, ginger, and cinnamon and bring to a boil. Cool and strain out spices.

3. After cherries are cool, place in a sieve and drain off juices, bruising the fruit gently in order to get as much flavor as possible; drain for 20 minutes or longer.

4. Combine cherry juice with spiced liquid and lemon juice, add sugar to taste, and chill. Serve garnished with a sprig of spearmint in each glass.

Makes about 2 quarts.

BLACK CHERRY RUM PUNCH

2   *quarts black cherry juice (see Index for Grape Juice and Other Wild Fruit Juices)*
1   *cup sugar*
½   *pint dark rum*
1   *quart ginger ale, chilled*
         Mint leaves for garnishing

1. Mix cooled black cherry juice with sugar and stir vigorously. Chill.

2. At serving time add rum and chilled ginger ale.

3. Serve in frosted crystal punch cups, each garnished with a sprig of fresh mint leaves.

Makes 10 servings.

ELDERBERRY FLOWER MILK ROB

This refreshing drink, English in origin, is one I made for years before discovering that it isn't exactly a "rob" as the dictionary defines that drink. But never mind— under any name it's delicious, and I hope you try it.

1 *quart milk*
8 *clusters of elderberry flowers, snipped from stems, washed, and drained*
½ *lemon, seeded and pulverized in electric blender, peel and all*
3 *tablespoons honey*
4 *tablespoons Cognac or other fine brandy Grated nutmeg*

1. Heat milk just to the boiling point, but do not boil.
2. Pour over elderberry flowers. Add lemon, honey, and Cognac and cool (don't chill).
3. Serve in glass punch cups. Sprinkle each serving with nutmeg.
Serves 8.

2. Pour into a sieve and press the fruit pulp and juice through the mesh.
3. Freeze in a shallow pan until mushy.
4. Spoon into crystal punch cups and fill cups with cold ginger ale. Garnish with cherries, if you like, and serve at once.
Serves 10.

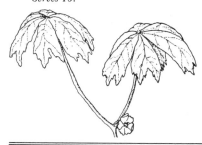

MAY APPLE (MANDRAKE) MAGIC PUNCH

Just looking at the leaves of this lovely plant gives me visions of fairies and elves and great magic. To smell the heady scent of the waxy blossoms and to watch the fruit form are indeed enchanting experiences, and when I first drank this sparkling punch the taste, too, was simply magical. I hope you like it.

2 *cups May apple fruit, washed, drained, and crushed*
  Water, as needed
2 *or 3 1-inch pieces of dried ginger root*
  Pinch of salt
½ *to 1 cup sugar, or to taste*
1 *quart ginger ale, chilled*
  Maraschino cherries for garnishing (optional)

1. In a saucepan cover May apples with water and add ginger and salt; bring slowly to a boil. Simmer for 20 minutes, add sugar, and set aside until cool, stirring occasionally.

MAYPOP PUNCH

2 *quarts maypops, washed and chopped or sliced*
1½ *cups sugar, or to taste*
  Pinch of salt
2 *cups water*
1 *cup Spearmint Tea,* chilled*
1 *cup heavy cream, whipped and sweetened*
  Spearmint sprigs for garnishing

1. Place maypops in a saucepan with sugar, salt, and water.
2. Bring slowly to a boil, reduce heat, cover, and simmer for 20 minutes, stirring frequently. Cool.
3. Pour fruit and juice into a colander. Drain off juice, but do not push pulp through the colander.
4. Refrigerate juice until icy cold.
5. At serving time, mix punch with the chilled spearmint tea and stir in whipped cream.
6. Serve in tall crystal glasses, each garnished with a sprig of spearmint.
Serves 5 to 6.

MINT PUNCH

2   cups (packed) of washed fresh,
        spearmint or peppermint leaves
2   quarts boiling water
1   cup Grape Juice,* well chilled
1½ cups superfine or regular granulated
        sugar
3   tablespoons lemon juice
1   quart ginger ale, chilled
    Mint leaves for garnishing

1. Chop mint leaves fine, cover with boiling water, and let stand, covered, for 10 minutes.

2. Strain and cool mint infusion, then set it in the refrigerator to chill.

3. Combine grape juice, sugar, and lemon juice, stirring until sugar is completely dissolved, and add to chilled infusion. Leave in refrigerator until serving time.

4. At serving time, pour the punch mixture and the ginger ale over a block of ice in a crystal or silver bowl and float a few mint leaves on the surface. Serve in individual punch cups about one-third full of cracked ice.

Makes about 3 ½ quarts.

SUMAC PUNCH

This tart punch, an improvement on the pioneers' "Indian lemonade," is a deep rosy-red color. It's a lovely drink when served in a tall crystal glass over crushed ice, garnished with a thin slice of lemon and a sprig of fresh spearmint. We often serve this punch at Christmas and Valentine's Day parties, as the color suits those seasons especially well.

2   quarts water
1   cup ripe sumac berries
1   tablespoon whole cloves
4   1-inch sticks of cinnamon, broken up
1½ to 2 cups sugar, to taste

1. Bring water to a boil; add sumac berries, cloves, and cinnamon, return to a boil, cover, lower heat, and simmer for 15 minutes.

2. Strain through a sieve lined with 3 layers of damp muslin or several layers of damp cheesecloth.

3. Add sugar to taste and chill. Serve cold.

Makes about 2 quarts.

STRAWBERRY COOLER

This chilled drink makes me glad when strawberry season comes. As there's no cooking involved, it tastes just like the fresh berries. You may want to freeze an ice-cube tray of the cooler and use the cubes in the glasses into which you pour the unfrozen part. This drink is particularly lovely to look at when served in stemmed crystal glasses, topped with a little whipped cream and a wild strawberry, if you like.

6   cups cold water
2   cups ripe wild strawberries, hulled and
        crushed
2   cups sugar
    Juice of 1 lemon

1. Mix 1 cup of the water with the berries.

2. Pour mixture into a fine sieve and press pulp through with a wooden spoon.

3. Add sugar, lemon juice, and remainder of water to the pulp.

4. Stir vigorously and chill.

Makes 8 servings.

STRAWBERRY DELIGHT

1 quart strawberry ice cream
¾ cup Strawberry Syrup*, chilled
1 quart ginger ale, chilled
  Whipped cream for garnishing (about
    ½ cup cream before whipping)
  Fresh strawberries and sugar for
    garnishing

1. Put scoops of ice cream in tall beverage glasses.
2. Combine strawberry syrup and ginger ale, pouring together gently.
3. Pour over ice cream and stir lightly, just until foamy.
4. Garnish each glass with a dab of whipped cream and top off with a fresh strawberry dipped in granulated sugar. Provide long-handled spoons for eating.
Serves 8.

GRAPE JUICE AND OTHER WILD FRUIT JUICES

These directions for grapes may be followed for making a beverage from wild plums, black cherries, blackberries, raspberries, huckleberries, or blueberries. The basic juice is not sweetened, so you can add sugar as required for various purposes.

2 to 3 quarts ripe wild grapes, washed
    and stemmed
  Water to cover well, at least 2 quarts

1. Bring grapes and water to a boil in a large pot over high heat, reduce heat, cover, and simmer for 20 minutes, or until skins have all split.
2. Crush grapes slightly with a potato masher and set aside to cool.

3. Strain off juice through a sieve, removing seeds, skin, and pulp.
4. The juice is now ready to use immediately or to can or freeze for future use.
Makes about 4 quarts.

GREENS AND FRUIT JUICE FOR BREAKFAST

This recipe makes enough breakfast juice for a family of five for most of a week, unless they find it irresistible and drink it all at once. The joy of this juice is that you can use sprigs of all kinds of greens as they first pop up in the early spring to make a really multi-flavored drink.

2 quarts boiling water
2 quarts of mixed greens, including some
    watercress, washed and drained
1 teaspoon salt
3 seedless oranges, blended to a pulp in an
    electric blender, peel and all
1 lemon, seeded and blended to a pulp in
    an electric blender, peel and all
¼ to ½ cup honey or to taste
  Apple juice, canned or bottled

1. Pour boiling water over the greens in a large pot; add salt and simmer, covered, for 20 minutes.
2. Strain mixture and reserve both the greens and the juice.
3. Add orange and lemon pulp to hot juice and sweeten with honey to taste.
4. Place greens 2 cups at a time in the container of an electric blender and purée.
5. Combine puréed greens and the sweetened liquid mixture and chill overnight.
6. Strain and add apple juice to make 1 gallon. Serve cold.
Makes 1 gallon.

TEAS: SPEARMINT, PEPPERMINT, BEE BALM, DITTANY, AND SWEET GOLDENROD

Soothing hot teas can be made from many wild plants as well as from the herbs that stand in your spice rack. The amount of these five tea plants you use is a personal thing—just as each person prefers his coffee weak or strong, so goes it for tea. The leaves of these tea plants can be dried and stored according to the individual plant entries in the field guide, so you'll always be ready to make a refreshing hot beverage. From one-half to one teaspoon of dried leaves per cup of boiling water is the usual amount, and the tea should be steeped, covered, for 10 minutes after water is poured over the leaves. Sweeten these teas to taste with honey or sugar.

If you make tea from freshly picked leaves of any of these plants, you'll need about twice the quantity of leaves for a given amount of water; otherwise, make the tea the same way, steeping it, covered, for 10 minutes.

Spearmint and peppermint teas, especially, are delicious when chilled and served over crushed ice, with a garnish of fresh mint leaves.

WILD GINGER TEA

4   *cups water*
1   *cup wild ginger roots, cleaned, scraped or scrubbed, and coarsely chopped*
12   *whole cloves*
4   *sticks of cinnamon for stirring*
    Honey for sweetening

1. Bring the water to a rolling boil in a saucepan and add ginger roots and cloves. Cover, lower heat, and simmer for 20 minutes.

2. Strain tea and serve in dainty china cups, each with a cinnamon stick for stirring in the honey for sweetening.

Serves 4.

SASSAFRAS TEA

Dried sassafras-root bark may be used for tea three times or perhaps even more, still retaining its flavor after repeated simmerings. After use, simply dry the bark again as if it were fresh. If you're in a hurry to make tea, just use more bark and simmer the tea for a shorter time. Our grandmothers used to give us this tea in the spring, to "thin our blood."

4   *cups water*
1   *tablespoon dried sassafras root bark (page 93)*
    Sugar to taste

1. Pour water over bark in a saucepan and bring to a boil over high heat.

2. Turn heat down and simmer, covered, for 20 minutes, or until the desired strength is reached.

3. Serve hot, sweetened to taste.

Serves 4.

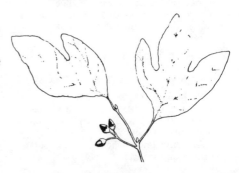

SPICED SASSAFRAS TEA

Serve this delicious drink in heavy mugs and spoon in honey to be stirred with the cinnamon sticks. Whether or not your blood needs thinning, I can promise you'll enjoy this tea. The sassafras infusion is the one also used for making candy.

> 4 cups water
> 2 cups strong Sassafras Infusion*
> ¼ teaspoon ground cloves
> ½ teaspoon ground cinnamon
> ¼ teaspoon ground ginger
>   Juice of 1 lemon
> 6 cinnamon sticks
>   Honey for sweetening

1. Bring water and infusion to a boil. Add spices and simmer, covered, for 10 minutes.
2. Add lemon juice and serve hot with cinnamon sticks for stirring in the honey.
Serves 6.

SPICED BEE BALM TEA

This tea is especially spicy and much akin to "Russian" tea. Our winters in Arkansas are fairly mild, so when we have a big snow it is a real treat. This tea is the one I serve to cold and chilled adults and children after a sledding expedition on Hunt's Hill or a snowy woodland walk. It not only tastes good but many an old-timer in our Ozark Mountains suggests that it prevents many of the ills that seem to follow too much exposure to cold weather. Whether or not this tea prevents colds and such I will not say, but it is certainly very soothing to scratchy throats, and well worth trying for its taste alone.

> 1 cup pineapple juice, or 1 cup Sumac Tea*

> 12 whole cloves
> 2   2-inch cinnamon sticks, coarsely broken
> 6   cups bee balm tea (see Teas)
> 1   cup brewed Pekoe or other black tea
> 2   tablespoons lemon juice
>   Honey or sugar for sweetening

1. Pour the pineapple juice into a 2-quart enameled or stainless-steel saucepan and bring to a boil.
2. Add cloves and cinnamon and simmer, covered, for 15 minutes.
3. Add bee-balm and Pekoe teas to the pineapple juice and reheat.
4. Strain out spices, add lemon juice, and serve hot with honey or sugar, if you like, for sweetening.
Serves 8.

SUMAC TEA

This perky pink tea is quite tangy and tart. Besides being welcome at teatime, it is especially good served with an egg or fish main course. The color ranges from pale pink to a deep rose to a brownish tint (for winter-picked berries), according to the deepness of the color of the berries to begin with.

> ½ cup ripe sumac berries
> 1   teaspoon whole cloves (about 20)
> 2   2-inch sticks cinnamon, broken up
> 2   quarts water
> ¼   cup honey, or to taste

1. Place sumac berries, cloves, and cinnamon in a saucepan, cover with water, and bring to a boil. Lower heat and simmer, covered, for 15 minutes.
2. Strain through a sieve lined with 2 or 3 layers of damp muslin or several layers of damp cheesecloth.
3. Add honey to taste and serve hot.
Makes 8 servings.

DANDELION ROOT "COFFEE"

The brew made from the roasted roots of dandelions has a distinctive flavor which is pleasing to many, either "straight" or mixed with regular coffee. I find that a percolator works best for making it.

> Water to fill coffee percolator to 8-cup mark
> ½ cup dried, roasted, and ground dandelion roots (page 46)
> Pinch of salt

1. Put water in percolator and put ground dandelion roots in basket. Sprinkle salt on roots.
2. Brew as you usually brew coffee, perking until you have the strength you like. Serve hot, with sugar and milk or cream.

> Makes 8 cups.

COFFEE WITH CHICORY

Most of us are familiar with Louisiana or Creole coffee, a dark-roast coffee to which dried, ground, and roasted chicory roots have been added for their special flavor. The Creoles consider coffee no good at all without chicory; they brew it half-and-half and serve it steaming, with hot milk and lots of sugar for sweetening.

> Water to fill percolator to 8-cup mark
> 4 tablespoons dried, ground, and roasted chicory roots (page 43)
> 4 tablespoons coffee, regular grind (use a dark roast, if preferred)

1. Put water in percolator and put ground chicory and coffee into percolator basket.

2. Brew as you usually brew coffee, perking as long as necessary to get the strength you like. Serve hot, with sugar and milk or cream.

> Makes 8 cups.

VIN DENT DE LION (DANDELION WINE)

One of the most enjoyable wine-making sprees we've had took place a spring or two ago, when my daughter Angel was home from the university, with several of her friends as guests. There were five or six of us working on the project, picking the flowers, snipping off the stems, measuring, pouring, and watching during the hour it takes for the water and flowers and fruits to cook. The wine starter is very fragrant as it cooks, both flowery and fruity—it does make one's mouth water with thoughts of the finished product. While the starter cooled we tested several other dandelion dishes, some of which appear in this book.

Working with a crowd, it was fun to strain and cool the starter and add yeast. Then I was on my own for the several weeks of waiting before the bottles could be corked and placed on their sides in my "wine cellar" (the closet of my ground-floor bedroom). Two weeks before Christmas I poured the first of the slightly cloudy, pale yellow wine for tasting. Heavy and a bit sweet, it has a fragrance reminiscent of spring, and a color only slightly less golden than the dandelions.

> 2 quarts freshly picked dandelion flowers in full bloom, washed and with all parts of the stems removed
> 4 quarts water
> 1 teaspoon ground or finely cut wild ginger root
> 2 seedless oranges, pulverized in an electric blender, peel and all

1 *lemon, seeded and pulverized in the*
   electric blender, peel and all
6 *cups sugar*
1 *envelope dry yeast or 1 cake fresh yeast*
½ *cup lukewarm water*

1. Combine dandelion flowers, water, ginger, oranges, lemon, and sugar in a large enameled kettle, bring to a boil, cover, lower heat, and simmer for 1 hour.

2. Strain into a 2-gallon crock through 2 layers of dampened muslin or several layers of dampened cheesecloth.

3. Cool until you can comfortably put a finger into the juice.

4. Dissolve yeast in lukewarm water and add to crock.

5. Let mixture stand for 1 week, undisturbed, with the crock covered with cheesecloth. Strain wine and pour into bottles, filling them just to the base of the neck.

6. Store bottles unsealed for 4 weeks, covered with a cloth.

7. Cork bottles and store at least until Christmas for full flavor. Decant the wine before serving it.

Makes about 2 gallons.

BLUEBERRY AND GRAPE WINE

This is a very old recipe of New England origin and was a favorite of many of our forebears.

4   *cups boiling water*
4   *quarts blueberries, rinsed and drained*
16 *cups sugar*
8   *cups Grape Juice**
4   *pounds seedless raisins*
2   *cups lukewarm water*
1   *cake of yeast or 1 envelope dry yeast*

1. Pour boiling water over berries.

When cool enough to handle, press out liquid through a sieve. Pour liquid into a stoneware crock; you should have about 2 quarts.

2. Add sugar, grape juice, raisins, lukewarm water, and yeast and mix thoroughly.

3. Cover with cheesecloth and let stand in a cool place for 21 days.

4. Strain and bottle wine. Stand bottles, uncorked and covered with cheesecloth, in a cool, dark place for 2 months.

5. Cork bottles tightly and store them on their sides for at least 2 months more. Decant before serving.

Makes about 4 quarts.

WILD GRAPE WINE

The alcoholic content of this heavy sweet purple wine may not equal that of its commercial counterpart, but the wine is delicious and heady. My Hungarian brother-in-law, Joe Denhoff, says that in Budapest his mother made this wine to be drunk young.

4   *quarts wild grapes, stemmed and washed*
4   *quarts water*
4   *cups sugar*

1. Place grapes in a stoneware crock, add water, and leave for 24 hours, covered with cheesecloth.

2. Crush grapes thoroughly and add sugar, stirring until dissolved.

3. Cover crock again with cheesecloth and let stand for 1 month, stirring every third day.

4. Strain, bottle the wine, and cork the bottles.

5. Lay bottles on their sides in a cool, dark place and allow to rest for at least 3 months before drinking.

Makes about 4 quarts

ELDERBERRY WINE

I never get even a sniff of this wine without visions of old ladies in lace, chatting and rocking while sipping and sewing — it's a very ladylike drink. Pale lavender-blue in color and just sweet enough, but with a bite — just the way I like little old ladies to be. I often pour a small crystal glass of elderberry wine, sit in a rocker, and dream of the time when I can just rock and sew and sip. More often, though, I serve it to drop-in company in small cut-glass fruit-juice glasses, accompanied by a slice of hot buttered nut or fruit bread. This is the type of homemade wine our grandmothers used medicinally for many an ailment.

 2 *quarts ripe elderberries, stripped from stems*
 4 *quarts water*
 4 *cups sugar*
 1 *piece of fresh wild ginger root or tropical ginger about 2 or 3 inches long, or a smaller root of dried ginger, cut or broken up*
 1 *teaspoon whole cloves*
 2 *envelopes dry yeast or 2 cakes fresh yeast*

1. Combine elderberries, water, sugar, ginger root, and cloves in a preserving kettle, bring to a boil, lower heat, cover, and simmer for half an hour.
2. Strain liquid into a 2-gallon crock. Let cool.
3. Add yeast and stir. Let mixture rest for 2 days, lightly covered with cloth.
4. After 2 days skim off any foam that has formed. Pour into a crockery demijohn or a small-necked glass bottle, cover with cheesecloth, and leave in a cool place until there is no hissing sound coming from the wine, about 2 weeks.
5. Put an airtight stopper in the jug or bottle and let the wine mature for at least 2 months before using.

6. If desired, line a funnel with filter paper and filter wine into smaller bottles, or just decant carefully without filtering. Cork tightly for storage.
Makes about 1 gallon.

RASPBERRY OR BLACKBERRY CORDIAL

This cordial recipe is an old British one that my neighbor at Tameweed brought to me years ago. It's supposed to be a sweet calmer of frayed nerves. I've made it for several years with total success. It has always been delicious, although the alcoholic content varies from batch to batch. We serve this thick, dark cordial in amethyst-colored liqueur glasses, and it's very pretty.

 2 *quarts fresh raspberries or blackberries*
 2 *cups boiling water*
 2 *cups sugar*

1. Crush the berries well with an old-time wooden potato masher or the bottom of a heavy bottle and put them into a small stoneware crock. Add water.
2. Cover crock with cheesecloth and set it in a warm place for 24 hours. Stir occasionally.
3. Push the berries and their liquid through a fine sieve to remove the seeds. Reserve the juice and discard pulp.
4. Add sugar to the sieved berries and stir well.
5. Stir again every 15 minutes for 1 hour (5 times altogether).
6. Strain mixture through dampened muslin or several layers of dampened cheesecloth.
7. Bottle cordial and cork bottles.
8. Place bottles on their sides and keep them in a cool, dark place for 4 months. Decant before using.
Makes 2 quarts.

PRESERVES, PICKLES, AND CONDIMENTS

JAMS

When a jam recipe calls for prepared fruit, prepare it as follows:

Use fully ripe fruit, washed and picked from stems, pitted if necessary, and crushed or cut up. Place it in an enamel or stainless-steel pan holding at least twice as much as the amount of fruit. Add water— to about a quarter of the depth of juicy fruits, halfway to the top of less juicy kinds, and enough barely to cover rather dry fruits. Place over medium heat and bring to a boil; lower heat and simmer for about 15 minutes or until fairly soft, stirring often enough to prevent sticking.

Pour fruit and juices into a colander or coarse sieve and with a wooden pestle or a large spoon force the pulp through. The yield of prepared fruit will depend on whether the raw fruit has large or numerous seeds and whether it's fairly fleshy— start with plenty of fruit, and if you end up with more pulp than you need for your recipe, you can always freeze the surplus and use it, with more fruit, another time. If the amount of pulp and juice isn't quite sufficient, a little water may be added; or another kind of fruit juice or pulp can be combined with the original fruit.

Good jam or fruit butter can often be made from the pulp remaining after the juice has been strained from fruit for jelly-making.

BLACK CHERRY JAM

4   cups prepared black cherries (see above)
1   box powdered pectin
5   cups sugar

1. In a large enameled or stainless-steel pot combine fruit and pectin and bring to a hard boil over high heat, stirring.

2. Add sugar and bring to a boil again, still stirring. Boil very hard for exactly 2 minutes, stirring constantly.

3. Remove from heat and skim off foam. Continue to stir and skim for 5 minutes.

4. Ladle into sterile jars or jelly glasses and seal.

Makes 7 half-pint jars.

GROUND CHERRY JAM

3½   cups fresh ground cherries, washed and
      well crushed
½   cup water
1   box powdered pectin
6   cups sugar

1. Mix ground cherries with water and
pectin and bring to a boil in a large
enameled or stainless-steel pot, stirring.
2. Add sugar and again bring to a boil,
stirring. Boil very hard for exactly 1½ minutes and remove from heat.
3. Cool for 10 minutes, stirring all the
while and skimming off any foam.
4. Pour into sterile jars or jelly glasses
and seal.

Makes about 6 half-pint jars.

MAYPOP (PASSION FRUIT) JAM

If you pick more maypops than you need
for this delectable jam, just stew them in a
little water for about 15 minutes, sweeten
them with honey, and serve the fruit,
chilled, as a dessert.

5   cups maypops, rinsed gently
½   cup lemon juice
     Water
1   box powdered pectin
7½   cups sugar

1. Measure maypops into an enameled
or stainless-steel pot and crush them
slightly. Add lemon juice, then water
barely to cover fruit. Bring to a boil, lower
heat, cover, and simmer for 15 minutes.
2. Strain through coarse sieve to
measure out 5 cups of pulp and juice.

3. Mix with the pectin in the preserving
pot. Bring to a boil stirring frequently.
4. Add sugar, return to a boil, and boil
very hard for 2 minutes, stirring constantly.
5. Remove from heat and stir, skimming off any foam, for 5 to 8 minutes.
6. Pour into sterile jars or jelly glasses
and seal.

Makes about 10 half-pint jars.

HUCKLEBERRY OR BLUEBERRY JAM

4   cups prepared fruit (see page 229)
2   tablespoons lemon juice
1   box powdered pectin
4   cups sugar

1. In a large enameled or stainless-steel
pot combine fruit, lemon juice, and pectin
and bring to a hard boil over high heat,
stirring frequently.
2. Add sugar and again bring to a boil,
stirring. Boil very hard for precisely 2 minutes, stirring constantly.
3. Remove from heat and skim off
foam. Continue to stir and skim for 5 minutes.
4. Ladle into sterile jars or jelly glasses
and seal.

Makes 7 half-pint jars.

STRAWBERRY, RASPBERRY, AND BLACKBERRY JAMS

The jams made from wild strawberries,
raspberries, and blackberries are much,
much better than either "bought" jams or
those made from garden fruits. However,

I have found no better recipes for these berry jams than the ones provided with commercial powdered or liquid pectin. I suggest you use these, as I do, simply substituting wild fruits for the domesticated ones.

MAY APPLE JAM

5 cups of coarsely chopped May apples
½ cup water
½ cup lemon juice
1 box powdered pectin
7 cups sugar

1. In a large enameled or stainless-steel pan combine May apples, water, and lemon juice. Bring to a boil, cover, lower heat, and simmer for 15 minutes, stirring occasionally.
2. Add pectin and bring to a boil again, stirring.
3. Add sugar and again bring to a boil, stirring. Boil very hard for exactly 2 minutes, stirring constantly.
4. Remove from heat. Stir and skim off foam for 7 minutes.
5. Ladle into sterile jars or jelly glasses and seal.
Makes 10 half-pint jars.

MULBERRY JAM

5 cups prepared fruit (page 229)
¼ cup lemon juice
1 box powdered pectin
7 cups sugar

1. Combine fruit, lemon juice, and pectin in a large enameled or stainless-steel pot and bring to a hard boil, stirring frequently.

2. Add sugar and again bring to a boil, still stirring. Boil very hard for 2 minutes exactly, stirring constantly.
3. Remove from the heat and stir and skim off any foam for 5 minutes.
4. Ladle into sterile jars or jelly glasses and seal.
Makes 8 half-pint jars.

PERSIMMON JAM

2 quarts ripe fresh persimmon pulp (page 229)
1 cup sugar
1 cup orange juice
Grated rind of 1 orange

1. Combine all ingredients in a 4-quart enameled or stainless-steel pan and cook over medium-high heat, stirring often until thickened, usually about 20 minutes.
2. Pour into sterilized half-pint jars and seal at once.
Makes about 6 half-pint jars.

WILD PLUM JAM

6 cups prepared fruit (see page 229)
1 box powdered pectin
8 cups sugar

1. In a large enameled or stainless-steel pan combine the fruit and pectin and bring to a hard boil, stirring frequently.
2. Add sugar and again bring to a boil, continuing to stir. Boil very hard for 1 minute precisely, stirring constantly.
3. Remove from heat and stir, skimming off any foam, for 5 minutes.
4. Ladle into sterile jars or jelly glasses and seal.
Makes 11 half-pint jars.

SUSAN'S PRICKLY PEAR JAM

    4 cups prickly pears, peeled and coarsely
         chopped
    ½ cup water
    1 cup lemon juice
    1 box powdered pectin
    7 cups sugar

1. Combine prickly pears, water, and lemon juice and mash until pulpy, using an old-fashioned wooden potato masher or, lacking that, the bottom of a bottle. You should have 5 cups of the mixture. If necessary, add a little water to make up the quantity.

2. Place pulp in a large enameled or stainless-steel pan, add pectin, and stir over medium-high heat until mixture boils.

3. Add sugar, bring to a boil again, and boil very hard for 2 minutes, stirring constantly.

4. Remove from heat and cool for 10 minutes, stirring constantly and skimming off any foam.

5. Ladle into sterile jars or jelly glasses and seal.

Makes about 8 half-pint jars.

SUNSHINE PRESERVE

Such wild fruits as blackberries, strawberries, and ground cherries may be preserved in this way. The berries need only be rinsed and drained, except for strawberries, which need to be hulled. Wash, drain, and crush ground cherries very lightly if you make this preserve with them.

    4 cups sugar

    ½ cup water, more or less
    4 cups prepared fruit (page 229)

1. In a saucepan dissolve sugar in as little water as possible and cook over high heat to the thread stage (230°).

2. Add fruit and simmer gently until tender. Do not stir.

3. Pour preserve into a large shallow pan or platter and cover with cheesecloth or glass.

4. Set in hot sunshine until preserve thickens, usually in 2 or 3 days. Bring inside each day at sundown.

5. When sufficiently thickened, put into sterilized jars and seal with paraffin.

Makes about 2 pints.

BLACK WALNUT CONSERVE

This goes well with venison or, for that matter, other full-flavored game or meat.

    ½ cup granulated sugar
    1½ cups brown sugar, packed
    4 cups water
    1 cup cider vinegar
    2 tablespoons honey
    ½ teaspoon each ground ginger, cloves,
         and allspice, whole mustard seed,
         and curry powder
         Grated peel of 1 lemon, yellow part
         only
    3 cups black walnut meats, in large
         pieces
    ½ cup dark rum

1. Combine the granulated sugar, brown sugar, water, vinegar, honey, spices, and lemon peel in a saucepan and boil until as thick as jam, stirring constantly.

2. Add black walnuts and simmer 5 minutes more.

3. Remove from heat and stir in rum.

4. Pour into sterilized half-pint jars and seal.

Makes about 4 half-pint jars.

BLUEBERRY OR HUCKLEBERRY CONSERVE

2 *cups water*
4 *cups sugar*
1 *lemon, thinly sliced and seeds removed*
½ *cup raisins*
1 *quart blueberries or huckleberries, washed and drained*

1. Bring water to a boil in a large enameled or stainless-steel pan and add sugar and lemon slices.
2. Bring to a boil, stirring, then lower heat and simmer for 5 minutes.
3. Add raisins and blueberries or huckleberries and cook, stirring often, until thickened, about 30 minutes.
4. Pour into sterilized jars and seal.
Makes about 4 half-pint jars.

WILD PLUM CONSERVE

3 *quarts washed and pitted wild plums*
1 *orange, thinly sliced, peel and all, and seeds removed*
2 *large oranges, peeled, seeded, and cut into half-inch bits*
2 *cups white raisins*

6 *cups sugar*
   Small amount of water, if needed
2 *cups coarsely chopped pecans*

1. Combine plums, orange slices, orange bits, raisins, and sugar in a large enameled or stainless-steel pot.
2. Bring to a boil, stirring constantly until sugar dissolves.
3. Lower heat and simmer for 30 minutes, stirring often, until mixture thickens. (If necessary during cooking, you may add a little water to prevent the fruit from sticking.)
4. Add nuts and cook 5 minutes longer.
5. Pour into sterilized jars and seal.
Makes about 12 half-pint jars.

RASPBERRY AND CHERRY CONSERVE

This recipe can be used for mulberries, which often ripen at the same time as cherries. In substituting mulberries for raspberries, add ¼ cup of lemon juice to make up for the lack of acid in the fruit.

4 *cups raspberries, rinsed and drained*
4 *cups sweet cherries (use a "tame" or garden variety)*
   Water
6 *cups sugar*

1. Press the raspberries through a sieve to remove some of the seeds.
2. Simmer cherries in a small amount of water. When soft, cool, then remove pits.
3. Mix sugar and fruits in a large enameled or stainless-steel pot and cook over low heat, stirring, until sugar has dissolved.
4. Raise heat and cook rapidly, stirring often, until thick, about 45 minutes.
5. Ladle into sterilized jars and seal.
Makes about 8 half-pint jars.

WILD GRAPE CONSERVE

2 *quarts wild grapes, washed and stemmed*
Water to cover fruit
Grated peel of 1 lemon
1 *teaspoon lemon juice*
¼ *teaspoon salt*
4 *cups sugar*
1 *cup chopped black walnuts*

1. Slip skins off grapes and set them aside.

2. Place grape pulp in a large stainless-steel or enameled pan, cover with water, and cook over high heat until softened, about 15 minutes.

3. Press pulp through a coarse sieve or a food mill to remove seeds.

4. Combine skins, grape pulp, grated lemon peel, lemon juice, and salt in the large pot and bring to a boil again.

5. Add sugar and again bring to a boil. Turn heat to low and simmer until mixture begins to thicken, stirring frequently.

6. Add nuts and continue cooking until conserve is as thick as you like it.

7. Pour into sterilized half-pint jars or glasses and seal with paraffin.
Makes about 5 half-pint jars.

BLACK HAW BUTTER

This isn't a very sweet butter—made with only a little sugar, it has more flavor, we think, than when it's made quite sweet.

2 *quarts black haw berries*
Water to cover fruit
½ *cup sugar*
¼ *teaspoon ground allspice*
2 *teaspoons ground cinnamon*
½ *teaspoon ground cloves*

1. In a large stainless-steel or enameled pan, bring black haws to a boil in water to cover. Lower heat and simmer for 30 minutes.

2. Pour into a colander and press pulp through.

3. Measure out 2 cups of pulp, adding a little water, if necessary, to make this amount, and return pulp to the large pan. Stir in sugar and spices.

4. Bring to a boil, lower heat, and simmer until smooth and spreadable, stirring constantly.

5. Pour into sterile jars and seal.
Makes about 5 half-pint jars.

WILD GRAPE BUTTER

This makes a delicious sandwich spread, and it can be used at breakfast on toast, pancakes, or waffles.

1 *cup water*
2 *quarts wild grapes, washed and stripped from stems*
2 *tablespoons grated orange peel*
2 *cups sugar*
½ *teaspoon ground cinnamon*
½ *teaspoon ground cloves*
¼ *teaspoon grated nutmeg*
¼ *teaspoon ground ginger, or 1 teaspoon grated fresh ginger root*

1. Add water to grapes, bring to a boil, and simmer 10 minutes, or until soft.

2. Pour grapes and juice into a colander and press pulp into a bowl.

3. Return pulp to an enameled or stainless-steel kettle and add orange peel, sugar, and spices.

4. Cook over medium-high heat, stirring constantly, for 10 to 15 minutes, or until thick.

5. Pour into sterile jars and seal.
Makes about 8 half-pint jars.

JELLIES

When a jelly recipe calls for the extracted juice of a fruit, prepare it this way:

Use fully ripe fruit, washed, picked from stems, and crushed slightly. Place the fruit in an enamel or stainless-steel pan holding at least twice as much as the amount of fruit. Add water—to about a quarter of the depth of very juicy fruits, halfway to the top of less juicy fruit, and water almost to cover if fruit is very firm or of a dry type (sumac berries or rose hips, for instance). Place pan over medium heat, uncovered, and bring fruit slowly to a boil. Turn heat down and simmer for about 15 minutes, stirring occasionally. Cool for 30 minutes, then pour into a jelly bag or a colander lined with several layers of damp cheesecloth and let juice drip through.

It's not always possible to judge in advance the exact yield of juice from the fruit. It depends upon the kind of fruit, how much water is added, and so on, but a rough rule is that a pound of fruit will produce a cupful of juice if a minimum of water is used (the less water, the better the flavor). If you don't have quite enough juice, a small amount of water may be added; or the imaginative cook may wish to use two kinds of juice. For example, if I don't have quite enough grape juice, I am quite likely to add a little plum juice.

If you like tart jellies, try using a combination of ripe and less than fully ripe fruit, or use a little lemon juice in place of part of the juice called for.

ELDERBERRY JELLY

Elderberry jelly is a very deep bluish-purple in color, so it is a delight to see as well as to taste.

3¾ cups elderberry juice, extracted from 3 to 4 pounds ripe elderberries (page 235)
¼ cup lemon juice
1 box powdered pectin
5 cups sugar

1. Measure elderberry juice into a large enameled or stainless-steel pan, add lemon juice and pectin, and bring to a boil, stirring, over high heat.

2. Add sugar and, still stirring, bring again to a full rolling boil. Boil very hard, stirring constantly, for exactly 2 minutes.

3. Set off heat and skim off foam.

4. Pour into sterile jars or jelly glasses and seal.

Makes about 5 half-pint jars.

ELDERBERRY AND GRAPE JELLY

2½ cups elderberry juice, extracted from about 2 to 2½ pounds ripe elderberries (page 235)
2½ cups wild grape juice, extracted from about 2 pounds ripe grapes (page 235)
1 box powdered pectin
¼ cup lemon juice
7 cups sugar

1. Mix the elderberry and grape juices with the pectin and lemon juice in a large enameled or stainless-steel pan and bring to a hard boil, stirring.

2. Add sugar and return, stirring constantly, to a hard boil that won't stir down. Boil for precisely 2 minutes, stirring all the while.

4. Set off heat and skim off foam.

5. Pour into sterile jelly jars or glasses and seal.

Makes about 6 half-pint jars.

ELDERBERRY AND SUMAC JELLY

This jelly belongs to a group of old-time jellies called "venison jelly," made of various fruits and served by our ancestors as an accompaniment to wild game, venison in particular. My family's favorite recipe for venison jelly is on page 239.

1¼ cups sumac berry extract, made from about 2½ cups ripe berries, that has been strained through 2 layers of cloth

2¼ cups elderberry juice, extracted from 2 to 2½ pounds ripe berries (page 235)

3 2-inch sticks cinnamon, broken up

1 teaspoon whole cloves

6 tablespoons cider vinegar

1 box powdered pectin

4½ cups sugar

1. Simmer the sumac and elderberry juices with the cinnamon and cloves, covered, for 15 minutes.

2. Strain, then measure out 2 cups of elderberry juice and 1 cup of sumac juice, add vinegar and pectin, and bring to a boil in a large enameled or stainless-steel pan, stirring.

3. Add sugar, return to a boil, stirring, and boil hard for exactly 2 minutes, stirring constantly.

4. Set off heat and skim.

5. Pour into sterilized jelly glasses or jars and seal.

Makes about 4 half-pint jars.

BEE BALM JELLY

This dark-green jelly is particularly good served with highly flavored kinds of game,

as well as with lamb and pork. Let it stand for at least a week to firm up before you use it.

1½ cups (packed) freshly picked bee balm leaves and flowers

3 cups water

1 box powdered pectin

4 cups sugar

2 or 3 drops green food coloring

1. Put bee balm leaves and flowers into a pot and crush slightly. Add water, bring to a boil, remove from heat, and let stand, covered, for 10 minutes.

2. Pour through a strainer and put the herb infusion into a large saucepan. You should have 3 cups.

3. Add pectin to infusion and bring to a boil over high heat, stirring.

4. Add sugar and, still stirring over high heat, bring to a hard rolling boil and boil for 2 minutes.

5. Stir in food coloring, skim off any foam, and pour jelly into sterile jars or glasses.

6. Let stand, covered with a cloth, for 1 week, then seal with paraffin.

Makes about 4 half-pint glasses or jars.

BLACK CHERRY JELLY

3½ cups black cherry juice, extracted from about 4 pounds of ripe cherries (page 235)

1 box powdered pectin

4½ cups sugar

1. Combine juice with pectin in a large enameled or stainless-steel pan and bring to a hard boil over high heat, stirring occasionally.

2. Add sugar and again bring to a hard boil, stirring. Boil for exactly 2 minutes, stirring constantly.

3. Remove from the heat and skim off any foam.

4. Pour at once into sterile jelly jars or glasses and seal.

Makes 5 half-pint glasses.

SPEARMINT JELLY

Spearmint jelly is traditionally eaten with lamb and mutton, but it's also particularly good with poultry.

2 *cups (well packed) fresh spearmint leaves, washed and drained*
3 *cups water*
1 *box powdered pectin*
4 *cups sugar*
2 *drops green food coloring*

1. Place spearmint leaves in a large saucepan, crush lightly, cover with water, and bring to a boil. Remove from heat and let stand, covered, for 15 minutes.

2. Pour through a strainer and measure 3 cups of the mint infusion into a large saucepan.

3. Add pectin and bring to a boil over high heat, stirring.

4. Add the sugar and food coloring and again bring mixture to a boil and boil hard for exactly 2 minutes, stirring.

5. Set off heat and skim off foam.

6. Pour jelly into sterile jelly glasses or jars. Cover jelly containers with a cloth and let stand 1 week, then seal with parafhn.

Makes about 4 half-pint jars.

SUSAN'S ROSE HIP JELLY

Rose hips, though not always thought of as a fruit, make fine jellies. The color of the jelly is pale pink to deep red, depending on the color of the hips used. Before making a batch of jelly, it is a good idea to taste an uncooked hip of each kind you pick to see whether you like the flavor. Some hips are tart and others sweet, so you may want to mix several types of hips to get a special flavor, or concentrate on one kind only.

4 *cups ripe rose hips, either wild or from the garden*
   Water to cover
1 *box powdered pectin*
3¾ *cups sugar*

1. Wash rose hips and crush them slightly with a rolling pin.

2. Cover hips with water in an enameled or stainless-steel pan and bring to a boil. Remove from heat, cover, and let stand until cool.

3. Strain through a sieve lined with several layers of damp cheesecloth and discard fruit. Strain infusion again through the rinsed cheesecloth.

4. Measure 3 cups of the infusion into the rinsed-out large pan and bring to a boil over high heat.

5. Add pectin and bring to a boil again, stirring.

6. Add sugar and bring to a hard rolling boil, stirring constantly; boil hard for 2 minutes exactly, stirring.

7. Pour into sterile jelly glasses or jars and seal.

Makes about 4 half-pint jars.

STRAWBERRY, RASPBERRY, AND BLACKBERRY JELLIES

If you want to make jelly from any of these wild fruits, do as I do—follow the recipes supplied with commercial powdered or bottled pectin—I've found no better way to make them. Just as with wild strawberry, raspberry, and blackberry jams, you'll find that the flavor will be far better than that of jellies made with "tame" fruits.

HUCKLEBERRY AND BLACKBERRY JELLY

1½   cups huckleberry juice, extracted from
        about 1 ½ quarts ripe berries
        (page 235)
2   cups blackberry juice, extracted from
        about 2 quarts berries
        (page 235)
1   box powdered pectin
4½   cups sugar

1. Combine huckleberry and black-berry juices with pectin in a large enam-eled or stainless-steel pan and bring to a hard boil over high heat, stirring occasion-ally.

2. Add sugar and again bring to a full rolling boil, stirring. Boil hard for exactly 1½ minutes, stirring all the while.

3. Remove from heat and skim off any foam.

4. Pour at once into sterile jelly glasses or jars and seal.

Makes about 5 half-pint glasses or jars.

HUCKLEBERRY OR BLUEBERRY JELLY

Follow the recipe for Black Cherry Jelly, substituting huckleberry or blueberry juice for black cherry juice. Taste the berry juice to see if it lacks tartness—if the flavor seems too tame, substitute from 2 to 4 tablespoons of lemon juice for the same amount of berry juice.

GROUND CHERRY JELLY

Follow the recipe for Black Cherry Jelly for a delicious clear lemon-yellow jelly made from ground cherries. If you'd like to increase the tartness of the jelly, substi-tute 2 to 4 tablespoons of lemon juice for an equal amount of the ground-cherry juice.

MAY APPLE JELLY

Follow the recipe for Wild Plum Jelly, sub-stituting May apples for the plums. This is a beautiful jelly, a clear sunshine yellow in color.

WILD GRAPE JELLY

For a refreshing topping for ice cream or a filling for crêpes or sandwiches, try the minted variation of this recipe.

5   cups grape juice, extracted from about
        4 to 5 pounds ripe grapes
        (page 235)
1   box powdered pectin
6½   cups sugar

1. Bring juice to a boil in a large enameled or stainless-steel pan, stir in pec-tin, and bring to a hard boil again, stirring.

2. Add sugar, stirring constantly, until a full rolling boil is reached. Boil very hard for 1½ minutes exactly, stirring constantly.

3. Set off heat and skim off foam.

4. Ladle into sterile jelly jars or glasses and seal.

Makes about 6 half-pint jars of jelly.

Minted Wild Grape Jelly

Place 1 half-pint jar of Wild Grape Jelly in the top of a double boiler over hot wa-ter. Add 1 tablespoon finely crumbled dried spearmint and stir constantly until jelly melts. Return to a scalded jelly jar and seal, or cover and store in refrigerator if jelly is to be used soon.

WILD PLUM JELLY

5 cups plum juice, extracted from 4 to 5
    pounds of ripe plums (page
    235)
1 box powdered pectin
7½ cups sugar

1. Combine plum juice and pectin in a
large stainless-steel or enameled kettle and
bring to a hard boil over high heat, stirring
occasionally.

2. Add sugar and again bring to a hard
boil, stirring. Boil hard for exactly 1 minute, stirring constantly.

3. Remove from heat and skim off
foam.

4. Pour into sterilized jars or glasses
and seal.

Makes 8 half-pint glasses.

Besides the syrups in this section, two
other good ones are by-products of making confections—see the recipes for Candied Ginger Root* and Candied Prickly
Pears.*

VENISON JELLY

This recipe for venison jelly has been
treasured in our family for years—it's our
favorite version of the old-fashioned
spiced jellies that go by this general name.

In the fall about squirrel-hunting time
we pick our ripe grapes and make up this
tart jelly to accompany the venison that's
sure to be brought in early in November.
The crisp fall weather, fresh venison, and
this jelly are sure signs that we'll have many
a fine autumn meal.

Venison jelly is also good with most
other dark game meats and with beef,
pork, and waterfowl. It's great in a
peanut-butter sandwich and as an ice-
cream topping as well.

8 quarts ripe wild grapes or Concord
    grapes, stemmed and washed
1 quart cider vinegar
¼ cup whole cloves
¼ cup stick cinnamon, broken up
12 cups sugar

1. Put grapes, vinegar, cloves, and cinnamon into an enameled or stainless-steel
kettle, heat to boiling, reduce heat to
medium, and cook until grapes are soft,
stirring occasionally.

2. Pour into a jelly bag or colander
lined with several layers of dampened
cheesecloth and let juice drip through. Return juice to the washed kettle. Bring to a
boil and boil for 20 minutes.

3. Measure out 10 cups of juice, combine with sugar in the kettle, and again
bring to a boil over high heat, stirring.
Boil, still stirring, for 5 minutes, or until
the jelly runs in a sheet from the edge of a
metal spoon (the jelly test).

4. Set off heat and skim off any foam.

5. Pour into sterile jelly glasses and seal.

Makes about 16 half-pint glasses.

SYRUPS

Besides the syrups in this section, two other good ones are by-products of making confections—see the recipes for Candied Ginger Root* and Candied Prickly Pears. *

MINT SYRUP

This is a delicious flavoring for fruit cup; add it to the fruit at least 2 hours before serving, and chill well.

- ½ cup (well packed) fresh spearmint leaves, washed and drained
- ½ cup water
- 1 cup sugar, or as needed
  Green food coloring

1. Boil spearmint, water, and sugar together for about 5 minutes.
2. Strain and taste; more sugar may be added if desired.
3. Add green food coloring to the syrup; cool.
4. Pour into sterile bottles or jars and seal, or store in the refrigerator until used.
   Makes about 1½ cups.

STRAWBERRY OR OTHER WILD BERRY OR GRAPE SYRUP

Make this syrup with other wild berries, too—blackberries, raspberries, blueberries, huckleberries, or mulberries—or with fine-flavored wild grapes. Taste the juice of any of these, and if it lacks tartness include a little lemon juice as part of the 3-cup quantity of berry or grape juice.

- 2 quarts wild strawberries, rinsed and hulled
- 4 cups water
- 1 box powdered pectin
- 4 cups sugar

1. Combine strawberries and water in a saucepan and heat to boiling.
2. Place in a fine wire sieve and drain off juice; do not stir or mash berries. Let juice cool.
3. Measure 3 cups juice and combine in an enameled or stainless-steel pan with the pectin.
4. Set over medium heat and bring just to a boil, stirring occasionally.
5. Add sugar and bring to a rolling boil. Boil 1 minute.
6. Cool syrup and bottle in sterile bottles or jars. Seal at once.
   Makes about 5 half-pint jars or bottles.

VIOLET SYRUP

After this syrup has been opened it is wise to keep it refrigerated to prevent mold. It's really fine on Cat-Tail Pollen Pancakes* or other light hot cakes. It will not have much taste of violets if wild violets are used, since they have very little fragrance, but the color is lively and the slight lemony flavor is pleasant.

- 2 cups (packed) violet blossoms, stemmed
- ½ cup water
- 2 cups sugar
- 1 tablespoon lemon extract (or violet flavoring extract, if you can find it)

1. Put violets in the jar of an electric blender with the water and blend on medium speed for 3 minutes, or till the flowers are in tiny particles.
2. Pour the violet purée into a saucepan, set it over medium heat, and add sugar and lemon or violet flavoring.
3. Bring just to a boil, then let cool until lukewarm.

4. Bring to a boil again, then strain through a very fine sieve, or a colander lined with cloth.

5. Bring to the boiling point, then pour into sterile bottles and cap closely.

Makes about ½ pint.

PICKLES AND CONDIMENTS

Here are some of my family's favorite pickles, relishes, and condiments.

SPICED PICKLED DAY-LILY BUDS

Let these spicy buds stand for a few weeks before using.

2   *quarts day lily buds, freshly boiled (page 144) and drained*
3   *cups white vinegar*
¾   *cup light-brown sugar, packed*
½   *teaspoon salt*
½   *teaspoon whole allspice*
2   *2-inch sticks cinnamon, broken up*
      10 to 12 whole cloves

1. Pack hot buds into 8 sterile half-pint canning jars.

2. Combine vinegar, brown sugar, salt, allspice, cinnamon, and cloves in a saucepan and bring to a boil; boil 3 minutes.

3. Pour pickling solution over buds, distributing spices equally. Seal at once.

Makes 8 half-pint jars.

ELDERBERRY "CAPERS"

This recipe makes "capers" fully as delicious as the imported kind. They're good

added to salads and to bland sauces, and they make a fine garnish.

2   *cups unripe elderberries or elder-flower buds, stems removed*
¼   *cup salt*
1   *cup water*
¼   *cup sugar*
1   *cup cider vinegar*

1. Wash the green berries or flower buds, drain well, and place in a sterile crock or jar.

2. Dissolve salt in water and pour over berries or buds. Cover with a cloth and let stand for 2 days.

3. Drain berries or buds and pour into 2 sterile half-pint canning jars.

4. Boil sugar and vinegar together for 2 or 3 minutes and pour into jars (jars should be filled to top) and seal at once.

Makes 2 half-pint jars.

POKE DILLS

2   *cups white vinegar*
1   *cup water*
¼   *cup sugar*
1   *teaspoon salt*
2   *fresh dill heads (unripe seed heads) or 2 tablespoons dried dill seed*
2   *quarts pokeweed stalks, cleaned, peeled, and cut into 4-inch lengths*

1. In an enameled or stainless-steel saucepan combine vinegar, water, sugar, and salt and bring to a boil; boil 3 minutes.

2. Meanwhile, put a head of dill or 1 tablespoon dill seed in each of 2 sterile quart-sized canning jars. Add poke stalks, standing them upright.

3. Pour boiling-hot liquid over poke to fill jars to top and seal at once.

4. Let stand at least 2 weeks before serving.

Makes 2 quarts.

PICKLED MUSHROOMS

We serve these pickled mushrooms with the appetizers at wild-food meals, or on the antipasto tray before a dinner of spaghetti, and sometimes with the first course when there is a dark-meat main dish.

    2   cups mushrooms (whole chanterelles or
            meadow mushrooms, or sliced oyster
            mushrooms or sulphur shelf)
    ¾   cup olive oil
    ½   cup wine vinegar
    ½   cup lemon juice
    ½   cup water
    4 or 5 wild garlic bulbs, chopped
    ½   cup wild onions (white parts), chopped
    1   teaspoon Dry Mustard,* commercial dry
            mustard, or dried wild mustard seed
            (page 80)
    3   small bay leaves
    2   teaspoons salt
    ½   teaspoon freshly ground pepper
    2   tablespoons packaged mixed pickling
            spice
    ½   cup sugar

1. Divide the mushrooms among 3 sterile half-pint canning jars.

2. Combine the oil, vinegar, lemon juice, water, garlic, onions, mustard powder or seed, bay leaves, salt, pepper, pickling spice, and sugar in a saucepan and bring to a boil; boil 3 minutes.

3. Pour over mushrooms, dividing spices, garlic, and onions among the jars, and seal. Store in refrigerator. The pickles may be used after a day or two and should be used within a very few days.

SPICED BURDOCK ROOTS

Let this spiced preserve or relish stand for at least two or three weeks before using.

    4   cups sliced burdock roots, precooked
            (page 140)
    1   cup cider vinegar
    ¾   cup granulated sugar
    ¾   cup brown sugar
    ½   cup water
    1   tablespoon mixed pickling spice
    1   2-inch stick cinnamon, broken up
    1   tablespoon salt

1. Place vinegar, sugars, water, spices, and salt in a stainless-steel or enameled pan and boil for 5 minutes.

2. Add burdock roots, cover, and simmer for 10 minutes.

3. Spoon into sterile jars and seal. *Makes about 4 half-pint jars.*

POKE AND MINT RELISH

This early-spring relish is just great with fish, frogs' legs, and poultry. It's too mild to accompany curry, we think.

    2   cups cider vinegar
    2   cups sugar
    1   teaspoon Dry Mustard* or commercial
            dry mustard
    1   teaspoon salt
    3 or 4 1-inch pieces of fresh ginger root,
            scrubbed and coarsely chopped
    6   cups pokeweed stalks, washed, peeled,
            and chopped fine in food grinder
    2   cups wild leeks (white parts), chopped
            fine in food grinder
    1   cup (packed) spearmint leaves, snipped
            coarsely with kitchen scissors
    ½   cup raisins

1. Bring vinegar to a boil in a large stainless-steel or enameled pan.

2. Stir in sugar, mustard, salt, and ginger, then add pokeweed, leeks, mint, and raisins.

3. Return to a boil, lower heat, and simmer 10 minutes.

4. Ladle into sterilized jars and seal. Let stand for 3 weeks before using.

Makes about 8 half-pint jars.

SPEARMINT RELISH

This uncooked relish is an old-time accompaniment for lamb, but it is equally good with other meats as well as with fish dishes and frogs' legs.

2 cups white vinegar
2 cups sugar
1½ teaspoons Dry Mustard* or commercial dry mustard
¼ teaspoon salt
2 large sweet apples, peels left on, cored and finely diced
1 medium-sized ripe tomato, scalded, peeled, and finely diced
½ cup wild onions or wild leeks, white parts only, finely chopped
½ cup white raisins, soaked in warm water for 15 minutes and drained
1 cup (packed) spearmint leaves, finely chopped or snipped with scissors

1. Bring vinegar to a boil in an enameled or stainless-steel kettle. Add sugar, mustard, and salt and set aside to cool.

2. Mix apples, tomato, onions or leeks, raisins, and spearmint.

3. Pour pickling solution over the vegetables, mix well, and spoon into hot sterile pint jars. Seal at once.

Makes 2 pints.

APPLE AND BLACK HAW CHUTNEY

1½ cups dark-brown sugar, packed
1½ cups red wine vinegar
2 teaspoons Dry Mustard* or commercial dry mustard
1 teaspoon ground cinnamon
1 teaspoon ground cloves
½ teaspoon salt
1 cup black haw pulp, prepared from about 1 quart fruit as described in recipe for Black Haw Butter*
2 large apples, peel left on, cored and chopped coarsely
1 cup wild onions, white parts only, chopped
1 cup raisins
3 medium-sized ripe tomatoes, scalded, peeled, and chopped coarsely
6 to 8 chopped dried figs (optional)

1. Mix brown sugar, vinegar, mustard, cinnamon, cloves, and salt in a large enameled or stainless-steel pot and bring to a boil.

2. Add black haw pulp, apples, onions, raisins, tomatoes, and figs.

3. Bring to a boil and cook, stirring, for 30 to 45 minutes, or until as thick as desired.

4. Pour into sterile pint jars and seal at once.

Makes ? pints.

WILD PLUM CHUTNEY

Especially good with lamb or pork, this is a deliciously spicy condiment. We like it mixed with cream cheese as a spread, too.

- 10 *cups wild plums, washed, pitted, and coarsely chopped*
- 4 *cups yellow or red onions, peeled and coarsely chopped*
- 8 *cups tart cooking apples, peeled, cored, and coarsely chopped*
- 3 *cups cider vinegar*
- 4 *cups dark-brown sugar, packed*
- 4 *cups granulated sugar*
- 1 *tablespoon ground allspice*
- 1 *tablespoon ground cloves*
- 1 *tablespoon ground ginger*
- ½ *teaspoon curry powder*
- 3 *tablespoons salt*

1. In a large enameled or stainless-steel pot combine the plums, onions, apples, and vinegar. Bring to the boiling point over high heat and stir in remaining ingredients.
2. Return mixture to a boil, reduce heat, and simmer, uncovered, for 1½ hours, stirring occasionally to prevent sticking.
3. Ladle into sterilized pint jars and seal immediately.
Makes about 10 pints.

DRY MUSTARD

- 1 *cup dried mustard seed (page 80)*
- 2 *tablespoons finely chopped wild onions, white parts only*
- 1 *teaspoon salt, or to taste*
- 2 *cups water*

1. Preheat oven to 200°.

2. Blend all ingredients in an electric blender until smooth.
3. Spread mustard paste thinly in a baking pan or on a cookie sheet and bake until dry, about 1½ hours.
4. Remove, cool, and pound into powder, using a mortar and pestle or an electric blender.
5. Store in an airtight jar or tin.
Makes about 1½ cups

PREPARED MUSTARD

Without the optional mayonnaise, this mustard keeps indefinitely in the refrigerator. The mayonnaise makes it milder and easier to spread, though it shortens its storage life somewhat.

- 1 *cup dried mustard seed (page 80) crushed coarsely with a rolling pin or in a mortar*
- 2 *tablespoons honey*
- 2 *tablespoons cider vinegar*
- 1 *tablespoon vegetable oil*
- ¼ *cup water*
- 1 *tablespoon mayonnaise (optional)*

1. Blend all ingredients in an electric blender until a smooth paste results.
2. Pour into a sterilized jar and store, covered, in the refrigerator.
Makes about 1½ cups.

MINT VINEGAR

This is a good vinegar to use with fruit salad or any green salad that includes pieces of orange or grapefruit, or in any vegetable dish calling for vinegar in which a minty flavor would be welcome.

- 2 *cups (packed) spearmint leaves, coarsely chopped*

1   *cup sugar*
1   *quart cider vinegar*

1. Place mint leaves in the bottom of an enameled or stainless-steel kettle and crush them thoroughly.

2. Add sugar and vinegar, bring to a boil, and simmer for 5 minutes.

3. Cool, then strain through cheesecloth and pour into sterile bottles. Cap or cork well.

Makes about 1 quart.

GARLIC VINEGAR

Using this pungent vinegar is an easy way to add garlic flavor to salads and vegetable dishes.

6   *wild garlic bulbs, white parts only,*
    washed, peeled, and crushed
    thoroughly in a mortar
1   *teaspoon salt*
1   *teaspoon ground cloves*
    Freshly ground pepper to taste
1   *teaspoon caraway seed, lightly bruised or*
    crushed
1   *quart red wine vinegar*

1. Put garlic into a wide-mouthed jar that has a tight-fitting lid.

2. Add salt, cloves, pepper, and caraway seed.

3. Heat wine vinegar just to simmering and pour into jar.

4. Cover tightly and let stand 1 week in a cool place, shaking occasionally.

5. Strain through cheesecloth and pour into sterile bottles and cork or cap well.

Makes about 1 quart.

CANDIES AND CONFECTIONS

BLACK WALNUT AND APPLE CANDY

This candy is not very sweet and it's a bit chewy, like gumdrops. It stores well in a cool place, but it's so good to eat that you may have trouble storing any for future use.

1½ envelopes (1 ½ tablespoons) unflavored gelatin
⅓ cup water
1½ tablespoons cornstarch
2 cups granulated sugar
1 cup thick applesauce (if necessary, cook down until it will mound up in a spoon, then measure)

4 tablespoons lemon-flavored gelatin dessert powder
½ cup black walnuts, finely chopped
Confectioners' sugar for final coating

1. Sprinkle unflavored gelatin into water and let soak for 5 minutes.
2. Combine cornstarch and granulated sugar and stir until well mixed.
3. Stir applesauce, sugar, and cornstarch together in a saucepan and bring to the boiling point.
4. Add soaked gelatin, then lemon gelatin powder, and stir until dissolved.
5. Cook slowly for 20 minutes over low heat, stirring constantly. Cool.
6. When cold add black walnuts. Turn into a buttered 8-inch square pan and let stand overnight. Then cut into 1-inch squares and roll each piece in confectioners' sugar.
7. Store, covered, in a cool place, with waxed paper between layers.

Makes about 5 dozen squares.

CANDIED GINGER ROOT AND GINGER SYRUP

1 cup water
1 cup wild ginger roots, well scrubbed and very coarsely chopped
½ cup sugar
Sugar for final coating

1. Bring water to a boil, add ginger, and simmer until tender, about 15 minutes.
2. Add sugar, stir until dissolved, and simmer 15 minutes.
3. Put syrup and ginger in a jar, cover, and let stand for 3 days.
4. Remove ginger from syrup, drain, and roll pieces generously in granulated sugar.
5. Store ginger, without packing it

down, in tightly covered jars for future use.

6. Bottle the drained syrup to use over pancakes or to flavor fruit mixtures.

Makes about 3 half-pint jars of candied root.

CANDIED MINT LEAVES

To make these delicious confections, follow the directions for Candied Violets* Rinse the leaves of spearmint or peppermint and pat them thoroughly dry with paper towels, then follow the same steps as for candied violets or candied rose or yucca petals. The oven time is about 30 to 40 minutes.

CANDIED PRICKLY PEARS AND PRICKLY PEAR SYRUP

The fruit will split open with a cheery pop while cooking. As the prickly pears continue to simmer they impart their flavor to the syrup, whose tangy taste is enhanced by a golden color. A very happy way to start the day is serving the syrup over crisp waffles with fresh butter. The fruit is a delicious nibble at any time.

- 2 *cups prickly pears, washed and with any thorns removed*
- 3 *quarts boiling water*
- ¾ *cup sugar*
- 1 *tablespoon lemon juice*
- 2 *1-inch pieces wild ginger root, dried or fresh*
- 2 *cups water*
- *Sugar for final coating*

1. Put prickly pears in a sieve, dunk them into the boiling water, and blanch for 2 minutes. Remove and set aside to drain, still in the sieve.

2. Place sugar, lemon juice, ginger root, and 2 cups water in a saucepan and add fruit. Gradually bring to a boil over medium heat, then reduce heat to a simmer and cook until the syrup is thick, 10 minutes or so. Set off heat.

3. Preheat oven to 200°.

4. Lift fruits gently from the syrup one at a time, using a slotted spoon. Allow each piece to drain well. Reserve syrup.

5. Coat fruit with granulated sugar, covering all surfaces, and place on waxed paper–covered cookie sheet.

6. Dry in 200° oven for 30 to 45 minutes, or until fruit is partially dried; it should be about as moist as candied citrus peel.

7. Strain the reserved syrup, adding a little water if too thick, and bottle for use over pancakes. Store candied fruit in a closed jar.

Makes about 1 pint each of fruit and syrup.

CANDIED BURDOCK

- *Juice of 1 lemon, strained*
- 1 *tablespoon shredded lemon peel*
- 1 *cup brown sugar (dark or light), packed*
- *Pinch of salt*
- ¼ *cup water*
- 2 *cups burdock flower stalks, precooked (page 140) and sliced in 3-inch lengths*
- *Granulated sugar for final coating*

1. Combine lemon juice, lemon peel, brown sugar, salt, and water and pour over the burdock in a saucepan. Bring to a boil and simmer until burdock becomes translucent, about 15 minutes.

2. Drain burdock pieces and lay them on waxed paper to cool.

3. Sprinkle burdock with granulated sugar and store, covered, as you would candied fruit peel.

Makes about 1 pound.

PERSIMMON CHEWS

1   cup dark-brown sugar, packed
1   cup uncooked persimmon pulp, fresh or
        frozen and thawed
1   cup black walnuts, chopped
2   egg yolks
1   tablespoon butter
¼   cup confectioners' sugar mixed with ¼
        cup finely chopped black walnuts

1. In the top of a double boiler combine brown sugar, persimmon pulp, black walnuts, egg yolks, and butter.

2. Place boiler top over base containing boiling water and cook for 25 minutes over medium heat, stirring once in a while.

3. Cool for about an hour.

4. Form into balls about the size of a walnut, roll in mixture of confectioners' sugar and nuts, and refrigerate for an hour or so before serving.

5. To store, pack in airtight tin with waxed paper between the layers and keep in a cool place.

Makes about 2 ½ dozen pieces.

SASSAFRAS INFUSION

The exact amount of infusion this recipe will make will depend on how strong you like it—use more or less water, simmer a longer or shorter time, or add water at the time of using it. Besides being used for candy (see the recipes that follow), this infusion can be the base for sassafras tea — just add boiling water until you have the strength you like.

1   cup dried sassafras root bark, (page
        93) crushed or shredded coarsely, or
        7 or 8 thumb-sized roots, bark and all
3   quarts water

1. In a 4-quart saucepan, simmer sassafras root bark or roots in water for about 30 minutes, or until water is deep rose-colored.

2. Strain and use at once, or store, covered, in the refrigerator.

Makes about 2 ½ quarts.

SASSAFRAS BRITTLE

This candy is clear and very hard. Young Julie Royal, who worked out these two recipes for sassafras candies, says if this clear hard candy is not boiled to 305°, or past the stage where it cracks when it's dropped into cold water, you could surely lose a filling from a tooth. It will not be hard and crystallized enough unless this temperature is reached.

2   cups Sassafras Infusion
3   cups sugar

1. Combine ingredients in a large saucepan and stir until sugar is dissolved.

2. Boil syrup without stirring until it reaches 305° on a candy thermometer, or is just past the hard-crack stage (brittle threads form when a little syrup is dropped into cold water).

3. Pour into a buttered 9-inch square pan and let stand until lukewarm.

4. Score into 1-inch squares and let cool. Break apart and serve, or store in closed plastic bags.

Makes about 1 ½ pounds.

ROYAL SASSAFRAS CANDY

This hard candy is granular in texture and is a lovely pale red color; it tastes strongly of sassafras.

2   cups Sassafras Infusion*
3   cups sugar

1. Combine ingredients, stir until sugar

dissolves, and boil without stirring in a large saucepan to 244° to 250° on a candy thermometer, or until a little syrup forms a firm ball when dropped into cold water.

2. Pour into a buttered 9-inch square pan.

3. While still warm, score into 1-inch squares. Let cool.

4. Break into squares and serve; or store in closed plastic bags.

Makes about 1 ½ pounds.

CANDIED VIOLETS OR CANDIED ROSE OR YUCCA PETALS

These lovely, frail confections can be kept for a year, or perhaps longer, when correctly stored. The violets tend to lose some color as they age, but if they are fully crystallized they remain tasty and delightful for use as a candy or as a decoration on desserts. Rose and yucca petals may also be candied this way. The yucca petals require a longer oven time, from 1 to 1½ hours.

2 *egg whites*
A large bunch of violets, stems and all
Granulated sugar, preferably superfine

1. Preheat oven to 200°.

2. Beat the egg whites with a wire whip just until frothy.

3. Pick up one violet at a time by its stem and dip it into the beaten egg whites, covering all surfaces. Then gently dip the violet into the sugar. Be sure all the petals are sugared, top and bottom.

4. Place each violet in turn on a cookie sheet covered with waxed paper and snip off the stem. Open the petals to their original shape, using a toothpick, and sprinkle flowers again with sugar if there are any uncoated spots.

5. Dry in a 200° oven for 30 to 40 minutes, or till the sugar crystallizes.

6. Gently lift the violets from the cookie sheet with a 2-tined fork or spatula. Sprinkle again with sugar if they appear syrupy to any degree.

7. Cool on racks and store in an airtight container. Be sure to put waxed paper between the layers of violets, which shouldn't touch each other.

Index

C

L

Y

Z